RL Fa~~~~

...for the lo~~~~

by Ray Gent and Tim Wilkinson

Best Wishes
Ray

1895, the year of shame,
When you northern folk changed the game.
Don't ever again feel surprise
As we, the Union, ostracise
Echoes of, 'ban the working class!
Never again touch our grass!'
The George Hotel was your epitaph,
Forever and ever to bear our wrath.
'But, m'lord, it was just an extra penny,
Compensation away from the spinning Jenny,'
Surely, it was never a crime
For one to be able to escape the grime?

Ray Gent February 2002

LONDON LEAGUE PUBLICATIONS LTD

RL Fanpower... for the love of League

Cover photo: Batley versus St Helens, courtesy Alex Service. Other photographs by Peter Lush except where otherwise credited and may not be reproduced without permission. All photos copyright to the photographer.

Cartoons by Darren 'Daza XIII' Broadhurst, Allan McKeown and Tim 'T-Dub' Wilkinson.

A CIP catalogue record for this book is available from the British Library.

First published in Great Britain in November 2002 by:
London League Publications Ltd. P.O. Box 10441, London E14 0SB

ISBN: 1-903659-01-9

Cover design by: Stuart Gent and Daniel Parker

Layout: Peter Lush

Printed and bound by: Catford Print Centre, PO Box 563, Catford,
                          London SE6 4PY

A share of any profits from the sale of this book will be given to good causes within Rugby League

Foreword (pass): Rugby League, alive and kicking

Alreet, folks, Rugby League here. Born 29 August 1895, but not sure of th' exact time, as I cawn't find me birth certificate. Best find it as them Welshies might need it one day.

Nay mind anyway, here I am, possibly 107 year old and still going strong. Strange one was me birth! Me mam was Rugby Union and me dad was workers' rights. Some months before no one down south knew me mam wuz up the duff, but all this broken-time kerfuffle brought it on! Happened in t' splendour of the famous old George Hotel, in th' historic mill town of Huddersfield. No common hospital for me: born in front of t' committee, in such magnificent surroundings.

Even from an early age I wuz a big celebrity up in t' north of England. Was paid to entertain those hard working northern folk, but that caused a bit of rumpus down south dust tha' know. Aye, it certainly mapped me life out good un' proper.

As me life progressed, I were courted by royalty, Prime Ministers, and other big wigs. Certainly made life interesting as I starred in the big time. That was me, down at yon Wembley every year. Shame it's no more - for now. Never did get married, mind you, though, I must have been naughty, as I now have offspring in good old Aussie, New Zealand, over t' Channel in France and all ower t' Pacific and many more places like Russia. Not bad for a good owd un.

Talking of France, our Pierre is still mithering about how the Hun stopped me from playing over in France. Them Nazis made the government there pinch all me brass, with nowt said then or since from them as played that 'other code of rugby'. Let em sup their Vichy watter, I'm still scrapping to get justice for that even now.

Still can't fathom out why some folk banned me, when in fact I were a celebrity and charmer to boot. Aye, it did happen, I'm afraid. Couldn't go in some clubs for a pint, not allowed to laik me talents on certain playing fields, even banned while serving King and Country.

Been many dramatic moments in me life but 2001 took the biscuit. Some doom mongers from t' media wouldn't let up telling all that would listen that I wuz about to die. It's true, me old muckers, Rugby League signed, sealed and delivered t' grave.

"Rest in peace", they said "glad t' see t' back of yer." Twelve column inches under.

I may be wobbly at the knees at times and kind of bang into meself now and then, but appen I'm still alive and full of fight yet. So what happened next has made me proud.

Me family started this petition off: 'Give our Rugby League a fair crack' and all that. It spread far and wide and even ended up on t' Sky telly. Some 30,000 folk eventually signed it. I never knew I had so many relatives and friends!

Anyway, enough of me for now, let's get up to date with this petition and see what else is up, cos I've heard there's a lot going on with good folk doing their bit to keep me going and help fight me corner with me.

Tha never knows, I might still be around to see in my two-hundredth birthday and receive a card off me owd mates Frank Keating and Stephen Jones - if they are still around scribbling their views.

Thanks for help in compiling material for this book to: rlfans.com and Totalrl.com websites and the Rugby League fraternity who inhabit them.

Thanks to Peter Lush and Dave Farrar of London League Publications Ltd for producing the book.

Thank you for the donation towards the cost of publishing the book from Jonathan 'Paley' Palethorpe, and to everyone who subscribed to the book in advance of publication.

Disclaimer

The views expressed in this book are not necessarily those of the publishers, London League Publications Ltd.

They are, however, those of the contributors, and the authors. It all seems honest and fair to us, so Ray and Tim will take any responsibility for them.

Anyone of a sensitive nature who is offended, affronted or who otherwise takes umbrage at anything they read in these pages, please feel free to contact either of the authors in the first instance.

This might be a struggle as by the time you read this they will both be residing in luxury caves in Tora Bora, Afghanistan.

However, if this is the case and you are a sensitive soul, frankly maybe you oughtn't to be involved in a game like rugby at all.

Introduction: New beginning, or a false dawn?

Rugby League exists in a crowded sporting landscape, dominated, often unfairly, by other codes, facing an ongoing struggle to achieve fair and proportionate media coverage and push out the geographical boundaries of its empire.

Much of this development and campaigning work is undertaken by enthusiasts, often out of a sense of injustice and bloody minded determination to spread the Rugby League gospel. This book doffs its cap to some of those efforts, past present and future.

Wow! What a year 2001 turned out to be. It was a roller coaster ride of fantasy and reality. The fantasy would be to be able to own a national newspaper so one could take great delight in giving Rugby League the limelight. However, what of the reality? Many national media outlets took a perverse delight in sounding the death knell for Rugby League and all but took it to the graveyard. 'Bury those Leaguies from the "other" code of rugby', was the war cry.

It seemed all League men and women, and the League cat were to be enticed through Rugby Union's pearly gates, draped forever in Fort Knox gold, ready for the glamorous Hollywood life style ahead. 'Forget the backwaters of Rugby League', cried the headlines, 'Come forth to be saved! Enjoy the opulence where one can shine like a beacon on the international stage', was the echo.

In reality only three prominent Rugby League players heeded the siren call and crossed the great divide to play Rugby Union from Rugby League. What of the three wise men that took the gifts on offer?

Jason Robinson was an instant hero in his new sport and suddenly the world and the universe knew about him. However, some in the Union game still seemed at first to begrudge Jason any glory, namely television commentator Stuart Barnes and former Union player and pundit Jeremy Guscott, both eventually forced to eat Wigan baked humble pie as Billy Whizz ran in the tries for the Union British Lions. In May, Jason was named Zurich Premiership Player of the Year and also the RFU Players' Player of the Year, having scored nine tries for Sale during the 2001-2002 season.

As for Iestyn Harris and Henry Paul matters were not so straightforward. Harris suffered the strain of getting to know his new game. Having been fast tracked onto the 'big stage' of Union internationals after an early record point scoring performance for his new club, Cardiff, he was subsequently dropped from the Welsh international scene after a series of try costing errors. The national coach who had been so keen to secure Iestyn's services for the Welsh game was replaced, and Iestyn went back into the ranks.

Henry Paul made goalkicking appearances for the England 'A' team and briefly the first team, again having Union stalwarts spluttering that he had been brought through too early, and his appearance for England being termed a 'disgrace'. Henry was subsequently fined a large sum of money for criticising the coaching methods at his club, Gloucester.

Rumour and unsubstantiated pub talk in early February 2002 mused on the two players returning to Rugby League. The latter had mixed feelings from League fans, with some for welcoming them back into the fold, whilst others suggested letting them stay and stew. Whatever the outcome, which will be in the book later, is it possible to have our cat back.

As for League internationals Keiron Cunningham, Leon Pryce, Kevin Sinfield, Kris Radlinski and others who had been head-hunted by the home Unions, they remained loyal to their native game and decided to stay with Rugby League. In fact it was scurrilously rumoured that Keiron was to start a birth certificate forging business for the young up and coming rugby code switchers. Keiron's Head Office was to be situated in Swansea, South Wales.

Did they do the right thing? Damned if they do, damned if they don't, those that did switch were either welcomed as converting pagans and feted for their success or hung from the yardarm as being 'technically deficient' or unable to master the oh so complex Union code.

Criticism was made of those who stayed as having 'failed to rise to the challenge' of the 'technical game'.

Let's not get too bitter too early, dear reader, but you can probably guess the journalist who penned that last quote - 'count his medals' (none of them for modesty!)

This book, as with its predecessor, has no particular bone to pick with Rugby Union - everyone should be free to enjoy their chosen sport without discrimination - but there are situations where comparisons have to be made, unfair treatment exposed and the different standards applied to the different codes highlighted.

Also, similarly to its predecessor, this book is written 'warts and all'. No fear or favour is shown to the greatest or humblest figure, friend or foe, whatever rank. Sorry if this puts anyone's nose out of joint but we write as we find. Anyone who feels they are above criticism or thinks they deserve special treatment might just need to reconsider that.

The fans are as important as anyone else in this game, not only paying at the turnstile, but also have an increasing role to play in campaigning and banging the drum for the game. By getting organised, fanpower can punch above its weight and make things happen. This book is written by some of those fans who have been prepared to go the extra mile for their favourite game, and makes no apologies if it causes anyone to blush.

Ray Gent and Tim Wilkinson
November 2002

Contents

About the authors

Ray Gent, who is currently a financial adviser, was born in St Helens and for many years lived opposite the old St Helens Recs club. He remembers many a Saturday afternoon spent watching the then mighty Pilkington Recs. Also as a youngster going in the ground to practice goal kicks and imagining being some famous player. However, the latter practice had the odd hazard or two such

Ray being interviewed at Westminster

as being chased off by the works security. Mid teens saw him eventually go and watch the Saints from which he is now a home and away supporter. The game is more than just a sport; it is a way of life and a passion. Long may Rugby League continue for future generations to enjoy.

Tim Wilkinson is a property surveyor, currently working in the broadcasting industry, after his 10 'Rugby League wilderness years' in London and the Midlands, Tim returned to the Headingley terraces in 1992 and like a manic street preacher, he remains obsessed by the vision of Rugby League's world domination. Although he should know better he can still occasionally be spotted hauling his dilapidated frame round in pursuit of the oval ball, regretting each of his 37 years.

Tim (on right) on the lookout for Rugby League in Morocco
(Photo: Courtesy Tim Wilkinson)

1. November 2001

What became of the great Media Petition?

The Media Petition was wound up in terms of signatures being collected at the final hooter of the third Ashes Test. The exercise was huge in respect of man-hours and perseverance for the handful of volunteers involved. It was never envisaged at the start of the campaign way back in May 2001 that 30,000 Rugby League fans would join in unison as one voice to say, 'Enough is Enough'. Given a chance to collectively vent their feelings at some of the media venom that had been directed at their sport, fans flocked to it.

Thanks once again has to be given to all those that contributed to the petition in terms of signing it, helping collect signatures and giving publicity.

The *St Helens Reporter* was at the forefront of positive publicity with John Yates giving more than was expected. Other papers to follow the band wagon publicity machine included: *The Independent*, via the popular Dave Hadfield, the *Liverpool Echo, Widnes Weekly News, Warrington Guardian, Hull Daily Mail, Yorkshire Evening Post* and *North Cumberland Times and Star*. *Rugby League Express* and *Rugby Leaguer*. Various internet sites were also helpful and supportive.

Radio listeners got the petition bug from BBC Radio Merseyside, GMR, Radio Humberside and Radio Leeds. Local stations to give some air time were WISH FM (the St Helens and Wigan local station) and Wire FM (the Warrington local radio station).

Finally, Sky TV did the petition proud by featuring it on their midweek magazine show *Rugby League World*. Filming was carried out at a Warrington versus Saints match and in my front room in Billinge. This really was the icing on the cake.

The story of the petition, the book entitled *The Petition – RL Fans Say Enough is Enough*, went to the publishers in January 2002. The book itself was a labour of love and a work of dedication and long hours, but was worth it in terms of placing in print what had gone on. It examined the way Rugby League is run, as well as the media attacks and the fans' responses.

It is no use criticising the media all the time when the game does shoot itself in the foot on occasions. A special thanks is extended to all the fans, as well as guest writers and cartoonists for making it a worthy effort. Many thanks must go to everyone who contributed, without whose help it wouldn't have been possible.

Initially 2,000 copies were printed and 1,450 were sold within the first couple of months of becoming available.

Many independent bookshops, Rugby League club shops and chains such as Sportspages, Waterstones, Ottakars and W. H. Smith stocked the book, the latter hosting book signing sessions.

Parliament now awaits the petition via the good office of David Hinchliffe MP. Media prominence is vital to handing the petition over to give it some clout, although we suspect that some media will mock it. This new book will document this process, month by month. So let's hope it goes well.

Signing on

Allan Reeve and his good wife Jackie were instrumental in collecting over 11,000 petition signatures along with son Arron and his friend Anthony. Allan has kindly penned a piece with his thoughts on the petition and comments from an article from Plymouth that should be blown out to sea.

"The first time that I bumped into Ray Gent he was in the 'wrong end' at Knowsley Road, home of the Saints. He approached me with petition board in hand to sign the media petition. The game at the time seemed to be reeling from one outbreak of bad news to another. Very little appeared to be written about it. Yet as a spectacle it was up there at the top.

Many fans at the time were up in arms, as per the many letters sent to the Rugby League press and aired on local radio. Yet what it needed was to ignite the fuse of protest against a backdrop of some wanting the game to be wiped off the sporting map. Even one highly rated local radio presenter cynically suggested the sport was 'getting the press it deserved.'

He missed the point though. We were getting the media coverage we didn't deserve. At that period of time you could read more about the 13-a-side code in the column inches (or should it be feet) of the Union journalists in the nationals than the paltry inches devoted to Rugby League.

I honestly believe that had Ray not felt so dissatisfied and incensed that he was motivated to do something about it, the situation would have got worse. As one who has spent hours collecting thousands of signatures at games, amateur and professional, as well as in pubs and clubs I know first hand how relieved some fans were that a counter attack was being driven forward.

From the help of signature collectors, local media and onwards to

2

Parliament the petition was indeed a credit to the game. And long may the game receive such dedication to the cause. The climate for Rugby League to go forward has never been better under its new leadership and there is a feeling in the game that the time to pull together is now. It is now ripe to get our 'own house in order' and move on with confidence under the new umbrella of 2003 when the new structure is instigated. We have, as many would agree 'been our worst enemy in the past.'

There will always be those bigots on both sides of the divide but because of the petition, the surrounding campaign and publicity it does indeed give us a platform to work from. The game will have to work hard to restore its image, especially in Plymouth. Yes indeed, Plymouth, where an *Evening Herald* reporter described League as a sport played exclusively by 'whippet breading northerners' in between breaks down the mine. Now who do you suppose would benefit from a lesson in good manners?

This was some cheap shot from someone who has total disregard for both our sport and way of life. To my mind regionalism is tantamount to racialism and should not be tolerated. There is also a danger that such people could indeed rise up the journalistic ladder to some national paper to continue on this unnecessary path of worthless articles. However, under the new climate that seems to have arrived from the petition he could indeed end up on the *Beano*, and good riddance. (no disrespect to the *Beano*.)"

First of many

A continuing theme through this book is the attitude of the BBC to our game and the many and various excuses given in response. With the long awaited on-off-on again Ashes Tour, critical to the game's parlous financial position at the time looming large, what surely represented a major sporting clash seemed to be being ignored.

Tim e-mailed the *BBC* during the week prior to the first test:
"Listening avidly to Radio 5 and watching BBC news as I usually do, it occurs that the BBC are not aware that the all conquering Australian Rugby League team are in town.

They play the first match of a three match series against Great Britain on Sunday, the first Ashes tour since 1994, which I believe BBC TV have secondary rights to.

All week I've heard all about the comings and goings of the England Rugby Union match (also against Australia on Saturday, good luck to them) and a horse that never wins. Today I've heard about Lennox Lewis's manager, allegations about a cricketer who might not be able to bowl straight and Goran Ivanisovich's foot.... but nothing so far about the League game.

I've just bought a new licence, begrudgingly so as BBC seldom mentions my favourite sport, even when they've got the rights to it.

Amongst the welter of banal football speculation we get daily I look forward to a decent preview on Friday night and during *Grandstand* on Saturday, and I'm sure the nation's broadcaster will not disappoint.

Best of British, Tim Wilkinson"

And a reply from Peter Salmon, *BBC*, on 8 November 2001: "We'll try not to let you down. There's a lot of sports around at the moment. It's a congested market...Peter"

And another on 12 November 2001: "Thank you for your recent e-mail regarding Rugby League coverage on BBC Television... I am sorry if you feel that we have been neglecting the Rugby League Ashes between Great Britain and Australia, most particularly in favour of the Rugby Union equivalent. We try to give a wide range of sporting activities as much air time as we can, and offer more range than other networked stations in this country. However, a number of major events take place at the same time and this, combined with the sheer variety of sports, makes it impossible for us to schedule coverage which will satisfy all the main audience groups, including of course those who dislike sport totally. Unfortunately, in the case of the Ashes, an additional problem is that the live coverage rights are owned exclusively by Sky, and so we are limited to previews and recorded highlights.

Nevertheless, I hope that you enjoyed the preview and highlights of the first League Ashes match on *Sunday Grandstand* on 11 November. Please be assured that your comments and preferences have been recorded for the benefit of senior management and the sports editorial department...Thank you for taking the trouble to contact the BBC. Regards, Neil McFarlane"

A regular excuse is to point the finger at *BSkyB*, as if to say 'if the BBC haven't got the primary television rights, it isn't important'. Well, they do not have the primary rights to lots of sports. Domestic league football (Sky, secondary rights ITV), English club Rugby Union (Sky), Celtic League Rugby Union (Eurosport), Ryder Cup golf (Sky), most Test cricket and horse racing (Channel 4 and Sky) and Formula One (ITV) etc, but those sports don't receive a media blackout. More of this later. In fact, much more.

4

Coincidence or fate?

When writing a book like this one it is important not only to cover serious issues, incorporating as many views as possible but also to try and keep a balance. Coincidence or fate gets Ray's old grey matter ticking over in a light-hearted way. These strange incidents provide some food for thought.

Firstly, there is the Media Petition itself. After getting to know Geoff Lee, who is the secretary of the Rugby League Supporters Association (RLSA) and successful novelist, I purchased his book *One Winter*. Lo and behold in the first chapter there was mention of a petition. (This particular petition was about the closing of the railways in the 1960s.)

Around the same period I happened to go into the St Helens town library and visit a section that I had never been in before. There on the shelf was a selection of books on Rugby League. On picking a book up and opening a page I was smitten with shock. In print was mention of the Media Petition that was handed into the BBC over 25 years ago. Yours truly was party to that petition and yet it was only during the 2001 Media Petition that I came across the article. That was eerie indeed.

Just a few days before travelling down to Parliament to hand over the Media Petition, June, my wife, and myself were driving through a local place to us called Upholland. June happened to spot the sign of the road, which was called Parliament Street. She came out with the comment that she hadn't noticed the name before, even though we had been through it hundreds of times. For the record, neither could I.

Two days later we went for a day out at the local beauty spot of Rivington, and in particular the quaint Rivington barn that is now a tearoom. We decided to pop into an art exhibition next door. Thirty paintings on display, and guess what? One was the Houses of Parliament. A coincidence?

While on a weekend break in North Wales another incident happened. On finding a bed and breakfast place to stay the night, it was a surprise to find the proprietor was an ardent Rugby Union fan. This was at the time when *The Petition - Enough is Enough* had just made its debut on the high street. Dave, the proprietor and myself had quite a chuckle at the coincidence, after all there were many, many places to stay and his was the first one that was chosen.

Adorning a dining room wall were several pictures of Rugby Union players, with the largest being Scott Gibbs, the Welsh Union international who played Rugby League with St Helens, my hometown club. Now here is another coincidence. On buying the *Daily Mirror* the same day, there on the front page was Scott Gibbs who it said was splitting up from his wife.

Another picture was truly a horror. It was taken by the *Western Mail*, and was of Gareth Jenkins having his eye gouged by an Argentinean player. The caption read: 'Unacceptable face of rugby'. (Union or League I wonder?)

Gerry, the proprietor, told me some good tales of his time in Tenby, South Wales. As a young lad, children were told that Rugby League people had curly horns and twisted tails. During some matches in the Principality, rumours would travel round that a League scout was present. Many times there was disappointment etched on his boyish face, as he couldn't find the person with horns and a tail.

Another story involved Narberth Rugby Union club's Hall of Fame. Many local lads that had come good in Union had their framed photos take pride of place. However, on one visit he was curious as to why there was a blank space, were once a picture frame appeared to have been. He was quietly escorted to the kitchen and shown the picture frame, now hung unceremoniously on the back of the door, with the player's image facing the door. Apparently the player had gone north to play 'another' sport and, as well as being barred from the club his picture was not worthy of exhibition.

...and one of Tim's

Every now and then the draft of this book (as did its predecessor) has had a good mauling, being edited and generally translated from Lancastrian into English. One of these occasions was on the beach in Minorca during May.

Having scribbled over the piece relating to the *Super League Show* and its nemesis - *Cagney and Lacey* repeats that are shown by non-northern BBC regions in preference to the *Super League Show* - I turned to my other holiday reading, *Notes from a Small Island*. This features an American, Bill Bryson, as he tours Britain prior to returning home to Ohio. He affectionately notes all he loves and hates about Britain, its people and places and its many and various idiosyncrasies. Remarkably, one of his repeating themes is his pet hate of... repeats of *Cagney and Lacey*. To quote Mr Bryson, "...this ancient programme that so besots the controller of BBC 1." Quite. Anyway, enough anecdotes and past events, what's happened since the Media Petition closed and *The Petition - Enough is Enough* went to the publishers?

6

2. December 2001

December brings the *BBC Sports Personality of the Year*, an annual two-hour plus summary of the sporting year, essential viewing for all sports fans to look forward to.

A full and eventful year for League, how did it get on? Tim saw it and like many others wasn't impressed.

Personality by-pass

Disappointingly, the entire Rugby League year was distilled into a three-minute comedy sketch where the Saints fan and comedian Johnny Vegas was shown in mock training with the Saints team. Whatever Mr Vegas' best intentions, it was difficult to see past the 'Rugby League is a game for fat northerners' stereotype.

There were only fleeting glimpses of the Challenge Cup, Super League Grand Final and Great Britain versus Australia Test series, the first of which Britain won in glorious style.

Passing mention of these season highlight events was made only by means of Mr Vegas holding up pieces of card, no detail, no explanation, and no background.

No interview with any Rugby League celebrities who might have been able to put some contextual flesh on these barest of bones. Nor mention that the season's Man of Steel (player of the year) was Paul Sculthorpe. Even St Helens failed to feature, having beaten Brisbane Broncos to become World Club Champions, the only British club side in any sport to be world champions during 2001, or mention of good luck to the Bradford Bulls who were soon to attempt the same barely a month later.

The whole sorry episode was over in three minutes, indeed anyone who had gone out to make a cup of tea could easily have missed the summary and would be none the wiser that a season of Rugby League had ever happened. The BBC has primary rights to broadcast the Challenge Cup and has acquired secondary rights from Sky for the other events, so the material to compose a substantive, informative and dignified Rugby League section of the programme was available.

Three major finals and the first Ashes Test series since 1994 deserved some sort of substantive coverage. Alas, it was seen as easier to belittle the season as a minor sideshow.

Contrast this to the first item on the programme, 20 odd minutes of tennis, in which the only British contribution was Tim Henman's semi-final defeat at Wimbledon. The tennis piece featured comprehensive interviews, action footage and an informative summary of the season, with plenty of time for a 'how did it feel' interview with Goran Ivanisovitch. Surely Rugby League merited a similar feature?

We all know Johnny Vegas' passion for the game of Rugby League and his club. I bet he didn't think that he would be duped into being the centre of attention and main feature of the BBC's summary of the season. The whole sorry episode even prompted comments from Maurice Lindsay regretting that the game had been made 'a figure of fun', and a press release from Super League (Europe) condemning the programme.

Given Maurice's reluctance to criticise the media, as we found in *Enough is Enough*, his comments raised an eyebrow or two.

Sadly typical of the BBC's attitude to Rugby League, and surely the low water mark of their coverage of the sport since the 'K9' incident back in Eddie Waring's era.

(For those too young, a stray dog got onto the pitch during a match at Headingley and excitedly joined in. The *Grandstand* producer saw the opportunity to ridicule the event by making a name caption for the dog, 'K9', after the robot dog on *Dr Who*.)

Thankfully, matters were looking set to improve.

Anyway, Merry Christmas.

'The M62 Game...?'

3. January 2002

Happy New Year.

Rugby League coverage is bound to be quieter during the Super League off season (although the exciting Northern Ford Premiership competition and amateur divisions continue to be played out with local media coverage only), so January seemed an opportune time to do some homework with the Press Complaints Commission. For the statistically minded, next is some research by John Finch into newspaper coverage since the beginning of the Super League era. To start with, a word from Gareth Roberts, Carlsberg-Tetley's sponsorship manager and Rugby League fan.

The smoothest beer in rugby

"Tetley's has been involved in sport for many years in various guises and continues to be proactive around its sponsorships. Although the title sponsorship of the Tetley's Super League was signed in 2000, previous to that the brand has had long associations with a number of the leading Rugby League clubs in the country. Leeds Rhinos is probably the best known, following a long-term agreement as main club sponsors that started back in 1994. However, it may not be widely known that Tetley's is also the 'official beer/supplier' at nine of the other 11 clubs that participate in the elite competition. That's 10 out of 12 clubs, a position we are extremely proud of. We are also heavily involved at the grass roots of the game an area touched on later in this section.

Let's not try and hide the fact that we do this for a reason. Tetley's invests in Rugby League to attract new drinkers. That's our objective. However, we also see ourselves as a key contributor to the game, not just financially, but to assist in delivering an experience that is second to none in sport. Once people sample the 'experience' they are hooked and will return, I know, because I've seen it.

People have different views of a sponsor, some so strong that they cannot see past the commercial reasons. However, it's now very clear that many sports just can not survive without them or certainly without the investment they make. That's the world we live these days and I can only see that increasing as time goes on. Where I see Tetley's being different to a number of sponsors out there, who are just there to get there name on a shirt or a title, is that we work extremely hard in various areas of the game to make it better. From match day branding to unique promotional campaigns, impactful advertising to an extensive PR programme, Tetley's invests further substantial sums supporting the sponsorship. That's why I firmly believe that Tetley's are a good sponsor. Yes we have to protect our rights and gain as much value as possible from our investment but at the end of the day it is business. However, I do see it in many ways to be our duty to support the game and work with those within it to achieve the sports objectives.

Two of the key areas around the sponsorship are the 'title' and the branding elements we gain at each match. My view is simple, during the time we are sponsors, the correct title of the competition is known as the Tetley's Super League. With a title sponsorship you would expect to get mentioned each time the Super League is talked about. This has been a struggle since day one and still does not happen consistently. We constantly battle against the incorrect use of the full title and get frustrated when it's not used at all. This may seem a bit petty but from a sponsors point of view the use of the title can deliver most of the value we pay for. It's about consistency and image and the 'correct' use is a return for our investment in the game.

It's also important that the game looks attractive so one of the first things we get involved in are the branded elements on the pitch. The 'look' of the game should be consistent, so every time someone comes to a game or watches it on television, they know it's a Tetley's Super League game and immediately thinks it should be a cracker. This part of the set up is now beginning to work quite well and I firmly believe that when all components are implemented the game looks so much better. Then I would say that wouldn't I, as it is all Tetley's. But, it confirms the message that there is a huge company as a partner, which is good for the image, and they are totally committed to making it look good.

Moving on, I talked earlier about the 'experience' and how people get hooked. I too have been converted from a mainly 'kiss ball' (football) follower to an avid Rugby League supporter, not bad for a person from Essex. But this shows the strength of the game and the marvellous spectacle it can be. In order for the game to secure its future, the sport needs to be marketed correctly and the experience delivered to a wider audience. We all know the matches are played in the north east and north west of the country but I know that those who watch the games on television are mainly in South Wales, the midlands and the south. This should be capitalised on and not just left as a statistic. Tetley's are trying to do their bit in reaching these people

10

by targeting these 'pockets' of interest around Britain through its natural outlet base with tailor made promotional activity. It's working for us but it could also work for the game.

Despite Sky's excellent presentation, week in week out, we also know that terrestrial coverage in any form will provide an audience of millions, again this should be one of the RFL's key objectives in developing the game in the future.

Back to our involvement in Rugby League. The title sponsorship of the elite competition provides Tetley's with a platform to build awareness of the brand. However, we also understand the importance of being involved at the grass roots of the sport. In September this year (2002), Tetley's renewed its sponsorship of the Yorkshire BARLA Cup and the Lancashire BARLA Cup and also continued its status as the Official Beer of Student Rugby League. This area is extremely important to us as it gives us a direct relationship with the 320 BARLA clubs and 70 plus Universities. Not only do we give financial support to BARLA and Student Rugby League, we can also provide a unique package to each Rugby League club tailor made to their requirements. This includes rugby equipment free of charge and support services that are second to none. Our objective here is to build the relationship with the club and work in partnership to develop their own business.

To the fans. Sometimes I feel that the fans of the game are underestimated. The previous book to this, *Enough is Enough* (that we later read was published in February 2002) clearly highlighted the extent of the fans' feelings and their commitment to the game. Rugby League has a great following of well behaved but passionate supporters, a huge plus for the game. Week in week out they turn out and create an atmosphere that cannot be beaten. They should be looked after, thanked and encouraged to speak up about the positives of the sport. They are marvellous ambassadors and should be treated accordingly. From a sponsor's point of view, it's great to be involved with a fan base that contributes so passionately and have a commitment to the team that they follow.

In finishing my section, I would like to summarise my views on our involvement. Hopefully the above has given a brief insight in to Tetley's status within the game. Simply, we sponsor with the objective to sell more beer. However, as it clearly shows we want to get under the skin of the game and work away at all levels. There are unique and beneficial packages available to all amateur and university Rugby League clubs. We are

11

committed to developing relationships with the premier clubs and their fans ensuring that everybody enjoys the experience on offer.

Tetley's too get frustrated on the lack coverage this sport gets and continue to do everything possible to address this area. However, I firmly believe that the key to the future success of the sport lies firmly with the governing bodies. They must ensure that the overall game is correctly marketed, building on the superb values it offers and the positives that already exist. If this is done effectively then fans will continue to be passionate and the game will gain the exposure it so richly deserves. They must also look after the partners in the game, whether it be Tetley's, SKY, Gilbert or any other investor, ensuring that they gain the highest value from their investment. By doing that they are then more likely to stick around and continue to invest in the game in the future.

This will be read after the Tetley's Super League Grand Final that took place on 19 October. I am sure we all have come away from the evening in Manchester with a 'wow' factor and a positive view of Tetley's Super League 2003.

Rugby League should be proud of what it's got to offer. Tetley's is proud to be its main sponsor.

A damp squib

Mention was made in *The Petition - Enough is Enough* about a fans' organisation being set up to continue to counter attack the media onslaught and to give Rugby League a positive and co-ordinated voice for media issues. Unfortunately, this never took off with only one meeting being held at the JJB complex in Wigan. A further meeting was scheduled for Yorkshire but was cancelled, and that was that. Perhaps another case of 'too many Rugby League cooks spoiling the broth.'

Still, out of this stalled start came rugby13.org. Jonty, a keen Barrow fan, had attended the one and only meeting, as well as a subsequent Rugby League Supporters Association meeting held in Salford. Here was a guy who was keen as mustard to continue the fight for justice and, true to his word, set up the rugby13.org web site.

This new site was to be used as a central 'meeting point' for fans to join forces in helping to stem the tidal wave of negative media against Rugby League. It was also envisaged for it to be used to promote the game and to try and win over certain media outlets for the benefit of the sport. It was to be tested sooner than expected and what a response from the fans….

12

Press complaints week. Week beginning 21 January 2002

A letter had gone out from Ray to Richard Caborn MP, the Minster for Sport during the Media Petition to notify him of the media attacks on Rugby League and seek his comments. This in turn was passed onto the Department of Culture, Media and Sport. A letter was received from Robin Millard from that Department suggesting that we made contact with the Press Complaints Commission. So a decision was made to organise a press complaints week to encourage Rugby League fans to write in and make their voices known as to what had gone on. This initiative was to start the week commencing the 21 January 2002.

This idea was to 'test the water' in terms of what could be achieved. Jonty set up an impressive web page with information of the campaign and some comment on the workings of the Commission. *League Express*, *Rugby Leaguer*, *Hull Daily Mail* and *Yorkshire Evening Post* were all contacted seeking publicity, as well as information being placed on the various League message boards.

Mention was made of 'testing the water' and this in fact was true in more ways than one. The Commission's function is to take in complaints about one particular piece of possible unsavoury journalism at a time and not about a mass complaint of many articles. It was also found out that the complaint had to be within one month of the supposedly offensive article being published. Now League fans' gripes are about many such press articles and not just one.

The response from the Commission was quickly followed up with many fans receiving a standard reply and booklet on how to complain. There was one complaint within the month, but as of 15 February no feedback had been received.

The exercise was still worthwhile in terms of galvanising fans together and to making fans aware what the Press Complaints Commission is all about. This though was not the end by a long chalk. Jonty was very impressed by the number of hits on the new site and encouraging e-mails from as far and wide as Ireland and France.

Footnote

It appears from replies to Rugby League fans that the Commission is a poor avenue of complaint. As we will see in Phil Stockton's article on Stephen Jones in February it is mentioned that the latter thinks Rugby League enjoys a ferocious devotion in one country, but is hardly played anywhere else on the planet. A reply from the Commission to a Rugby League fan suggested this was okay, as long at it was a personal view. Quite frankly this is a shocking state of affairs in that the comment is clearly not true, yet deemed acceptable by the regulatory authority for press honesty.

It transpires that during June the country's Prime Minister has taken the press to task for 'dishonest' media coverage, among others his highest profile complaint being about his role in the Queen Mother's funeral. Whatever the truth of the matter, the Press Complaints Commission would seem to be a toothless tiger, even when the complaint comes from the Prime Minister.

A letter to Parliament (oh no, not again!)

It was decided to write to the new Press Officer of the Parliamentary All Party Group of Rugby League MPs. This was to give Mr Cunningham MP an insight into what has gone on.

"Dear Mr Cunningham,

No doubt you will be aware of the media petition that took place last year. The petition finished with 30,000 signatories signing it and will be handed into Parliament in February. Further developments from David Hinchliffe MP are awaited.

During the course of the petition a letter was sent to the Minister for Sport, Richard Caborn MP, about the way many media outlets were attacking the game of Rugby League. Eventually I received a letter from a Robin Millard suggesting contacting the Press Complaints Commission. During the past week an exercise was undertaken to test the water in relation to the Commission. Hundreds of fans were urged to write in and make a complaint at the unfair treatment, as well as any offensive articles.

We are now receiving responses back, which show the limitations of the Commission. Any complaint has to be received within one month of the article. There is no agenda to handle mass complaints.

From a conversation with the Commission, I was then referred back to the Culture Department. So here we go to and fro. As for Robin Millard, he was only a temp and has now left.

Attempts are being made to find out if anyone has had a successful claim regarding the PCC in relation to Rugby League. Has anyone within your group had any success, or maybe know of a successful claim?

There is a new organisation being set up to try and tackle the media. You can go into rugby13.org/press for details. If it is at all possible could the fans be informed from time to time on matters within the group of Rugby League MPs? This would at least keep them in touch with your work and successes.

Yours sincerely,

Ray Gent"

Footnote

Lord Wakenham, Head of the Press Complaints Commission was forced to resign from the Press Complaints Commission during our campaign over the Enron scandal in the USA.

More media: *The Times*, *The Independent* and Rugby League

As 'a lover of the Greatest Game, a life long supporter of Leeds and a director of Derby City RLFC,' John Finch contributes his thorough and enlightening study of two of our quality broadsheet newspapers.

"Nothing seems to get Rugby League supporters more animated than the perceived treatment of their favourite sport by the media; the press in general and the BBC in particular.

No one can deny that Rugby League is attacked in the press by Rugby Union writers. This often puzzles and annoys fans who cannot understand why just one particular sport, one they often love with a passion, should be singled out in this way.

If a tennis writer used the same phrases to condemn table tennis he would simply be laughed at and the editor would seriously consider his future. However, the *Sunday Times* seems happy to publish any amount of invective from Stephen Jones. Frank Keating in the *Guardian* and more recently Chris Hewett in the *Independent* have wasted whole articles condemning a sport about which it seems to me they know next to nothing and predict its imminent demise with obvious glee. Hewett to this day, when writing about the make up of a Union team, can refer to 'the latest refugee from Rugby League land.'

The complaint against the BBC is harder to pin down and has more to do with omission by editors and presenters rather than openly hostile attacks, although features in the 'is Rugby League dying?' vein are not unknown.

15

Data Collection

I first started to collect some newspaper data for Jeremy Shires when he was running the 'Media XIII' campaign and which he needed to present to the Parliamentary Rugby League Group several years ago. I thought then that the biggest problem facing anyone making a case for the under representation of Rugby League was how do you determine what constitutes fair and equal treatment? How do you measure the popularity of a sport and even if you could, should newspapers match it with column inches?

Premiership football clubs cannot build stadia big enough yet the latest figures show a precipitous drop in people actually playing the game. Rugby Union points to its packed grounds for international matches and now claims spectators for the Zurich Premiership exceed those in Super League. Rugby League fans can nit-pick about Union always adding in season ticket holders and free tickets being handed out. On the plus side for League they can point to good television audiences, a rise in registered players and national spread of the game, thanks to the Rugby League Conference, together with the highest number of people qualified to coach the game since 1895.

As none appeared to exist, I felt it might be interesting to collect data to establish whether Rugby League was better or worse off compared to rival sports over a period of time. At least this would be a good starting point.

The data was collected from microfiche copies of the London edition of *The Times* in the local library. This is not as easy as it sounds, some pages have seven columns others eight, the pages on the fiche are not in precise order and it would be almost impossible without doubling the time taken to know if one was missing. However, the space given to four major sports, cricket, football, Rugby League and Rugby Union was measured in column inches as best as I could. This included pictures and sport specific articles but omitted results tables, fantasy leagues and the like.

I took as my starting point the launch of Super League on *Sky* TV on 28 February 1996 and measured the first full weekend in each month in the season, i.e. Friday, Saturday and Monday, from March to November from 1996 to 2001. This naturally missed weekend specific events such as the Challenge Cup final when it moved from the first weekend in May to the last in April and I hope that this applies to the other sports and even itself out.

The results

Five studies compared Rugby League coverage against other sports.

16

Study One. *The Times*: space given to cricket, football, Rugby League and Rugby Union using data for the first month in the collection series, March, year on year between 1996 and 2001.

The results show the not wholly unexpected increase in football coverage, with cricket just about hanging on to static space and a healthy year on year growth for Rugby Union. Rugby League appears to show a tiny growth in the last three years, but the step change in 1999 reflects the changing start of the Super League season rather than anything else.

Study Two. *The Times*: annual space given to cricket, football, Rugby League and Rugby Union. Looking at the total space given to the four sports across the Rugby League season, March to November, year on year.

Trend analysis shows that the space given to football has doubled in the period 1996 to 2001 and analysis of the monthly data simply confirms what is common knowledge, that is football is a now a year round sport. Cricket has increased its coverage from approximately 4,500 to 6,000 inches as befits a summer sport and Rugby Union from 3,000 to 4,500 inches mainly as a result of increased international activity in March and April and the Rugby Union World Cup in 1999. Rugby League coverage remains flat across the six years covered.

All this is against a background of increased space given to sport in general with most broadsheet newspapers having a separate sports supplement at the weekend. Thus it is important to look at the effect of this increased space.

Study Three: *The Times*: annual space given to cricket, football, Rugby League and Rugby Union, the space given to the four sports as a percentage of the total space given to the four.

Trend analysis shows that football increases its share from 49 per cent to 59 per cent, cricket has a marked decline in share from 27 per cent to 21 per cent and Rugby Union, without its mid-season months of December to February remains constant at 17 per cent. Rugby League however shows a decline of 2 percent across the years, a massive third of its percentage share of the space.

All the *Times* measurements, however, can give no indication to the qualitative coverage given to Rugby League and an immense amount of time would be needed to provide the detail required. I felt though that it should be possible to spend a few minutes a day to provide these data from my own daily paper, the *Independent*. Prior to the Keating article this would have been the *Guardian*, but a strong letter to the editor at the time had to be backed up with action and I hope they regret losing a reader loyal from as far back as his student days.

I chose the *Independent* as it boasts Dave Hadfield, one of our sport's best writers, as its Rugby League correspondent. To a certain degree, however, a writer can only be as good as the space allocated to him and on many days Hadfield can do no more than state the 'headline' facts as can be found on *Ceefax*. It is obvious that in the Rugby Union season Hewett is given considerably more space to lavish his views on the sport and players he obviously loves.

Study Four. *The Independent*: space given to Rugby League and Rugby Union in 2002 using the space given each month for the past year as gathered on a daily basis with the same conditions as outlined for *The Times*.

The peaks in the Rugby League coverage coincide with the highlights of the calendar, the Grand Final in October, the Ashes series in November and the Challenge cup in April. Anomalies in July and August seem at present to have more to do with the timing of the correspondents' holidays than the activity in the sport.

Study Five. *The Independent*: space given to Rugby League and Rugby Union respectively. Even Rugby League's main events are out covered by routine Rugby Union. Union also has highlights at this time of year and Rugby League space is pushed below 25 per cent of all space given to rugby generally Only when Rugby Union is 'on holiday' does Rugby League claim over 50 per cent of the space.

As found with *The Times*, bald column inches tell only a part of the story and in an attempt to make some qualitative assessment on an empirical basis I measured simply the number of pictures, interviews and profiles of players, coaches and owners for the two codes. Many 'mini profiles' and quotes are found buried in articles and I stipulated that they had to be stand alone interviews and profiles as I judged these are what gives the sport credence in the eyes of the disinterested reader.

Summary and Conclusions

As these studies demonstrate, over a six-year period Rugby League has struggled to maintain its share of space across the key months of March to November

Although the actual space given to the sport over the period remained constant, there is a worrying fall in 2001. Unless the New Zealand test series

18

can command greater than normal coverage this downward trend will no doubt continue in 2002.

Sport in general has received more space over the period and the other three sports have increased their column inches accordingly. Taking the percentage space given to each sport provides a method to show which sports are doing well and which are not. In 2001 Rugby League received less than 4 per cent of the total space given to cricket, football and the two codes of rugby, down from fractionally over 6 per cent in 1996. Rugby League is therefore one of the losers.

It is not possible to give precise reasons for this relative decline, but it seems that the day to day fare of the Super League is not commanding the same attention it once did in *The Times*. The heady days of the launch of Super League, the early success of London with stars such as Shaun Edwards and Martin Offiah are over.

The increase in column inches in 2000 was as a result of the Rugby League World Cup and other peaks can be detected on a monthly basis for events such as the World Club Challenge in 1997 and the New Zealand tourists in 1998, but these come along all too rarely compared with the other three sports to make a major impression on the annual figures.

The space given to the Ashes series in 2001 was not enough to compensate for the decline in the reporting of day to day activity in the sport. The impact of world cups can be seen in the figures of all four sports but long term the space given to Rugby League has remained static whilst all other sports have expanded around it.

The more detailed daily analysis in *The Independent* cannot as yet detect long term trends, but quite clearly Rugby League comes second to Rugby Union as measured in column inches. It can be said, however, that Rugby League is usually present on a daily basis, but only the high profile events of November and April push the space given to it anywhere near 1,000 column inches for the whole month. Unfortunately these are also high profile months for the other code so the share commanded by Rugby League remains at 20 to 25 per cent, similar to the rest of the season. I had in fact expected this percentage to be worse than this and it does indicate that one daily paper at least takes the sport seriously. For comparison, the proportion of rugby space given to Rugby League by the *Times* is of the order of 15 to 17 per cent.

It is in the qualitative measurements, however, that Rugby League fares badly in *The Independent*. Only the Challenge Cup and the Ashes Series pushed the monthly total of pictures above 10 whereas Rugby Union had 25 or more pictures in five out of the 13 months recorded. This is compounded by the paucity of interviews and profiles and again these nearly always accompany the high profile events of both sports, such as internationals or cup finals. I am convinced that it is these qualitative factors by which the general sporting public primarily assess the 'desirability' of a sport over the long term.

The ultimate conclusion is depressingly familiar. Rugby League must make a concerted effort to raise its general profile with good quality, positive news stories. It needs a regular competitive international calendar if it is to maintain its position relative to other sports and achieve the national profile that its fans crave. Internationals of one form or another are coming to dominate the other three sports. Apart from the two major domestic events in Rugby League it is the internationals that gain the attention of the newspapers and achieve increased quantitative and qualitative coverage.

Rugby League must follow the others or the day to day happenings of our sport will eventually be relegated to the results section of most newspapers and our stars, who we know to have few equals for skill, fitness and athleticism, will remain anonymous to all but their devotees."

Stevo, Stevo...!

Lauren Rose from the Bradford Bulls fans' message board, comments "I think Rugby League has hit the midlands, 'cos when Villa played Leeds, a bald Danny Mills was hit by the chant by Villa fans of 'Stevo, Stevo...,' so it looks like it gets recognition in other areas."

Schoolboy Rugby League, then and now

A poignant piece now from Jim Forshaw:

"On 28 August 1961, I walked into St Anselm's school in Boardman's Lane, St Helens, and at the startlingly young age of 20, commenced a teaching career which was to last 41 years, most of it in that building. Now, as I write (September 2002), I have just entered my 42nd year in the profession. Officially, I retired in 1992, but I have been asked to do a lot of part-time work during these last 10 years, so I am still a working teacher.

Just over three months before I started work, on 13 May 1961, I had watched Saints beat Wigan in the cup final at Wembley. It was the famous van Vollenhoven final and I, like so many other Saints' supporters and the game's fans, gloried in what was a magnificent occasion. Until quite recently, I kept the following day's Sunday papers, in which southern-based sports writers wrote in glowing terms about what they had seen as a great sporting spectacle. (A little bit different from what they write these days).

To follow Rugby League in those days was an absolute joy; there were at least a dozen strong teams, and each had its stars and characters. At Saints, we had players like Austin Rhodes, Tom van Vollenhoven, Mick Sullivan, Alex Murphy, Alan Prescott, Dick Huddart and Vince Karalius, and the most unsung hero of them all, Wilf Smith. Matches were almost always on Saturday afternoons; the first team at home one week and the 'A' team the next. Even the 'A' team would attract 4,000 or 5,000 spectators, and most would stay after the final whistle until the first team score came through.

The enthusiasm for Rugby League in the early 1960s was not just confined to spectating. All over St Helens little games went on in the streets and on wasteland almost every evening till it went dark. Lads from the various streets and districts used to organise teams and challenge similar teams from other areas. On Sunday afternoons, young men (and some not so young) would come out of the pubs and play in similar games. Rugby League was the sport in St Helens then, and Saints were the team.

It was in this atmosphere that I started my teaching career. My main responsibility was to impart some knowledge of our country's glorious history into those young Blackbrook and Parr minds. But what I couldn't wait to do was to get involved in the school's sport, and in particular to organise and coach the lads in Rugby League. A great friend of mine, Trevor Simms, started at St Anselms at that same time as PE teacher, and together, we held trials and selected teams in preparation for the new schoolboy season. In those days, to play rugby for your school was a great honour for any lad, and we had over 40 boys at each one of those first trials. There were only about 50 lads in each year group, so the interest was great and it was the ambition of almost every one of them to play for their school. Unfortunately, that is not the case today, but more about that later.

I was given responsibility for the younger boys, known as 'first years' in those days, (Year 7 today), and to say that they were enthusiastic would be a considerable understatement. We held the trials and picked the team, and prepared for our first match, a friendly against Parr Central away. I can still, even after 40 years, name every lad in every position in that side. In fact I still have a framed photograph of that particular team. Having helped to select them, then coach them, I held the naïve belief that there wasn't any other under-12 team in the town that could live with them. So we went to Parr Central for our first match. We lost 20-5, and were lucky to get five.

We lost some other games in that first season as well, but the enthusiasm never lessened and we got better as the season progressed. We reached the final of the Pennington Cup, the school's first ever final. We played Parr Central (again) at Knowsley Road, and lost again, this time only 9-5. It was a wonderful experience playing at Knowsley Road in our first season, and the fact that we lost didn't matter. Just 12 months later, as under-13s, that side won the school's first rugby trophy, beating St. Cuthberts at Merton Bank in the Waring Cup final.

One of the second-row forwards in that team was Alan Gwilliam, presently mine host at my favourite watering hole, Greenall's social club in Alder Hey Road, St Helens. I asked Alan what he remembered about those days. Not only could he recall the names of every one of his team-mates, he remembered the reserves as well. He also reminded me that he broke his arm in that first match against Parr Central and complained vehemently that the nurse in the hospital re-set it without an anaesthetic. But the most important comment he made concerned the pride he felt in representing his school. It was the same for all the lads who played then. Their one ambition was to get into the school team, and if they were good enough, to represent their town. That was something they and their families were really proud of.

Which brings me on nicely to the subject of schools representative rugby. I first watched St Helens schoolboys play around 1952. I was 10 years old then and I don't remember much about the game except that it was played at City Road, Leigh Schoolboys were the opponents, and Frank Carlton scored a great try. As a schoolboy myself during the 1950s, I watched some great schoolboy players, such as Norman Wills, the Mulcahy brothers, Jackie Pimblett and Derek Brown. The latter two went on to earn some success with Saints at professional level.

My own involvement with the St Helens schools set up started in 1962. I was asked to be a selector for the under-13 team, which I considered to be a great honour for someone so young and inexperienced. The interest was so great, and the competition for places in the teams so intense, that each town team had two coaches and no fewer than five selectors. Trials took place at Merton Bank. Following the under-13 trial, the under-15s came out and I was absolutely amazed at the sheer size of them. I remember the under-13s being well beaten by Wigan, but the under-15s beat Wigan quite easily.

School and town rugby

And so began an interest in inter-school and inter-town rugby, which was to last over 40 years. I have watched or been involved with every St Helens schoolboy side, at all age groups, throughout that time. I have seen many great matches, and one or two which I would sooner forget. Perhaps the most bizarre match I ever watched took place in March 1968 at The Boulevard in Hull. St Helens had a great side that season, and we expected to win the English Schools' cup. This newly introduced competition was the equivalent of the Challenge Cup as far as school lads were concerned, and having beaten Wigan Schools at Central Park in an earlier round, we travelled to meet Hull Schools in the semi-final feeling extremely confident.

The two half-backs who played for St Helens that day, Tommy O'Neill and Ken Kelly, were the best two half-backs, as a pair, that I have ever seen in schoolboy rugby. However, even their undoubted skills and class could not overcome a penalty count of 24 to one in Hull's favour and we lost by 9-8. The local press got hold of the story and expressed incredulity that any team of lads could be treated in that way, but it happened, and in spite of many protests, we were out. In fact we were out for the next three years because we withdrew from the competition in protest the following season and didn't enter again until the 1971-72 season.

During the early 1970s, however, things improved considerably. Under the guidance of Mike Ellis, undoubtedly the most successful coach that St Helens Schools ever had, the under-16 teams (the school leaving age having been raised in 1974) had three glorious years. The 1974 team won the ESRL cup, beating Leigh Schools in the final at Hilton Park. Brian Case, Ian Potter, Brian Parkes and a young Chris Arkwright were amongst a number

23

of outstanding players in that team. The following year, Chris captained the side that won the ESRL championship, and in 1976 the ESRL cup was won again. This time Knowsley Road was the venue as Oldham Schools were defeated by a side captained by Derek Traynor and including Steve Peters, who went on to play professionally for Saints. That 1976 win was the last time that the Saints under-16 town team won that prestigious competition. For an area like St Helens, steeped as it is in Rugby League history, tradition and passion, it seems incredible that 26 years have gone by without the premier schoolboy trophy coming back to the town. But there are reasons for it and I will outline them later in this piece. Suffice to say, none of the reasons have anything to do with the efforts put in over the years by a succession of dedicated teachers and enthusiasts

Chairman

The pinnacle of my own involvement with schoolboy Rugby League came in 1992 when I had the great honour to become chairman of the English Schools' Rugby League Association. During the first year of my two-year tenure of office, I hosted the schools international test match between England and France at Knowsley Road. England won 42-14, and which wasn't surprising with the number of current stars who played in that team. Gary Broadbent (now with Salford), Robert Smyth (Warrington), Francis Cummins (Leeds), Ian Knott (Wakefield), Sean Long (St Helens), Kieron Cunningham (St Helens) and Andy Leatham (Swinton).

The following year I lead the ESRL team on their tour of France and again the international match was convincingly won, this time by 40-0. Paul Sculthorpe captained that side, and other notable players that year were Daryl Cardis (Halifax), Gavin Brown (Doncaster), Wes Rogers (Rochdale), Rob Roberts (Huddersfield) and Adam Hughes (Widnes). Incidentally, the Sculthorpe family hold a rather remarkable record in schools international rugby. Paul captained that 1994 team, and two years later his younger brother Danny captained the 1996 team. No other family has provided two England Schools captains, and it is extremely unlikely to happen in the future because the Rugby Football League has recently taken steps to end all schools representative football. But more about that later.

I am often asked to name the best schoolboy player I have seen during the 40 years or so that I have been involved in the game. There have been so many great players. To help me to grasp the nettle, as it were, I asked a number of my long serving colleagues to name the three best schoolboy

24

players that they had ever watched.

Ray Unsworth, the present English Schools secretary, has been involved in schools rugby for nearly 50 years. His three were Jackie Edwards, Alex Murphy and Shaun Edwards. Jackie and Shaun, of course, are father and son. The next was Roy Knowles, who has almost as much experience in schools Rugby League as Ray. He chose Dennis Betts, Shaun Edwards and Kevin Sinfield. Dennis McHugh, who has also spent over 40 years connected to schools Rugby League, including 13 years as England Schools coach, was my third choice and he chose Shaun Edwards, Paul Sculthorpe and Kevin Sinfield. And my choices would be Chris Arkwright, Shaun Edwards and Kevin Sinfield.

Of the four of us, only Ray has a clear memory of Jackie Edwards and Alex Murphy playing at school level. He says that he didn't really have to think about it as far as those two were concerned; they were by far the best two schoolboy players that he ever watched. I myself have a very vague recollection of a game played at City Road, St Helens, in the early 1950s. It was the *Daily Dispatch* final between St Austins of St Helens and All Saints of Wigan. Alex Murphy played in that game, but it was a long time ago and all I remember is that All Saints won and the four half backs who played that evening all went on to play at international level as professionals. They were Keith Holden and David Bolton of All Saints, and Austin Rhodes and Alex Murphy of St Austins. I am reliably informed that the crowd on City Road for that game was in the region of 8,000.

What has happened to schools Rugby League in recent years? I often get stopped in the street and asked. The answer is quite long and involved so my well-meaning questioners usually walk away either confused or frustrated. I think I first detected a change in the late 1960s. Certainly by the early 1970s, the attitude of many boys to playing the game had altered for the worse. Although many were still very keen, there was a growing number who showed little interest in schools' rugby and preferred to do other things with their time. I clearly remember a boy from my own school who was big, strong, fast and skilful, and could kick goals from anywhere, confronting his teacher and telling him that he had no interest in playing for the school. I believe that all schools could quote examples like that.

And this, of course, filtered through to town team level. Boys of good ability who played for their school under sufferance had no intention of turning up on a Saturday morning to represent their town if they had the choice. So by the late 1970s, the St Helens town sides were rarely

25

representative of the true rugby talent we had in the schools. On many occasions, teachers would pace up and down in Birchley Street, (the meeting point for the coach to away matches) waiting for boys to turn up. And quite often they didn't. Teachers sometimes went round to boys' houses for them so that we had 13 to travel. There were times when St Helens Schools travelled to important away fixtures with less than a full complement of players. Jim O'Reilly (another great stalwart of St Helens schools rugby) travelled to play a very powerful Hull schools side with just 12 players.

This of course answers the question I posed earlier as to why our senior side has not won the ESRL trophy for so long. Over the years, some of the best boys we had playing rugby for either their school or their BARLA club never ever played for the town team. The problem was not quite so bad at the younger age groups (under-13 and under-11), but even there, especially under-13, there were some problems.

St Helens

In the early 1990s, St Helens schools became a force again and the present situation in our town is quite healthy. But other areas are still suffering. Many established Rugby League towns did not run under-16 teams at schools level throughout the 1980s and 1990s. And the irony of the situation is that there were more opportunities for playing the game then than ever there were in the halcyon days of the 1950s and 1960s. ESRL introduced and administrated more competitions, both regional and national, but the take-up was not what it should have been. The one association which is probably beyond criticism as far as all this is concerned is Wigan Schools. They were always very strong at every age group (and still are) and maintained their strength by managing to continue a policy which kept their town teams at the top of their agenda. Thursday afternoon was always used as town team training time. All schools agreed to not to arrange inter-school fixtures at that time. And that became a tradition that they kept for many years. We never managed to do that in St Helens.

There are several factors to account for this decline in interest in playing schools rugby. The first one involved the changing social habits which occurred during the 1960s. Boys around that era increasingly found that they had many more things to do with their time, and much more spending money in their pockets. Many of them therefore began to focus on other things rather than Rugby League or sports in general, greatly to their own detriment. Attempting, as teachers, to convince them of the error of their

26

ways usually ended in disappointing failure.

The sporting curriculum in schools changed as well, from about the early 1970s onwards. Whereas previously, games lessons for boys had just involved rugby and football, many more activities began to be introduced into the curriculum. Sports like badminton, table tennis, basketball and even squash became quite common in schools, so fewer and fewer lads were playing rugby during school time.

In 1974, BARLA was created and began to provide well-organised youth rugby right across the age spectrum from seven to 17. This was bound to impact on schools rugby. Lads decided that they could get all the rugby they needed playing for their clubs, with no 'sirs' to tell them what to do.

The final factor was the disappearance of many of the traditional Rugby League playing schools. In St Helens, for example, we lost secondary sector schools, like Holy Cross and St Austins, many years ago, and with the best will in the world, the schools that replaced them did not have the same Rugby League traditions. In addition to that, we are now without such great Rugby League playing schools as Robins Lane, Rivington Road and Parr Central. I am sure that the situation is much the same in other towns. The whole education scenario has changed, and as a result, much of that rivalry that years ago made the schools Rugby League scene so interesting and enjoyable has disappeared.

And what of the future? The inter-schools situation, as far as St Helens goes, is still relatively healthy. The old, well-established cup competitions (Pennington, Waring, Marsden, Ellison and Walsh) are still much valued and competed for with as much enthusiasm as ever they were. In addition to that, schools can now enter the regional and national competitions which were introduced by ESRL a few years ago. So, for example, as well as playing against other schools in its own town or area, a school can play a meaningful, competitive match against a school from Barrow or Cumbria, and then go on to play a Castleford school, or a Hull school. To illustrate the health of inter-schools rugby in St Helens, I know of one school that played no less than 60 games in a season just a year or two ago. That averages out at 12 games for every year group. And if that school is playing so many games, other schools must be quite well involved as well.

The Rugby Football League has quite recently taken town team rugby away from the schools associations. All youth representative rugby is now organised by bodies known as Service Areas. This is quite a new concept, so it is too early to pass any kind of judgement on it. Suffice to say that we have probably seen the last of Wigan Schools verses St Helens Schools, or indeed, Wigan Schools verses anything or anybody. Wigan Schoolboys, like St Helens Schoolboys, or Leigh Schoolboys, or indeed any town schoolboy side, have ceased to exist. Those who want to watch representative rugby at schools age will have to watch the Wigan Service Area playing against the Service area from where ever, or to be more precise, the Wigan and Leigh Service Area playing against whoever, because Leigh haven't been given a Service Area of their own. Doesn't sound quite the same, does it? But who knows, it might prove to be the answer. Only time will tell.

As for me, I'm left with just my memories, and I wouldn't change them for anything."

4. February 2002

February features the explosive opening of the professional Rugby League season, the World Club Challenge, and its predictable dousing with cold water from you know who at the *Sunday Times* (count his medals for Rugby League, won't take long).

It continues with a grilling of the BBC regarding their refusal to broadcast one of the few top quality sports they have the rights to.

The Petition - Enough is Enough takes its bow in the pantheon of literature.

World Club Challenge?

The first of February 2002 was World Club Challenge time. Bradford Bulls of Great Britain and Newcastle Knights of Australia met for the title of World Club Champions. Bradford qualified by beating Wigan in the Grand Final at Old Trafford in October 2001 before a 60,000 crowd. The Knights beat Parramatta in the Aussie Grand Final to have the right to compete.

The match was played in a downpour at a near capacity McAlpine Stadium, Huddersfield, which was eventually won convincingly by the Bulls. This followed on from St Helens beating the Brisbane Broncos in the previous year's final. All in all British teams have fared well in inter-country challenges, as past winners include Wigan three times and Widnes once. I suppose it makes up for the Ashes Test series that Australia have dominated since Roman times, or so it seems.

Now what of the media in a new year? Phil Stockton of Aberdeen catches up again with his old foe Stephen Jones of the *Sunday Times*.

Belgian stilt walking

"On Friday 1 February 2002 Bradford succeeded St Helens in becoming Rugby League's World Club Champions with a convincing victory over the NRL champions, the Newcastle Knights, at Huddersfield's McAlpine Stadium. A great achievement, not only for the Bulls and British Rugby League, but also for British sport in general.

The Australians' killer psyche has equipped them to produce world champions in many sports including cricket, hockey, netball, both codes of rugby and deliver enough defeats to all kinds of British teams to establish them as our sporting Nemesis. To vanquish an Australian team for a world

29

title in any sport is always a great victory but to do it in arguably the Australians' own national game is an achievement that all genuine British sporting fans should applaud and be proud of.

However, not all eyes in the British media saw Bradford's achievement in such glowing terms. The Rugby Union journalist Stephen Jones judged it a little differently in an article printed in the ensuing edition of the *Sunday Times*. The gist of the piece was that the title World Champions was meaningless, a bit over blown, but harmless fun. To make his point he lumped Bradford in with the recently crowned American Football Superbowl champions, stating that neither team really deserved to be called more than 'king dog of the kennel in their own backyard'. Well perhaps if Mr Jones ever 'strays' into the Bulls' backyard he can advise them of their overblown title. Perhaps they will put him straight on a few things too. Also Newcastle and Bradford are separated by over 10,000 miles - how big does he want the backyard to be?

He attempted to make the point that there was only local interest in the match by stating that joy of the result was confined to Huddersfield. Well some of it surely overflowed into Bradford, the rest of Yorkshire, Lancashire, Cumbria (these old counties alone account for a quarter of the English population) and beyond - I can personally testify to joy in Aberdeen (350 miles away).

These comments are in line with Jones' familiar theme that League has failed to appeal to a global audience and, like a number of other sports, is only followed by localised minorities of fans. Because of who he is, the subtext is that Rugby Union is a global game and can of course boast true world champions.

Regarding Bradford's World Champion credentials, he went on to question, which countries contested the title, when were they knocked out and then to emphasise his point he cheekily questioned which pool the Welsh team were in? I doubt that there are many sporting titles (if any) that are actually contested by all the countries that the title would strictly suggest should be included. And for overblown titles surely he need look no further than any further than his very own Rugby Union.

For example, Union's European Cup comprises teams from six countries; by Jones' own reasoning surely it's an exaggeration to crown any team European Champions in a competition in which only six out of over forty European countries are actually represented (less than 15%).

Moving along to the more modestly titled Five Nations, oh apologies, now Six Nations. Yes in a feeble effort at expansion, Italy has been included in this illustrious competition. A competition that boasts so many titles, from the Triple Crown to the Calcutta Cup (I wonder which pool the Indian team were in for that one?), that almost everyone is guaranteed a trophy. Yes folks nobody goes home empty-handed, well apart from Italy that is, who have won precisely one game since their inclusion and at the present rate will soon possess more wooden spoons than Delia Smith. That is probably a little cruel and demeans the undoubted efforts of the Italians but it demonstrates how easy it is to belittle anyone's efforts if you are so inclined.

But surely the most boastful of all is the Rugby (sic) World Cup. In the first place this is a title they don't even own as the RFL have the copyright to it. Secondly, the title suggests that, not only are countries from around the globe included, but also all codes of rugby are represented. It surely begs the question: when were the Kangaroos Rugby League team knocked out?

It is interesting that he catalogues American Football and League together because of an ironic twist in all this. It was Jack Gibson who significantly raised the standard of Australian Rugby League in the 1970s (and thus the rest of the game) by utilising American Football approaches to fitness and technique, particularly defensive patterns and tackling.

These defensive techniques were more recently imported into the Australian Union team by way of ex-League coach John Muggleton. Thus equipped, they conceded only one try in the whole of the 1999 Union World Cup on their way to becoming world champions (though the Kangaroos may have something to say about that). Food for thought when what you consider to be minority sports are over 20 years ahead of your own.

Back to the article, he argues that League has a great following in one country, but is played hardly elsewhere. This is incorrect, Rugby League has 20 countries in its world rankings and a further 13 listed unranked. The fact that teams from two different countries contested the WCC surely tests the very logic of his assertion.

He states that the Rugby League and American Football players belong with the Sumo wrestlers of Japan, the stilt walkers of Belgium, the Rules footballers of Australia and the Gaelic footballers and hurlers of Ireland. He catalogues League with Sumo Wrestling and Belgian stilt walking. The first has the popular image of fat blokes lumbering against each other (I know Sumo is more skilful and involved but that's an incorrect popular perception) and I have no idea what Belgian stilt walking is, but

31

clowns immediately come to mind. (I bet if the Australians took up stilt walking they'd be world champions at it, though). Here Jones attempts to associate League with the ridiculous.

What I also find curious is that he lumps Rugby League in with sports that really are principally played in one country. All sports are played on the world stage to varying degrees - I suspect that even football is not played by every nation on Earth but along with the likes of athletics and boxing can be considered at the higher end of the geographical popularity stakes. In contrast there are sports largely confined to a single country. The majority of sports fall between these two extremes. Rugby League is in this middle ground along with Rugby Union, hockey, rowing, cycling etc. All these sports boast what are widely regarded as legitimate world champions and League is no different, so why try and belittle Bradford's achievement?

Anyway, just who is Stephen Jones and what has motivated him to launch these attacks on our game?

When I initially became aware of Stephen Jones a couple of years ago I thought he was your archetypal, public school type, rah rah, hack, not just because of his attacks on League but also the tone of some of his other articles which seemed fawningly sycophantic over all things English Rugby Union. It then turns out that he is in fact Welsh. I hope he will forgive this mistake, because as an Englishman living in Scotland, I know how strongly the Celts identify with their roots. Despite his claims however, I cannot help feeling he as at least a little 'Celtic-ly challenged.'

Finally, having recently read a piece in his book *Midnight Rugby*, it would appear that all is not well in the 15-a-side code. He apparently asked 20 of his colleagues on a recent tour of South Africa if they were still in love with the sport and surroundings. It appears that all 20 were not prepared to give an unequivocal yes.

The above question was in response to Rugby Union going professional and as a consequence the game seemed less appealing and more severe. He finished by questioning if they were just more tired. Certainly the Rugby League family are tired of you Mr Jones, whoever you are."

Footnotes

This last paragraph isn't meant to be 'Union bashing' but is an interesting and very rare antidote to the usual 'booming Union, League dying' spin so often peddled as 'fact'.

On the subject of the WCC, the New Zealand Warriors, based in Auckland, play in the Australian NRL and therefore did indeed participate in the qualifying competition.

Mad March

Well, if the *Sunday Times* isn't enthusiastic about the return of the Rugby League season, what does the *Guardian* think? Matt Anniss analyses a piece written by the *Guardian's* own Grim Reaper, Frank Keating.

"The month of March is one of joyous celebration for us die-hard Leaguies. As the bitter cold of winter turns into the weak sunshine of spring, the start of Super League has us rubbing our hands with glee. Even for supporters of clubs outside the top flight, there's plenty to look forward to, including the semi-finals of the Challenge Cup, the culmination of the amateur season and the continuing drama of the Northern Ford Premiership.

Sadly, not everyone shares our excitement. Down in the newsrooms of

Wapping, Farringdon and Fleet Street, our rejoicing is matched only by the frenzied sharpening of knives. The start of Super League, you say? Sounds like a prime opportunity to stick the boot into Rugby League!

With depressing inevitability, our friends in Fleet Street rarely miss this golden opportunity to belittle the Greatest Game. This year, we had high hopes that things would be different. Since the petition campaign and Ray's tireless work to ensure fair media coverage, things have improved measurably - though sadly not enough to stop the annual ritual of Super League bashing.

Ironically, it was on the eve of the petition's Parliament presentation that the attacks begun. Predictably, it was our old friend Frank Keating who nipped in there first, devoting much of his *Guardian* column of 25th February to his thoughts on the forthcoming Super League season. Somewhat unsurprisingly, our Frank predicted the demise of the Greatest Game, choosing to paint a bleak picture of the state of our sport. To summarise, this year is make or break for League - if it fails to attract a higher profile outside the heartlands, it will die. Super League's television viewing figures, he argued, were poor, and needed to improve for Sky to even contemplate offering TGG a new contract in 2003.

As he put it: "this time there is not only the routine and bitter sporting rivalry with the ancient Union foe but Super League will also come under enormous pressure to fashion a realistic and telling profile (that is, realistic and telling viewing figures) against not only the usual high octane sporting calendar of any summer, but in 2002 against a June totally awash with the football World Cup and ditto July with the Commonwealth Games being held in its own heartlands 'backyard'."

Perhaps he has a point? I mean, there's not much evidence to support our counter argument, is there? Sky's own viewing figures suggest that Rugby League matches - both domestic and international - are among their highest-watched sports events, behind only England football games, selected Premiership soccer matches and Ryder Cup golf. Meanwhile, Challenge Cup matches on the BBC regularly attract several million viewers (significantly more than Heineken Cup Union games, the most heavily advertised television sports event in living memory) – the majority of these outside the so-called 'heartlands'.

What Keating conveniently ignores is the issue of the value of sports rights, and specifically the value of Super League to Sky. By recent standards, the amount paid for exclusive coverage of the Super League is a pittance. It is certainly considerably less than that paid for coverage of Union's Zurich Premiership, which pulls in far fewer viewers. In this respect, Rugby League is terrific value for broadcasters. In an age when many media companies are beginning to realise they've paid over the odds for sports that just don't deliver the viewers, Rugby League looks in a relatively strong position. The real test will come when the television contract is renegotiated in 2003, of course – then we'll find out just how important League is to BSkyB.

To be fair to Keating, this wasn't one of his most viscious articles, and he did make some valid points. He highlighted the stupidity of playing televised games on Friday and Saturday nights, thus making it difficult to get coverage in the following day's papers – something the more media savvy of us have been moaning about for ages.

What Keating has stumbled upon is something many of us have been banging on about for years: if there were prizes for 'shooting yourself in the foot', then Rugby League would scoop the lot.

Take this classic from Bradford Bulls skipper Robbie Paul. As Keating's inflammatory and patronising article hit the news stands, the New Zealand international was using a Bulls pre-season press conference to outline his fears for the game in this country. "If the game doesn't go forward it will die a slow death," he said, going on to explain that a new injection of cash, energy and "direction" was needed to stop the rot. "It's something I'm very emotional about because I love this sport and I want it to continue to grow."

His (selected) criticisms were obviously well meant, and they are undoubtedly valid, but the timing was appalling. Once again, the start of the British game's showpiece competition was overshadowed by headlines of entirely the wrong sort. How can we expect to persuade a new audience that our sport truly is 'The Greatest Game' when predictions of the game's demise fill the sports pages of broadsheet and tabloid newspapers? Frank Keating and his ilk rarely need an excuse to stick the boot in, so why give him the ammunition? Unless, of course, we really do want to sign our death warrant. I'll leave it to you, Mr Lewis, and the rest of the able felons at Red Hall. Actually, on the other hand…"

Bread and Butter Competition (without the jam): The BBC and the *Super League Show*.

While collecting petition signatures it was quite common to come across fans that had travelled far and wide to watch a game of professional Rugby

League. These are the same fans that don't seem to exist when it comes to being able to watch the *Super League Show* in their region. Then what about the Challenge Cup Final that is shown on a national basis and attracted an audience of around 4.5 million? Surely the same ethos should then be applied to this programme. What a load of baloney!

How about where the game is played on an amateur basis, or does this not count?

The BBC broadcasts a programme called the *Super League Show* that is transmitted in the Sunday morning regional 'opt out'. This show gives a preview and analysis of the Rugby League games that have been played in the Super League, and are to be played that day. However, it is only shown in the north and north west regions of England. League fans in other parts of the UK have to put up with repeats of *Cagney and Lacey, Star Trek* or some other ancient time filling programme.

Via the 13.org, website many e-mails have been sent to Peter Salmon, Head Controller of Sport at the BBC about the injustice of fans having to miss out. (In fact many fans tape the show and then send it to umpteen relatives and friends around the country. Yes it is a fact that we northerners do have friends and relatives outside of our stronghold.)

It has always seemed strange that many replies (if one does get one) have been contradictory. A quote from a message board (no hard copy) suggests Peter Salmon saying in an e-mail: "I'm afraid we can't at present expand our output. BSkyB are the exclusive rights holders for the competition and consequently can't show any action on terrestrial television. We can show the *Super League Show* as an opt out in the two northern regions thanks to a sub licensing agreement with Sky, but again that agreement precludes national coverage."

The above has supposedly been blown apart with an e-mail from Vic Wakeling, Managing Director at Sky Sports. "We have allowed the BBC in the north to use footage for highlight purposes, only to help in the promotion of the game. There is no geographical limit, and we have not received any requests for use from any BBC region."

So what's the truth? Ask for yourself at peter.salmon@bbc.com. Lots more about this in July.

E-mailing the BBC

Here are some of the e-mails to the BBC about the *Super League Show*. These are only a few of many that are winging their way in February 2002.

Saint Billinge (who he?)

"For some time now Rugby League fans have been told that the *Super League Show* can only be shown in the northern regions because of contracts with Sky TV. It seems this was blown out of the water by an e-mail sent to a fan from a Sky producer who has said it could go nationwide but no one from the BBC has made a request.

It does seem strange that someone at the BBC is now changing their mind in another e-mail saying that that it is only shown in the northern regions as that it where the most interest is. This comment is a strange one when in fact the Challenge Cup is shown nationwide.

Further to this, Rugby League has a thriving Rugby League Conference with teams in such places as Cardiff, South Norfolk, Ipswich, Sunderland, Birmingham, Coventry and London. There are around 48 colleges and universities playing the sport nationwide, as well 170 amateur and armed forces teams. It is a fact that Rugby League is played in every county in England, as well as teams in Scotland, Ireland and Wales.

A Media Petition was organised last year against the way certain media outlets attack and discriminate against Rugby League. 30,000 fans signed it and it will go to Parliament soon. It was noticeable that many signatories travel far and wide to watch a professional game of Rugby League, as well as supporting the amateur game.

Why is it then that certain media outlets continue to bracket the game as a sport for them 'up there'?

Come on the BBC show some courage and fair play and help spread the word about a fine sport that has had to suffer over 100 years of discrimination."

Northampton Saint.

"Why don't you broadcast the Super League Show nationwide?

By not doing so you are being inconsistent – when showing Challenge Cup games, you show them nationwide. Despite claiming to have a commitment to the game of Rugby League, the BBC is treating it like an embarrassing cousin who is best regarded as out-of-sight, out-of-mind.

I am confident the programme would generate better viewing figures than your current schedule."

London Saint.

"I am writing to complain about the *Super League Show* not being shown nationwide. I am a St. Helens fan exiled in London and until recently didn't know the programme existed on the BBC. Rugby League gets a raw deal from the media in this country (very Union biased), which is down right unfair on the second most popular spectator sport in the UK".

Doghead

"Dear Mr Salmon,
Further evidence of the popularity of Rugby League in Britain and Ireland Rugby League playing towns or cities in Great Britain & Ireland. Many of these places have multiple clubs and have multiple teams within those clubs across multiple villages... For example on the amateur list: In Leeds area ARL there are 135 teams registered with BARLA (British Amateur Rugby League Association), and the team from Drighlington ARLFC for example runs 11 sub teams every weekend. - In London ARL area there are 21 teams registered and London Skolars ARLFC run 6 sub teams.

Some towns may run teams in more than one area of Rugby League and therefore may appear in different sections.

Super League: St Helens, London, Warrington, Leeds, Bradford, Salford, Halifax, Castleford, Wigan, Hull, Widnes, Wakefield.

Northern Ford Premiership: Huddersfield, Gateshead, Oldham, Sheffield, Workington, Barrow, Batley, Keighley, Whitehaven, Hunslet, Hull, Chorley, Leigh, Rochdale, Swinton, Featherstone, Doncaster, Dewsbury.

Rugby League Conference (England and Wales): Hemel Hempstead, Cardiff, Crawley, North London, West London, South London, Worcester, St Albans, Oxford, Cambridge, Bedford, Kingston, Rotherham, Gloucester, Nottingham, Ipswich, Coventry, Leicester, Birmingham, Crewe, Chester, Derby, Wolverhampton, Bridlington, Newcastle, Sunderland, Durham, Teeside, Manchester, Luton.

Ireland Conference League: Dublin Blues, Dublin City, Churchtown, Clontarf, Cork, Carbury, West Coast, Suir Valley.

Scotland Conference League: Glasgow, Edinburgh, Lockerbie, Portobello, Boness, Alexandria, Clyde.

Universities (England and Wales): Warrington, Leicester, Leeds, Liverpool, Teesside, Loughborough, Cardiff, Birmingham, Nottingham, Lincoln, Crewe, Oxford, Cambridge, Luton, Hertfordshire, Northampton, Bedford, Cheltenham, Stafford, Durham, Newcastle, Northumbria, Sunderland, Portsmouth, Brighton, London, Greenwich, Manchester, Chester, Lancaster, Salford, Glamorgan, Swansea, Bristol, Exeter, Barnsley, Sheffield, Bradford, Hull, York, Huddersfield.

BARLA: York, Workington, Woodlesford, Wigton, Wigan, Wibsey, Whitehaven,

Warrington, Wallsend, Wakefield, Ulverston, Twickenham, Todmorden, Thetford, Telford, Swansea, Surrey, Sunderland, Suffolk, Stoke on Trent, Stirlingshire, Stainland, St Helens, St Albans, Sowerby, Southampton, Southport, Sheffield, South Shiels, Sharlston, Selby, Scarborough, Salford, Rochdale, Redhill, Preston, Pontypridd, Portsmouth, Pontefract, Plymouth, Penrith, Oxford, Ormskirk, Oldham, Nottingham, Normanton, Newcastle Upon Tyne, Newmarket, New Elvet, Morecambe, Moorends, Mirfield, Millom, Middlesborough, Maryport, Manchester, Luton, Loughborough, London, Liversedge, Liverpool, Littleborough, Lincoln, Leyland, Lenton, Leigh , Leicester, Leeds, Lancaster, Knottingley, Kingston Upon Hull, Keighley, Jarrow, Isleworth, Huntington, Hull, Huddersfield, Horsforth, Hindley, Heslington, Hemel Hempstead, Headington, Halifax, Guisley, Cockermouth, Gloucester, Glasgow, Fleetwood, Filey, Featherstone, Exeter, Eltham, Elland, Egremont, Edinburgh, Eccles, Earby, Doncaster, Dewsbury, Derby, Dalton-in- Furness, Durham, Cyncoed, Coventry, Colne, Clifton, Cleator Moor, Choohiro, Chester, Cheltenham, Castleford, Carlisle, Cambridge, Bury, Burtonwood, Burnley, Brotherton, Bristol, Brighouse, Bradford, Bolton, Blackpool, Birmingham, Binley, Bingley, Beverley, Bedford, Batley, Barrow-in-Furness, Barnsley, Bailrigg, Askam-in-Furness, Annan, Alsager, Alexandria, Accrington and others.

Armed Forces / Services: RAF Bruggen, RAF Wittering, RAF Cottesmore, RAF Coningsby, RAF Aldergrove, RAF Leeming, RAF Honington Centurians, RAF Brize Norton, NAVY Royal Marines (Plymouth), NAVY HMS Collingwood, NAVY Portsmouth Command, NAVY Scottish Command, ARMY Light Dragoons, ARMY Fort Blockhouse, ARMY 38 Engineer Regiment, ARMY 2 Signals Regiment, ARMY 1 KORBR, ARMY Sennelager Stags ARLFC, ARMY 1 QLR ARLFC, ARMY 36 Engineer Regiment, ARMY QRH ARLFC, ARMY 3 BN REME, ARMY 7 Signal Regiment, ARMY 35 Engineer Regiment ARLFC, ARMY 26 Regiment Royal Artillery, ARMY 7 Royal Horse Artillery, ARMY 11 Signals Regiment, ARMY 1 PWO ARLFC, ARMY 2nd Battalion Royal Green Jackets, ARMY 47 Regiment RA, ARMY RDG, ARMY 25 Engineer Regiment, ARMY 28 Engineer Regiment ARLFC, ARMY 1 RRW, ARMY 3 RSME ARLFC, ARMY 10 Regt RLC, ARMY SEAE, ARMY 2 RRF ARLFC, ARMY 1 RSME ARLFC, ARMY 2 Close Support Regiment Royal Logistics Corp, ARMY 30 Signal Regiment, ARMY 6 Supply Regiment RLC ARLFC, ARMY Rheindhlen Lions Rugby League, ARMY SEME London Met Police.

And not forgetting Cynon Valley Cougars.

A Northern only sport? I don't think so it gets bigger and better every season.

A. Whittle"

(Stats supplied by Paul Cunliffe of the Rugby League Supporters Association and John Grime, a student.)

Over 95 per cent of the English population now live within half an hour's drive of a Rugby League team. Over 45 per cent have one in their own town or city.

Add in the many supporters who like Rugby League *per se* around the country and there seems no reasonable excuse not to show the *Super League Show* across Britain. Apologies if anyone has been missed off this ever growing list, as we are sure many are.

No point fighting!

Just as this book has been started there was an article in the *Daily Star* by (Rugby League) writer Peter Wilson. This is in response to a press release from Paul Cunliffe of the RLSA as to why the *Super League Show* was not being shown nationwide.

Peter Wilson wrote: "There are some causes worth fighting for - but I am not sure the latest taken up by the Rugby League Supporters Association is one of them. They want the BBC to screen their *Super League Show* nationwide rather than in the north alone.

But the fact is that all but one of the Super League clubs are in the north; the exception being the Broncos, who still have to establish themselves in London.

I suspect the Beeb will suffer the complaints from little pockets of 'disschuffeds' of Cheltenham and Basingstoke rather than slot in what they see as a northern sports programme on a Sunday morning."

I don't suppose it matters to Peter Wilson that there are many people around the country that wouldn't mind at least having the programme tried out to see what response it got.

Wasn't it Peter Jackson of the *Daily Mail* on 12 February 2002 suggesting that Rugby League wouldn't mind the publicity that Rugby Union receives? This was in response to Leicester Tigers RFC complaining about the bad press Martin Johnson (Leicester and England Rugby Union captain) received in regards to a punch on an opposing player. He said: "Ah yes, blame those beastly television people from Sky whose millions keep the club game afloat, and those newspapers whose daily coverage of the sport is something Rugby League would kill for."

Apparently, Martin Johnson got himself in deep water, not only with regards to the punch but also with the media. Stephen Bierley of the *Guardian* also had a scathing report with a headline of "An amateurish game that still demands an eye for an eye." It starts with: "Rugby Union is intrinsically a game of institutionalised covert court violence, where the strong look after the not so strong behind closed doors of the ruck, the maul and scrum. It is the code of the barracks or prison wing, where anybody who steps out of line is swiftly and silently dealt with on the basis of an eye for an

40

eye. Officialdom looks the other way, happy not to get involved, knowing that the unwritten law of retribution makes life that little bit easier."

The trouble is that some players - and the England team captain is the latest example - will insist on acting the amateur fathead and throwing punches under the nose of the referee." It goes on to mention "yellow and red cards were introduced to try and stop foul play but concealed thuggery still goes on, with the cards of little use."

Yes indeed. If Rugby League were given substantial positive publicity on an ongoing basis it would benefit the game immensely.

A change in the weather

Like a head of corn blowing in the wind, Peter Jackson of the *Daily Mail*, 26 February 2002 was this time in good League form for a change. He praised the Rugby League disciplinary system in an article headed: "If League can throw the book at its bad boys in just four days, why can't Union?" The thread of the article was to question the Martin Johnson saga of not being instantly disciplined by the RFU, but being strung out to enable him to play against France in an international.

It appears that the drama is rumbling on into a fourth week, whereas in League it would have been done and dusted within the week. It also questions why League can find a high court judge to chair its panel at a day's notice when Union cannot. Peter Jackson finishes with "Rugby League 1 Rugby Union 0." Maybe not quite in terms of what League has had to put up with, but still a smack in the nose for Stephen Jones of the *Sunday Times* who suggested some while back that Union has nothing to gain from League.

French in the Commonwealth Games

Still in February, Ray French, the current BBC Rugby League commentator and journalist has started the 'rugby' topic again on the BBC website. An all-action picture of Jason Robinson, a Rugby Union convert from Rugby League in 2001 is pictured in action to publicise the 'rugby sevens' tournament at the forthcoming 2002 Commonwealth games to be held in Manchester. He queries if League players Kris Radlinski, Shaun Long, Paul Sculthorpe and Paul Deacon will be starring in the tournament.

"Of course not!" is his reply. "It's the same discrimination, which kept the 13-a-side code out of the armed forces, universities and colleges for over

41

100 years and is now keeping the sport out of the Commonwealth games."

The term 'rugby' is becoming a sensitive point with regard to League fans. It totally confuses the general public into thinking that there is only one kind of rugby. David Hinchliffe MP questioned the Minister for Sport, Richard Caborn MP, about a statement he made. This went along the lines of "Rugby sevens is governed by the Rugby Football Union in England."

The reply was sweet. "They do for Rugby Union, Mr Caborn, but they don't for Rugby League. Rugby Union sevens is governed by the RFU and not rugby sevens." England, Ireland, Scotland, Wales, South Africa, Australia, New Zealand, Canada, Cook Islands, Samoa, Fiji and Tonga are all eligible to take part in the Rugby Union Sevens, yet don't all these countries also play Rugby League?

Monday, 18 February: An historic day

The day was as grim as a Leigh miner just surfacing from the pit, evening time as black as his face.

It was cold and wet, yet Ray was as excited as a thousand Christmases put together. It was now time to pick up his books with Roger Grime. Anticipation was to the fore, with a degree of uncertainty as to what was ahead. Would the book be all he had dreamed of?

After getting slightly lost in the Manchester streets, we eventually arrived at the printers, with Andy the publisher showing a sign of relief with a mop of the brow that we had arrived. After loading up it was on our way back.

On returning to Roger's it was time to have a good look at the finished article, and I must say what a great effort from Andy at Parrs Wood Press and the printers.

After delivering a few that night I spent all of the next day either delivering or posting and eventually waiting for some feedback on my first book. Can I say in print that I was eventually overwhelmed by the fans feedback? Listed below are a few comments.

Razorjack: "This book is a must for anyone who cares about the game of Rugby League. If you haven't yet bought your copy, I urge you to do so now.

It is a very professionally produced and a great contribution to our cause. Don't let all the hard work go unrewarded."

WKH: "Keith and I received your book this morning, started reading it on the train. Highly absorbing read, summarising what we've had to put up with lately makes my blood boil."

MR. WKH (or alias the Judge now gone from shipping tycoon to selling pies): "Typical isn't it, I don't get to read it first. Everything I buy for myself, my wife WKH takes it from wherever I leave it for a minute, and I don't see it for a few days. Hope she reads the book quicker as the 'quick' glance I had this morning was very encouraging and it looks like a 'belter'."

South Wales Saint: "Got to agree the book is an absolute cracking read. I only got back home late last night to find the book had been delivered. As I was tired, I thought I'd have a quick flip through just to see what it was like. Over an hour later, I was still there reading. It's a professionally produced book, which is sometimes humorous, sometimes sad (when put down in black and white the bigoted opinions of some folk just beggar belief), often thought-provoking and always entertaining from cover to cover."

XYZ: "I'll be honest now, I've never read a book in my life cover to cover but… if you were at all interested in this I would *highly* recommend it. I will have to admit that I was laughing at times, so there is humour in there too."

Jack Whittaker: "This book is a 'must have' for anyone who cares about the game of Rugby League. If you haven't bought a copy, then I urge you to do so now."

There were many more great comments – and not without a fight or two for first read. Hope I haven't caused any matrimonial splits, else it maybe a lawyer job?

I'll have six

Wendy Neal, a client of Ray's, decided to secretly order three books, one was for Bernard, her partner, and one each for their respective fathers. All three books had been paid for in advance by Wendy with names to be printed inside in the subscribers list pages. Anyway, when the books were delivered, and being so busy, they were put through their letter box by yours truly without thinking. A few days later a letter was received from Bernard, and what a laugh.

Bernard had sent me another cheque for the books and to say that he had given one away, while another was to go to his club, Chorley RUFC. I quickly had to make an apologetic phone call to say that the two other books were meant for dads. Suffice to say another book had to be ordered. It is a fact that the couple are like passing ships in the night, and even if they lived on a desert island they would still pass each other by.

I did question why an ardent amateur Rugby League player was now playing Rugby Union? 'The old bones won't take to playing League anymore' came the response. I didn't think that Bernard would ever go out to pasture, which is no offence to our Rugby Union counterparts.

Challenge Cup cheer from *The Times* and *Guardian*

The Challenge Cup now includes four French teams and their inclusion has generated interest both here and in France.

Widnes are back in the top flight, promoted this year to Super League, after six years in the NFP, introducing a fresh impetus to a competition that was perhaps getting stale for the want of some new blood.

Vikings set out to conquer all over again

Christopher Irvine wrote in *The Times* in February 2002: "In the seven years since Widnes last featured on *Grandstand*, the impressive, council-built Halton Stadium is far from the only difference. The Cheshire club, which flirted with financial ruin even in the good times, is back on an even keel. In retrospect, missing the Super League cut was the best thing to happen to Widnes, for the six years that it has taken them to rejoin the elite has been about putting right the mess of the past..."

"With Widnes also featuring on television in their opening Super League fixture at home to St Helens next Saturday, the club is making the most of the exposure. Sponsors have been flocking to get on board and there is keen expectation in the Rugby League-mad town, despite a generation having passed since the glory era and more modest ambitions in the present day..."

"Jason Demetriou, a young Australian threequarter, who turned up at Widnes to chance his luck and was a cornerstone of last year's success, said: 'You just don't play rugby here, you get involved in the whole club and the town. Widnes takes a hold of you... Widnes back in a Challenge Cup final has got everyone there dreaming'."

Wigan get the royal treatment on French trip
Challenge Cup gives Treiziste a chance to show their credentials

Andy Wilson wrote in *The Guardian* on 23 February 2002: "They found the foyer of the team hotel packed with autograph-hunters. Then yesterday morning Andy Farrell awoke to find his salary printed in Euros in the local *L'Indépendant* newspaper - a first, for Farrell and Rugby League.

The visit of 'la célèbre équipe de Wigan' in 'la prestigieuse Cup Anglaise' has provided France's battling treizistes with easily their biggest day since they successfully hosted a group in the 2000 World Cup.

The match is significant not only for UTC but for the French game in general: it comes at a time when their campaign to return to the Super League is gathering momentum. More than four years have passed since Paris St Germain, the club who gave the Super League its European dimension and kicked off the summer era by beating Sheffield in front of an 18,000 crowd at the Charlety Stadium, were kicked out to make way for Huddersfield.

...Now Maurice Lindsay, and many other Super League power brokers that have looked enviously at the success of Union's European Cup, believe the time is right for the French to return.' I don't know whether their playing standards will handle Super League or not,' he added, 'because they are not full-time professionals. But the simple truth is, if you want to develop the game in France, you have to put a team in a European League'."

Excellent articles from the two newspapers, yet what of the BBC? The Saturday game between Warrington and Saints was shown on BBC, yet didn't get a mention in the evening sports news desk.

Maurice's mischief

On the eve of the new Super League season, what better than to wheel out a northern stereotype to provide a negative spoiler?

Maurice Bamford, the former Great Britain coach from 1984 to 1986 was quoted by the BBC on 28 February 2002 as saying: "British Rugby League will relinquish its status as full-time and return to largely being an amateur sport." A fervent traditionalist, Bamford believes the switch to summer rugby and the advent of full time professionalism in 1996 will one day come back to haunt the game.

"I maintain that one day the amateur game will be the saviour of Rugby League football." It seems his opinion is that the game has become too reliant on Sky TV money and overseas players. "When all the television monies have been exhausted and the foolish spenders are skint, I feel the game will return to the amateur ways once again."

The response from some fans was a metaphorical rolling of the eyes – 'better in my day' Maurice again!' Typically, on the eve of Super League VII, this follows on from similar outbursts from the likes of Maurice and other ex-players and coaches at such times. At the end of the day negative comments like this can't do our game any good – but who prompts them and why?

To quote Allan Reeve from *The Petition - Enough is Enough*: "doing your dirty washing in public... sums up what damage can be done to the game." It's interesting to hear what former characters - players and coaches - have to say, but it's a shame when their purpose extends little further than for a ready and reliable source of negative 'rentaquotes'.

(Note: Maurice's book is called '*Memoirs of a Blood and Thunder Coach*' and is widely available from good bookshops.)

'The M62 Game...?'

46

5. March 2002

An eventful month for Rugby League. Ray monitors the launch of the Super League VII season, the Challenge Cup, responds to Mr Barnes' (and others') untimely swipe at the game and spins the yarn of the submission of the Media Petition to Parliament.

Rugby League hits the back page

The first match of the Super League season has come and gone with a first win in the Super League era for the Bradford Bulls at the new home of Wigan in front of a 14,000 crowd. Now for the aftermath, did it register with Fleet Street?

The *Daily Mail*, on Saturday 2 March 2002, had a picture of a Bradford Bulls player on the back page, as well as a report inside. This had several League fans visiting the cardiac unit of their local hospitals and booking appointments at the opticians. What made it even more surprising was the fact that it was on the same day as the France versus England Rugby Union international, incidentally won by France 20-15. This would normally swallow up the much of the sports section, just behind football.

Even more good news was that there were several other good articles in the *Daily Mirror, Sun, Daily Express* and many more papers. What is interesting is that the match kicked off at 8pm on a Friday evening when many tell us that it is too late for the press to give a report the next day. Still, well done the press on this occasion.

However, it still appears that many outside of the heartlands still don't get much coverage of Rugby League. The one notable exception is the *Metro* free paper that by all accounts is fabulous as far as Rugby League goes, and is in fact in the *Daily Mail* stable. In fact the *Metro* went on to sponsor the London Broncos, so well done the *Metro*.

Obviously the *Independent* is another Rugby League friendly paper that is well received by fans.

Catch a falling star

Taken from the Bradford Bulls website in March, a balanced view which should have had Mr Ackford's ears burning.

"I am writing concerning an article written by Paul Ackford on the 3 March 2002, about England's so called 'grand slump'.

I was disgusted by certain comments concerning Henry Paul in this article. I fail to see how Paul Ackford can say Henry Paul was out of his depth and that Woodward 'seriously wounded' England by picking him, he, like all of the team, made mistakes, but unlike some he also made some good runs, showed quick handling and eagerness.

On one occasion Paul got himself into a great try scoring position, but as so often happens in his Union career, he failed to receive the ball from his teammate. How can anyone excel when he seldom gets the ball? Ackford seems to overlook the fact that France scored no tries after the arrival of Paul, that England scored almost immediately after Paul's appearance and also that Wilkinson, supposed nation's hero, did not have his greatest game ever.

Well actually the article says 'Wilkinson was simply not allowed to play,' which I agree with but then it continues saying 'he will be richer for the experience, and all credit to him for never giving up.' Yet when it comes to Paul, who just happens to be a New Zealander and former Rugby League star, it's 'Paul was out of his depth.'

On important occasions when England was pressing it was Paul's errors, which clogged up promising attacks. 'Picking him was a disaster.' The article fails to say that he gave it his all, he did no worse than any other player and was rarely given an opportunity to show his talents on the ball, as more often than not he was the missed out man.

Next time maybe Mr Ackford should look to the so-called stars of the England team, namely a certain Johnson (who should not have even been playing, maybe justice was done in England losing?) and Wilkinson, and that's just for starters.

Some reporters disgust me with their tendency to blame the least recognised people in the team (who do as much, if not more than the recognised players) and condone the so-called stars' below average performances.

Yet again Paul's talent has been put to waste, which seems to be the story of his Union career so far. All I can say is Henry, we (League fans) know you can do it, you haven't anything to prove to us and you are much more appreciated in League!

Hannah Mason (aged 14)"

Strange how one minute you are being hailed as the next Union international great, while next you are taking the journalistic flack. At least Hannah doesn't bare any grudges as far as Henry Paul switching to Union.

Would that the anti-League journalists in our national papers would be as open minded.

Talking of an ill wind - James Lowes

It is very seldom that one hears of players publicly commenting on their opposite numbers in the other code, but a rare exception from James Lowes, Bradford, Ireland and Great Britain hooker, as published on the Bradford Bulls website during March.

Lowes criticised Stuart Barnes for his comments on Henry Paul's performance for the England Union team. He argued that Barnes would never accept League players in Union, and had "only just grudgingly started giving Jason Robinson any praise at all. He didn't give any constructive criticism of Henry at all; he just bagged him all the time."

Lowes felt that Barnes, in his opinion, was "the worst commentator on any sport I have heard".

Strong stuff, Jimmy. I wonder what Chris Caisley, his Chairman, thought, given that he also runs Wakefield Rugby Union club?

Simon Barnes writes to Parliament

Seemingly short of an original current subject Simon Barnes of the *Times* penned another League-bashing article (11 March 2002) about the state of Rugby League and goes to show that an ill wind, as above, just blows and blows.

The article starts with his having just finished a letter to the All-Parliamentary Group of Rugby League MPs, when on a whim, he switched television channel during the half time of the Newcastle versus Arsenal match to see the goings on at the London Broncos versus Wigan Rugby League game. He is quoted as saying "The match appeared to be taking place in a warehouse used for the storage of stadium seating."

It goes on to question why David Hinchliffe MP could find the time to take Mr Barnes to task for suggesting that Rugby League is about to be swallowed up by Rugby Union, when there are far more important issues such as trying to solve the Third World debt, halting the ecological holocaust and achieving world peace. (all in one go I presume?)

It continues smirking that he (Simon Barnes) read too much into the fact

49

that Jason Robinson, Henry Paul and Iestyn Harris left Rugby League and won international recognition at Union. It mentions other players that have since left Rugby League to go back to the game of Union. (see my reply for details)

Mention is made that Rugby Union was behind Rugby League in terms of defensive strategy but since gaining several League coaches, it has now changed. It appears from the text that he is saying that Union is now appearing to be more like League. There is a short mention of the Johnson affair in that Union still need to learn more about disciplinary procedures.

It wonders if Henry Paul would become home sick for the M62 corridor, when in fact he is going to the Far East to play Rugby Union sevens. He quotes a statistic that: "The BBC gets an average of 1.9 million viewers for club Rugby League: for big Union international they get six million". (I wonder if by club Rugby League he meant Challenge Cup – if so his stats are sadly wayward from the BBC's own, and as we have established, the BBC don't show regular club League games nationally to draw any stats from.). Ill researched or just misleading?

All in all we are back to the argument that League can't compete against Union and will ultimately end up as a fusion of the two codes. (Now who has said that before? Yawn, yawn.)

Now I don't suppose my reply will have him choking on his cornflakes but I did have a laugh writing it?

"Dear Sir,

Early indications suggest that the *Media Petition* book is selling well. It now appears that some scribes who scribble rubbish are fighting to get included in the follow-up book. No doubt you must have bought a copy and realised that that one of your articles is included, although I must admit that [in my opinion] you lack the talent to be another Stephen Jones or Frank Keating.

You mentioned in your article on 11 March 2002 that the Broncos versus Wigan match shown live on television appeared to be in a stadium used for the storage of stadium seating. The actual attendance being 4,284. However, did you know that the impressive Headingley stadium had a lock out for the Leeds Tykes versus Bristol Rugby Union game on the same weekend? Someone must have forgot to open up several gates, as the attendance was just over 2,200. I suppose next time you could provide a locksmith.

What about the rest of Rugby League's fixtures for the said period. Over 10,000 attended the St Helens versus Salford game on the Friday, while

Bradford had 13,876. 8,192 watched the Castleford game, 8,091 at Hull and 4,159 at Halifax. In fact the Bradford game produced a larger attendance that than either of the major Union semi-finals. A mere League match gaining more support than major Union semi-finals.

Now what of Henry Paul? You say he has been chosen for England for the Hong Kong and Beijing Rugby Union sevens tournament and should not miss the M62 corridor. Strange one this, as some of your fellow journalists crucified the man for his performance against France in a full England shirt. Comment was made that the sevens tournament was in fact relegation for him.

Mention is made of Scott Gibbs, David Young, Allan Bateman, Scott Quinnell and Alan Tait going back to Rugby Union. But surely some of these players were past their best at the time. In any event, it is a good job that Rugby Union changed the rules to allow such players to grace the Union game once again. I take it you have forgot about the ban that was imposed for over 100 years?

Lastly, if David Hinchliffe MP found the time from a busy workload of saving the world to 'upbraid' you in relation to say that Rugby League is not a dying sport, then how do you manage to find time writing articles that are not informative, or well written? Maybe you should join David Hinchliffe MP and write about the Third World debt, achieving world peace and solving the ecological holocaust. But then again I just wonder if you have the brain like David Hinchliffe MP to perform on a higher stage? Still, I could give you a mention in the next book to liven up your life.

Yours sincerely, Ray Gent"

No reply from Simon. Like so many others, in my opinion, a big man behind his keyboard.

A fan responds

KOL, a Bradford fan was stung into a reply:

"The comments made by Simon Barnes on the subject of Rugby League are in my view disgrace to your publication. His comments are that of a comic and maybe he should consider a switch of career.

From what I assumed to be an articulate, informed, intelligent and unbiased newspaper, here we are presented what I consider to be comments like those of a five year old child, and a misinformed one at that.

I follow all types of sport and like many southern dwellers, have been exposed to the game of Rugby League through Sky television and can appreciate the following it gets. Does Mr Barnes know that Rugby League is the second most watched sport, at a domestic level in Britain?

His comments on Mr H. Paul are also unfounded. Does he realise that Mr Paul travelled extensively throughout the south west Pacific with his New Zealand national Rugby League team. Also, he is currently unhappy with the Rugby Union training set up, calling it 'a step backwards'.

Maybe, Mr Barnes would rather like to comment on Mr I. Harris, the decay of Welsh Rugby Union and the hardship the RFU are enduring following the conversion to professionalism.

Finally, he may wish to comment on how the Rev Frank Marshall (aka The Witch Doctor of professionalism) would turn in his grave to see his beloved Rugby Union players receiving a full time salary.

An apology is expected from Mr Barnes on his [in my view] ignorance."

Doubt if KOL got a reply either.

Saints or sinners?

During March, Stuart Duffy, the Bradford Bulls' media manager penned a brilliant article about the petition and book for the Bradford versus Warrington programme. Likewise, Peter Roe the Wakefield coach gave a great account of the book on the Wakefield website and Ray French wrote a very good article in the *Rugby Leaguer*. Brian Kelly, chief executive of St Helens and Eammon McManus, the new chairman, generously came forward with some monetary help with regards to the travel costs to London for the petition hand over day in Parliament.

Many clubs decided to sell the book but others declined for their own reasons. There were still some in the game that spurned or opposed the petition and all that can be said is that they are entitled to their opinion, even if it is out of step with so many of their paying customers.

And now for Parliament: The march south

From its humble beginning in May 2001, the Media Petition grew in stature as the word was spread by internet, local newspapers, local radio and onto Sky TV. It eventually amassed 30,000 plus signatories and was indeed a magnificent achievement by all those that contributed.

It will never change the world, and there will still be those who make it their business to downgrade the game of Rugby League, but it will act as a marker for the Rugby League family in future years. It was indeed an historic occasion in the patchwork tapestry of 'The Greatest Game'.

Although it had an uncertain start in terms of how many would sign it, there was always an inner belief by those involved that it would reach the high echelons of power. As the Speaker of the House of Commons would eventually speak of it no detractor could say it fell short. And so my friends, here is an account of progress to its final destination on the 20 March 2001.

Ray's tale unravels commencing the Tuesday before 20 March. It was to be an early start, as I had to tidy some personal office work up, as well as finalise several matters to do with the petition. Contact was made with the *Widnes Weekly News, Warrington Guardian, Yorkshire Evening Post* and *Hull Daily Mail*. Being that busy I had forgot about the press release that had been issued from the Rugby League Supporters Association. And, without warning, a telephone call was received from the BBC. The enquirer asked about the petition handover the next day, so that it could be included on the BBC website, and it must be said that it was very impressive.

From the above, an early lunch had to be cancelled due to Alan Robb of Radio 5 Live requesting an interview for 12.15pm. Contact was also made with David Hinchliffe MP regarding some publicity with *BBC Look North* in Yorkshire. Once contact was made, there was a request to see if some information could be delivered to the Leeds studio. They wanted a copy of *The Petition - Enough is Enough* and some press articles that had been gathered over the previous year. As I was journeying over to stay with Geoff Lee of Shipley near Bradford before travelling down to London, I said I would deliver them to a courier later on. There was also the matter of contacting Angela Powers at Sky TV to finalise the filming.

The morning progressed at a hectic pace, akin to a marathon, as more phone calls were received, as well as trying to catch up with work. Eventually the journey to Yorkshire commenced, and what a mad dash is was to get there on time. It was certainly a pleasure to arrive at Geoff's and put my feet up.

Parliament day arrives - the journey

It's 6.30 am on 20 March 2002 and time for the big event for Rugby League. 30,000 voices (in spirit) are travelling down to good old London town for the Media Petition hand-over. After a quick shower and shave it's panic time. Seem to have misplaced my car keys and credit cards. Geoff joined in the search but no luck. Then it dawned on me that I had called at the bank the night before and realised that they were in my coat under the stairs. In the panic Geoff nearly burnt the house down, as he had forgotten that the toaster was on.

Now off to Shipley railway station via a brisk walk through the town. Could do with a donkey to carry the very heavy books of signatures. More panic, as we couldn't find how to buy a ticket. However, there in front of us was a machine that took a 10p coin for an entry ticket onto the platform. Payment could be made on the train, or at Leeds.

Arriving at Leeds railway station all appears bedlam, as folk scurry here and there like demented mice. Is this the real world that I am sheltered from in tranquil Billinge? Anyway, there was a short wait for Cliff Spracklen to arrive who was journeying down with me. Having met Cliff and had a quick drink, it was time for a shifty into W. H. Smith to see if *The Petition - Enough is Enough* was on sale. I made a quick note in my diary that it wasn't in, and to notify Geoff (who had now set off back to Shipley) on my return. Geoff has been spending much of his time on whistle-stop tours to top up any book outlets with the petition book and his novel *One Spring*.

The train journey to Kings Cross in London eventually got underway at 9.05am. After a couple of hours whiling our time away, it was now getting close to our destination. Ben from Sky TV was waiting on the station with a cameraman. As we approached the station it was time to take my coat off to reveal my Saints top (nicely ironed by June), whilst Cliff put on his bumblebee Bramley shirt. While talking to Ben on the mobile phone to discuss the filming I noticed all the 'suits' on the train trying to tune into what was going on. It appeared from their inquisitive faces that they thought it might be something like *Where the heart is*, the popular ITV drama, or something similar. I'm sure some were thinking 'Drat. Should have brought the old rugger shirt.'

Filming duly completed on arrival, it was then down into the Underground to catch a train. This was to be a complete laugh. Having not been down on the tube for an eternity, it was indeed an experience from hell. I say hell, as you go so far down that I'm sure you pass Old Nick at the halfway point. As for the escalators, well I didn't know the rules. On going down, Cliff was on the right, with yours truly on the left. Suddenly, a rather gruff voice shouted: 'Move to the right, move to the right.' As I moved over, one hundred gazelles in pin stripe suits suddenly raced past. Apparently the right is reserved for the slow coaches of society... and Rugby League fans.

As for the tube train itself, they are so packed that it seems like an advert for some sardine company. There is a sign saying: 'Beware of Pickpockets'.

54

They could flipping well pinch your trousers and you couldn't do anything about it.

Finally, it seems that getting a seat is nigh impossible on some trains. Rumour has it that many commuters put a towel on a seat the night before. And finally, had a scary moment in that I temporally lost sight of Cliff. "Now which tunnel did he disappear down?" was my panic stricken thought, as it seemed that there was a labyrinth of passageways.

Arrival and onward

Arriving at Lancaster Gate station, it was then onto the Columbia Hotel for a quick shower, cup of tea and then onto the House of Commons via once more on the underground assault course. It has to be said that the sunshine had disappeared to be replaced by a grey, overcast day, with plenty of drizzle.

Emerging from the sardine train feeling like a surfacing miner, Parliament was now in full view, as Cliff and I walked round to St. Stephens entrance were everyone was scheduled to meet up at 2.30. Eventually several fans from the London area joined us, including two from the South London Storm RLFC. After a short wait, and with Sky TV now being present, David Hinchliffe MP for Wakefield, Andy Burnham MP for Leigh, Tony Cunningham MP for Workington, Lindsay Hoyle MP for Chorley, Helen Southworth MP for Warrington South joined us, as well as Lord Hoyle and Lord Lofthouse.

Filming and interviewing then started to take place amongst the many inquisitive public that were milling around the area. Suddenly, even more camera crew arrived on the busy scene. There were some from *BBC Look North*, as well as BBC 1. After more interviews and photos it was indeed a job well done. Thanks must also go to Peter Lush, London League Publications Ltd's photographer and to the other media representatives present. At last the petition had arrived and received good publicity.

After the publicity event, it was time for a few drinks with the other fans and then onto Sportspages in Charing Cross Road. This shop is indeed stocked well with Rugby League books and trade papers. In fact Charing Cross Road overflows with bookshops.

On journeying back to the hotel there was an amusing incident on the underground. After Cliff had gone through the ticket barrier, it was my turn. On placing my 'ticket' through the machine I found the gate would not open. Several failures later, and after receiving a few 'tuts' from commuters, I realised to my embarrassment that I had been putting in a business card obtained from Sportspages. The train ticket was still in my pocket.

A capital evening out

Once back at the hotel there was not much time to relax, as we had to be back at Parliament to meet David Hinchliffe MP to witness the petition being handed into Parliament. Once arriving at Parliament it was off to the Strangers Bar for a couple of drinks and a chat and then onto the restaurant for a meal accompanied by David Hinchliffe MP and Andy Burnham MP. After a delicious meal of prawn and mussel soup, pork, potatoes and veg, plus cheese and biscuits (all accompanied by some red wine - not bad for a 'staff canteen'!) it was nearing the time for David Hinchliffe MP to hand over the petition in the Commons. At around 9.50pm he mentioned that a vote that had been going on previously about another matter should now have been finished, so off he went, later to be followed by Andy Burnham MP, Cliff and myself. We were off to the gallery to witness the event. However....

It appeared that the vote never took place and so the Speaker of the House shouted out 'Petition' sooner than expected. As David had made a call to the loo he was still outside of Chambers and had to make a mad dash, huffing and puffing, lugging the books of signatures into the Chamber. David told us that this caused hoots of laughter from the Speaker. It also meant that we did not witness the petition being placed in the 'box', but there it was.

House of Commons Motion 1023 25 March 2002

"That this House welcomes the presentation to Parliament of a petition signed by over 30,000 supporters of rugby league calling for the promotion of fair and constructive media coverage of the sport; shares their concern over a series of recent examples of inaccurate, ill-informed and damaging commentary in some sections of the media by London-based journalists with little or no knowledge of rugby league; notes that the popularity of rugby league is such that it is now played regularly in all counties of the United Kingdom and in the Republic of Ireland, with clubs at amateur, semi-professional, professional, student and armed forces levels and can no longer be characterised as a purely northern regional sport; commends this important supporters' initiative; and calls upon the Secretary of State for Culture, Media and Sport to make every effort to ensure that rugby league is covered in the media in a balanced, accurate and informed manner."
(from Hansard)

Once David was out of the Chamber it was back into the Strangers Bar for more drinks. This time we ventured out onto the terrace, and on a still, dry night, the atmosphere was superb.

The magnificent Parliament buildings, stunningly crafted in a time gone by, was a picture of excellence as it glimmered from the search lighting. On the other side of the river the mighty 'London Eye' gently turned, as Father Thames flowed serenely by.

It all seemed a long way from Billinge and collecting the first few signatures.

All in all a successful day for Rugby League with 30,000 supporters finally having their say in Parliament.

Parliamentary snippets

Now enshrined in public record, the Media Petition has now been included in Hansard (see above). This is a daily record of events in the House of Parliament. David Hinchliffe MP sent me a copy, which thanks is given for. The volume is 382 No. 120, with the Media Petition mentioned on page 408.

Finally, on the way back from Shipley I made a stop at 'Dick Turpin's' chuck wagon for one of his famous double burgers. Travelling west, it is just past East Marton in a lay-by on the A59. Well worth a visit if you are passing. Restaurant tips as well.

Now to follow up the presentation to Parliament with a circular to the national media to let them all know about it.

That can be April's little job!

Presenting the Media Petition to Parliament: Cliff Spracklen (left) and Ray Gent with David Hinchliffe MP and Lord Geoffrey Lofthouse at St Stephens Entrance

The Media Petition: David Hinchliffe MP being interviewed by Sky Sports. Ray Gent is talking to Helen Southworth MP

6. April 2002

After the flurry of activity in March, time to draw breath, then follow up with the real crunch, a volley to the various media outlets that the Media Petition was aimed at, letting them know about the petition and its findings.

Let's also see who thought it was worth reporting. The television debate continued with an unexpected ally appearing.

Towards the end of April an audacious idea bore fruit, a tour to England by teams from Russia and Tartarstan, organised by Niel Wood of the Student Rugby League.

Finally…a ceasefire?

Time to saddle up again.

Having now presented the petition to Parliament, the next exercise was to circulate our Rugby League indifferent media to explain exactly what had been achieved during the petition exercise and seek their response.

The following letter was circulated by Ray to all London based national and 'non heartland' regional newspapers, BBC Television, Granada and Yorkshire TV, as well as all other major television stations, national radio stations, and many local media outlets. The letter was also sent to media outlets in Northern Ireland, Scotland and Wales. It will be interesting to find out who will reply As well as the letter, other interesting 'points arising' information was attached, as per the appendix in *The Petition - Enough is Enough.*

All or nothing will be revealed later in the book!

Fair Media for Rugby League

"Dear Sir,

Please find enclosed a summary of the media petition that was recently submitted to Parliament via the good office of David Hinchliffe MP with the support of 80 plus MPs.

The petition reached its target of 30,000 signatories demonstrating that Rugby League fans will not continue to put up with their game being downgraded, attacked or ignored by some areas of the national media.

There are some media outlets that do give decent coverage to the game, for which thanks is given. However, whilst constructive criticism, or reporting of bad news is acceptable, during the course of 2001 some attacks were so bitter, dishonest and misleading, often pre-written before a big match or final, as to lead to the conclusion that some media organisations have a prescribed anti-Rugby League agenda.

The petition was not against the freedom of the press or other media outlets, but more of a marker to say that Rugby League fans are saying: 'enough is enough.' Indeed many Rugby League fans spoken to have given up buying national newspapers.

Moving forward, Rugby League and the national media need to exist in a co-operative manner and try and iron out any differences. It would be appreciated, if indeed your organisation cares for the sport, to let me on behalf of the fans' Fair Media for Rugby League campaign, or John Huxley (media manager at the Rugby Football League, Red Hall, Leeds) know your views on this matter.

The book that was written about the Media Petition is selling very well with 1,400 copies sold in the first few weeks, reaching the Sportspages' Top 10 list and engendering media attention as far away as New Zealand. The follow up will be out next year and I would like to offer your organisation the opportunity to give your views for inclusion. Only the *Sunday Times*, via Alex Butler the sports editor, cared to respond last year.

Please take a few moments to read the summary and it may be useful to pass this to your sports editor, who may well have underestimated the damage that negative or scant treatment of Rugby League can do to circulation. I look forward to hearing from you.

Yours faithfully."

Little Response

Very little in the way of response, apart from a couple of acknowledgement post cards from the *Daily Telegraph* and PCC and somewhat confused acknowledgement letters from the *Daily Mail* and *Evening Standard*.

The main prize though is not provoking a response from individual papers and broadcasters, but achieving a change in mindset, however gradual.

Better still though, by mid April the volume of Rugby League coverage has improved and the steady flow of one off 'dying game' attacks seem to have been staunched.

Might it just be the case that the message that Rugby League bashing loses circulation has got through to one or two newspapers? We can't prove it, and are gradually turning blue through holding our breaths, but maybe a few quiet words have been exchanged in Fleet Street with the message to 'lay off Rugby League'.

Let's hope it's not one of the false dawns the Fleet Street sports editors kept telling us Rugby League is forever having.

Programme news

There was an interesting article by David Lawrenson of the *Sunday Times* in the Saints versus Wigan match day programme on the 1 April 2002.

He mentions being impressed with the new 'Saints Experience'. Brian Kelly, the newly appointed Saints chief executive introduced this family orientated promotion, to try and increase the crowd figures at the Saints. David suggests this initiative is just at the right time as the game of Rugby League comes under more media attack, and in particular, the Simon Barnes article mentioned earlier. He did once think that Rugby League fans were paranoid about media coverage of their sport but was now not so sure. "How else can you explain the vitriol that has been poured on the game by observers who often have never seen a live game and seem to trot out statements which have no basis in fact?" was his comment.

David Lawrenson isn't against constructive criticism like many others, but biased, uninformed comment is another matter. He puts into question the ethics of someone like Simon Barnes of *The Times* (see previous comments) writing from the comfort of an armchair on a match he conveniently switched channels for during the half time of a football match, and described as "Looking like it was played in a warehouse used for the storage of stadium seating." Yet nothing of the fact that Leeds Tykes versus Bristol Rugby Union match attracted barely 2,200 fans to Headingley the same weekend, half that of the Wigan versus London Broncos Rugby League game he is so quick to mock.

The Simon Barnes article went on to suggest that League is about to be swallowed up by Union by comparing BBC viewing figures for Union international attendances to League's club games. David mentions that the figures have already been called into question but why let the facts spoil a good story?

David wrote that it wouldn't be a bad idea for journalists to relinquish the armchair and go to visit the people who watch, play and enjoy the sport at the likes of St Helens, Wigan, Bradford, Hull, Castleford etc. But no, far easier to do it from the comfort of your own home.

As a young journalist, David had a tough news editor on the *St Helens Reporter* by the name Ray Moore. Apparently, Ray used to throw some stories back at him with the comment of 'get some bloody balance in it'. And with that, more interviews had to be undertaken.

It is suggested that Mr Barnes wouldn't last five minutes with Ray Moore, nor to the fact that you don't see these journalists having a go at speedway, basketball, ice hockey etc, so why Rugby League? "No, Rugby League is a soft target, particularly for those based in the south many of whom have a negative view of the north anyway," suggests David.

He also penned a hilarious piece based on *Monty Python*'s famous 'dead parrot' sketch. Imagine thousands of fans turning up at the JJB, Knowsley Road or Headingley only to be told: "Sorry, this game is dead, it is deceased, it's gone to meet its maker, now run along and watch Orrell, Liverpool St. Helens and Leeds Tykes."

Is it possible that Rugby League fans could club together for a pair of shoes for Mr. Barnes to replace his carpet slippers, and then he would have no excuse for not making a visit 'oop north'? Given the understandable reticence by some journalists to comment publicly on this subject, David's candour and forthright comments are even more welcome

Footnote

David does suggest writing to the newspaper editors in a rational way about any offensive articles, or lack of Rugby League coverage, and if there is no joy, then to buy another paper. As discovered chatting to petition signatories, already many fans have given up buying national newspapers, whilst some editors seem to shy away from replying to correspondence on this subject.

Express delivery

It's no secret that the Media Petition wasn't exactly front page news as far as some parts of the Rugby League trade press were concerned. No reason given but by September we could guess why.

At the risk of airing dirty washing here, the article on one leading publication's stance has been deleted and replaced with two proverbs.

'Manners maketh man.'

'Least said, soonest mended.'

*I wonder who's with us in
the trenches today Tim ?*

Meet the Rugby Football League

Also in April, John Huxley, the RFL's media manager, made a visit to 'Gent Towers' to have a chat about events. Thanks must go to John, as it is nice to be able to communicate with those that work in the game in a direct and human way.

We discussed several issues, including the need to upgrade the RFL web site, communication and bridge building with the media. Also getting the *Super League Show* shown nationally (a meeting had been arranged with Peter Salmon), trying to get more Rugby League personalities on television shows and trying to have a central communication point where clubs can feed in positive news items for release by the RFL. More on this later to see how events mapped out.

There was also a brief talk about Richard Lewis, a former Lawn Tennis Association official, who was due to take over the running of the Rugby Football League from 1 May 2002. Being one who has no 'baggage' so to speak, it will be interesting as to how he motivates his new troops into positive moves forward.

One journalist suggested that this was Rugby League's 'last chance saloon', in that it had to succeed. Now where have we heard these comments from before? It appears that we have enough 'last chance saloons' to build our own 'wild west' town. 'Drinks on me folks'.

Community spirit

Elsewhere in sport it appears that, half way through April, all is not well with the Nationwide Football League. The sponsorship from ITV Digital appears to be under review, with the likelihood of a reduced amount or nothing at all. Granada and Carlton TV did come under attack from one journalist who suggested that it would have a massive impact on those smaller football communities. "Football is at the heart of many communities and it could be that many could go to the wall." It went on to comment that it would be a disaster for those that have nothing else to take them away from their computers

Now isn't the game of Rugby League part of many similar communities? Yet here we have a situation in reverse in that some journalists would have the Rugby League game die. It appears from some areas of the media that Rugby League is not a welcome part of our nation's sporting landscape.

To Russia and back

Niel Wood of the Student Rugby League tells his story of how a dream can come true, against all probability.

"Ever had a great idea? I have. It was born out of a desire to repay hospitality and turned into a mammoth effort on behalf of real Rugby League fans.

When the Student Rugby League visited Tatarstan and its capital, Kazan in September 2001 with 104 players and officials representing Scotland, Ireland, Wales and England, we were overwhelmed by the reception and hospitality shown to us.

From the greeting party with almost the whole of the town that met us at 7:00am as we stepped off the overnight train, through the 16,000 people who attended the opening game to the final Vodka send off on the train station, we were met with surprises. The biggest surprise of all is that these people play Rugby League and do it very well without much help from anyone.

The 2000 Rugby League World Cup has had a very bad press, but let me tell you the contacts made at that tournament were of real value. The Student Rugby League was in need of an overseas venue to send England, Scotland, Ireland and Wales in order to prepare for the next World Cup. Where to go? Russia had been very keen to receive tours after the World Cup so I emailed and asked them.

From that point on it was a roller coaster ride, which saw the depths of despair and the heights of joy. Yes they would like to host it and could it be a European Cup? Why not? Contact was made with France but they would not enter as it was not an 'officially sanctioned RLIF event.' The Russians in the meantime came back with the answer that Moscow was no good but the Mayor of Kazan was very keen. Where is Kazan?

Kazan is the capital of Tatarstan a Russian Republic 500 miles to the east of Moscow. This seemed a challenge but the Mayor was keen so we couldn't let him down could we? We raised the cash, travelled via London, Moscow and overnight train to Kazan and the rest is history.

There were many in the party who had their lives changed by the event. Stefan Hopewell has formed the Russian Connection solely to promote the exchange of ideas and culture between young people of Russia and Great Britain and he uses Rugby League as the medium of exchange. It was obvious that these people are desperate for international contact and that they love Rugby League. We should not get carried away and think that Rugby League is the national sport, it is not but it is popular among some and in particular the young. What is popular, however, is overseas visitors. They are rare and a novelty and as such their appearance is treasured.

But how good are the Tatars and the Russians? I felt that the international competition could be fuelled by inclusion into the Challenge Cup so I suggested this to the RFL. They were very receptive but it was too late for 2002 so Plan B was hatched: 'bring them over for a tour, play against a couple of professional sides, but it can't cost the RFL anything.' OK let's give it a go.

'The M62 Game...?'

I put together a budget that showed a way in which we were not relying upon great gates to underwrite the tour - a familiar failing in the past. The budget was imaginative to say the least with some unusual headings for professional sport. There was 'sponsorship' and 'gate receipts' and 'programmes' but also there was 'local authority' and 'fans' appeal'.

I am a regular visitor to the Totalrl.com message board and I see the passion with which supporters discuss issues and the great ideas that they come up with. Some are frankly unworkable but many deserve a good hearing. If I could harness a significant number of these to buy into the project then I could prove to the RFL a real desire for international competition. So I put a message on the board asking for support in the shape of paying up front for a 'season ticket' at £10 per head. I was encouraged by the responses, at least enough to start approaching clubs and local authorities.

The clubs responded well with Dewsbury and Workington straight out of the blocks. Hull KR came along with some persuasion and Sheffield were keen, but felt that they needed some guarantees from the RFL, which they would not give. The dates were set for the Challenge Cup weekend, which ruled out the Lancashire clubs as they were scheduled to have league fixtures, then came the Rhinos' fantastic performance against the Bulls. Would the Bulls take a game against some Russians given that they had an unexpected free week over the Challenge Cup period? Abi Ekoku could see the possibilities straight away and agreed to host a game at Odsal. The pieces were in place we had tourists, hosts and some fan support.

The local authorities were key and came up trumps. All four came into the event with cash donations towards the cost of the tour. Hull City Council, Allerdale Council, Kirklees Council and Bradford Council all pledged funds.

Then came a break from Neal Coupland and Cathie Hessian, RFL's sponsorship chasers. Damart had a desire to add to their sponsorship of the Bulls and could see the value of this event. One meeting and we had agreement. Sponsorship, local authorities and fan support all secured we awaited the RFL decision. After a weeks delay and daily calls to Russia to keep them informed, the go ahead was given by Nigel Wood who could see that the project had merit but was also a risk.

Accommodation was an essential element to this tour. It had to be in the right place at the right price. Scoutdyke Outdoor Pursuits Centre was not the first choice, but what a good one it was. In picturesque South Yorkshire, overlooking a reservoir with adjacent pitch for training, a welcoming manager and as much food as they could eat. All at the right price.

The scores are now history and the fact that it happened at all is due to the efforts and commitment of many people, but the true test is whether the exercise proved that a Russian team can come into the Challenge Cup and support their domestic game for years to come.

The whole Rugby League community can take credit for the Damart Russian Tour, but it was the 80 odd fans who dug into their pockets and sent cheques that was the encouragement to carry on. When the two teams marched onto the playing surface at Murrayfield to receive their fantastic ovation, I think that the point was proven. It does cost a lot to put on international football but the benefits it brings to players, officials, administrators and fans is beyond money.

I would never advocate international football at all costs, I would however, suggest that it needs to be given the highest priority and that means having the courage to give something a go. It is also a mistake to do things in isolation so the Damart Russian Tour should only be the start of a programme and all the sums and adding up should be done after a few more events and let's see then if international football returns a profit. I do not know but I think that it will."

Rugby (Union) Special

The issue of disparity of television coverage of the respective codes rumbles on through April, and here is one individual, Chris Gallagher's, take on it.

Chris is a Wigan-exile now living in London and has become quite frustrated that he can't see the *Super League Show* as it isn't being broadcast nationwide. Chris has taken on board a personal crusade to try and rectify the situation, especially with the fact that Rugby Union's version is broadcast to a wider audience.

"It started as a good-natured argument with a colleague. We were discussing the merits of Union and League earlier in the day, and the conversation hadn't been concluded. My Union supporting colleague recommended I looked at an old link regarding the relaunch of the BBC's *Rugby Special* programme. It was a question and answer session with Pat Younge, the head of BBC's rugby programmes, and my friend was using it to back up his own opinions.

After my colleague had left, I continued reading the rest of the article. I noticed that one Rugby League fan, (Paul, UK) had a question accepted and Pat's reply was given. Paul's initial question was 'As the show is called *Rugby Special*, how much of the show will cover Rugby League issues?' a question that Rugby League fans have been asking for years.

Pat's reply caused a red mist in me. I'll reproduce the first two sentences here: "Not very much, because it's a Rugby Union show. **Rugby League has sold its soul** to Sky, and it has to live with that."

To me, the two sports seemed to be in the same situation with one noticeable difference. Both sports have their domestic leagues covered on Sky, both sports have international teams covered on Sky, both sports have occasional live matches shown on BBC and both sports have highlights shown on the BBC.

The difference is that *Rugby Special* is broadcast nationally, and has been for years. The last nationally broadcast, weekly highlight show for Rugby League games was during the 1960s, I believe.

Another member of the Totalrl.com forum, 'Ed I Tackle', pointed out another part of the same interview, detailing the BBC's desire to secure the entire Rugby Union Six Nations competition (which the BBC has since secured). Rugby Union's domestic competition is also under contract to Sky currently, but there is still a national programme with highlights for it. It seems the 'selling their soul' argument is good for the goose, but not for the gander.

There followed a number of e-mails between Pat and myself, who, credit to him, was big enough to reply. He could have quite easily binned my first mail, which I admit was harshly worded.

So, Pat replied, and the e-mails continued between us. The upshot, at time of writing is this; it transpires that the contract is between BBC North and the relevant authorities, not the whole of the BBC, hence no national broadcast. The question of whether Rugby League highlights can be broadcast nationally is still unanswered, despite evidence from senior members on the administrative side of Rugby League saying that it is available, and always has been.

I suggested that Pat might like to check the Rugby League contracts to confirm this, but that idea wasn't met with much enthusiasm. However, he did admit 'it may be possible for other BBC regions to get access to that material if there's demand.'

Demand? Funny you should say that ...

Another section of the interview was by a viewer who was questioning the proportion of technical analysis. The end of Pat's reply was that "this isn't ratings-driven - if we were worried about ratings we'd put on a game show - this is much more about providing rugby fans with a proper service." Now, this is not really an issue at the time of writing, but certainly something to remember if the BBC play the 'demand' card as a reason not to broadcast the *Super League Show* nationwide.

Even forgetting Pat's comments for a second, I don't believe that that demand will be an issue. If you look at recent viewing figures, I understand that the numbers watching the Rugby League Challenge Cup games are consistently higher than Union's Heineken Cup matches, and even some Six Nations matches, the jewel in the BBC's Rugby Union crown, and in a normal year, the sport they promote most.

Add to that the fact that Rugby League has four of the six best-supported rugby clubs in the country, London Broncos' presence in the top echelons of the domestic competition and the growing Rugby League scene in London and the south - I could go on...(for more information on the Rugby League scene in London, there is another article in Chapter 8 of this book about it, by an extremely talented, handsome writer).

So, back to the question of broadcast rights: Pat suggested that we try and get the relevant parties to talk to each other about this, rather than everything being co-ordinated through me (shame - I quite fancied being the next Richard Lewis). With that in mind, a letter was written regarding the situation and distributed to relevant parties at the RFL, Super League, the BBC, David Hinchliffe MP, and of course, the authors of this book,

The main thrust of the letter is to ask the RFL to try and overcome any hurdles, which might prevent an Rugby League show, similar in content, length and budget to *Rugby Special.* It also requested that official pressure backed up this fan's little 'crusade.'

Progress

Since the letters went out, although I can't report anything concrete, three things have happened.

Firstly, I've had contact from Super League, informing me that there are *no regional restrictions* on Super League being broadcast nationwide. In fact, the original intention of releasing the broadcast rights was for them to be broadcast nationwide.

Secondly, a letter from David Hinchliffe MP saying that Peter Salmon, BBC's Head of Sport, and Pat's boss, would be invited to a future meeting to discuss this and other issues.

Thirdly, a letter from the RFL thanking me for my letter. They expressed sympathy, and said that Richard Lewis had seen the letter. The issues were expected to be discussed in the next meeting between the Rugby Football League and the BBC - meetings which happen regularly.

They are 'clearly anxious to expand terrestrial Rugby League' and 'hope that your work together with our efforts, will encourage the BBC to re-examine the position regarding the *Super League Show.*'

As I say in the last line of my letter to Pat: 'Here's hoping that I can add to the viewing figures of the *Super League Show* in the very near future.'

More about this in July.

Balding - Best Coverage
(or Bring Back Claire)

So, it's to be a Wigan versus St Helens Challenge Cup Final after the two sides defeated Castleford and Leeds respectively in the semi-finals. There is sure to be a warm welcome for both sides in bonny Scotland, and in particular, Edinburgh, home of Murrayfield where the game is to be played. Now, what of the match presentation of the semi-finals by the BBC?

It wouldn't be the BBC, would it, if their match coverage didn't attract criticism from League fans. A large banner constantly flashed up the news that the US Masters golf was on the other side, and a constant stream of football scores distracted in the corner of the screen (would that happen during a high profile football or Six Nations game?)

However, more positively, this weekend was a revelation in one respect. Claire Balding, better known for her work in horse racing, was an instant hit with many fans regarding her presentation of both games. Her refreshing attitude to a sport she confesses to know little about was top drawer. For once we had someone who can give the other side of Rugby League to the likes of Stephen Jones, Frank Keating, Simon Barnes and others who we - and most League fans believe - let their own personal 'baggage' prejudice the way they view the sport.

We hope it lasts!

A further surprise was an article by Claire in the *Evening Standard* on 18 April 2002, spotted by Mick Ayres, a Saints fan living in the 'Smoke'; and what a classic.

Clare had spent the weekend at the Rugby League Challenge Cup semi-finals in Leeds and Wigan and thoroughly enjoyed the experience. Having watched only a handful of Rugby League matches before, she had done plenty of homework and had few nerve-filled nightmares, worried that she "would be vilified as a posh, southern bird who knew nothing about Rugby League." As it turned out, she could not have been felt more welcome if her hosts had "laid out a red carpet and given me a bouquet of flowers". Claire professed to be "overwhelmed by the warmth of the people, the accessibility and eloquence of both players and coaches and the quality of the action on the pitch".

She felt "the relentless physicality of the game means that the players have to have stamina levels unheard of in other sports and the fans appreciate the effort displayed on their behalf without resorting to mindless abuse of the opposition or of the opposing fans."

She also found it curious that fans frequently swap ends at half-time and was struck with the "joyful, noisy family atmosphere."

An impartial view from within the BBC Sports Department - bring back Claire. Back over to you, the BBC, for national coverage of the *Super League Show.*

Time for a challenge

Ray wrote during Challenge Cup final week ahead of the 'Clash of the Titans', or so the Wigan and Saints fans would have you believe. There was going to be a media watch, as in *The Petition - Enough is Enough*, but sadly, other events took the game by storm.

Ian Millward, the St Helens coach, created much controversy by naming a virtual reserve strength team for the league match against the Bradford Bulls on the Saturday before the final.

Millward made a statement at a press conference before the said game that he had many injured players and suggested the RFL (who were represented) send a physio to check matters out. To add fuel to a growing fire the Saints played the last 25 minutes with only 12 players on the park, with no substitute going on to replace a player taken off.

This didn't go down well with Chris Caisley, the Bulls' chairman, who called an impromptu post match press conference of his own, claiming the crowd was down around 3,000 to around 14,000 as a result, putting the club's receipts £35,000 out of pocket. (Later in May, a similarly high profile game between Bradford and Wigan drew a 13,300 crowd.)

Calls of fines, deducted league points and reprimand vibrated around the game of Rugby League. It all seemed to reach fever pitch, as even the fans went to a war of words against each other.

In their wisdom the RFL sent out a request for the club to submit information about events not later than the Wednesday before the final, ahead of any possible enquiry. This didn't go down well with the Saints club who were immersed in the task ahead of them in getting the club ready for the final. It certainly was a challenging time in more ways than one. The Saints did eventually receive a £25,000 fine, later withdrawn after an arbitration hearing.

No matter who is right or wrong on the above, the game came out of it all minus some credibility and in retrospect it could have been handled in a better way.

The dust settled and by August a sort of peace had been declared, with the following press statements:-

Eamonn McManus, Saints' chairman, stated: "Saints and Bradford are each committed to providing world-class Rugby League in a friendly and entertaining environment. Bradford are always very welcome at Knowsley Road and our own supporters will be looking forward immensely to the return trip to the Bradford & Bingley Stadium.

The best of luck to Bradford and their supporters for the rest of the season. It's going to be a thriller and we are all privileged to be part of the most knowledgeable, passionate and well-behaved supporters in the world."

Chris Caisley, the Bradford Bulls chairman said: "Saints and ourselves have agreed to draw a line under some of the recent off-field differences between our two clubs which have tended to detract from the excellent quality of the on-field performances. I look forward to warmly welcoming St Helens and their supporters to the Bradford & Bingley Stadium at Valley Parade. It is a game not to be missed."

A sorry episode.

Although there was no media-watch prior to the final, there was a fantastic Rugby League article in the *Guardian* on the Monday after the Bradford versus Saints match. It covered nearly two pages and was about

73

Keiron Cunningham, the St Helens forward. It was well researched and written and was a credit to the paper after it had come in for some criticism from Rugby League fans during the petition campaign. An e-mail campaign was started to encourage fans to write in and congratulate the paper. Well-done Jim White and the sports editor at the *Guardian*.

As for the final, the Challenge Cup went to Wigan with a 21-12 victory. As for the crowd of just over 62,100, it was 5,000 short of capacity. However, when we look back at a previous clash that attracted 95,000 fans, then we do wonder if the Challenge Cup competition is in need of a bit of 'spit and polish'?

The *Scotsman*, however, was full of praise for the event and Rugby League supporters. By all accounts they had 'drunk a fair bucket', been no trouble to the local plods and appealed to the locals with their down to earth attitude (in contrast apparently, to followers of another sport who, apparently, often appear 'snooty' when visiting Edinburgh.)

As with the 2000 Challenge Cup final and various other games staged north of the border, when Rugby League visits Scotland it tends to make news there, a point worth noting.

7. May 2002

The smearing and malicious attacks by national newspapers had dried up for the time being, so time now for some more examples of fanpower and personal stories from various Leaguies at different points along the Rugby League road to Damascus (just past the M62 Brighouse turn off).

The end of May also saw the end of the *Rugby Leaguer* newspaper as we knew it, as its title was acquired by League Publications Limited and merged with *League Express*.

Radio Ga Ga

But first the implausible spectacle of our 'medal winning' friend, frothing that the BBC sell Rugby Union short. On the planetrugby.com website, Stephen Jones had a long diatribe attacking Radio 5 Live for what he felt was its inadequate coverage of Union's Heineken Cup semi-final and the domination of football in the sports coverage that day. Earth calling Jones! This is exactly what Rugby League fans have been going on about for years! Maybe the nation's appetite for Rugby Union isn't as voracious as he's been telling the nation every Sunday.

Mr Jones does have a point that there is more to sport than football. Radio 5 Live is an award winning broadcaster and knows best, still 'count their medals.'

In at the deep end

Mick Dyer (Chairman M) spends much of his time helping out at his local swimming club, yet when it came to the game of Rugby League, he jumped in at the deep end and was immediately smitten.

Initial contact was made with Mick via the Totalrl.com message board were he offered to help distribute some *The Petition - Enough is Enough* book flyers. We actually bumped into each other during the 2002 Challenge Cup semi-final between the Saints and Leeds and I asked if he would write a short article for this book. This he duly did at the beginning of May. Let Mick explain how he became involved with League in a city that hosts so much top class senior sport, but so far, little Rugby League.

"I was born and bred in Leicester, living 20 minutes walk from both Leicester Tigers and Leicester City. I watched both on a regular basis, and everything was right in my sporting world. That world began to crumble in the nineties when I became disillusioned with the direction association football was taking. In my opinion it won't be long before it is a non-contact sport. I turned my attention solely to the Leicester Tigers RUFC and was happy to go to Welford Road whenever I could. That was until the new Millennium and a new dawn.

At the beginning of the year 2000 I had *Sky Sports* installed, and one evening I decided to watch a Super League game for the first time. I can't remember who it was between, but I was impressed with what I saw - the commitment of the players, the atmosphere in the grounds, and the pace and skill of the game - it soon had me wanting more. I don't think I missed a televised game all season. In fact I was hooked!

Now we all need a team to follow and during that first season the team that stood out to me was St Helens. Who will ever forget the championship play-off game between the Saints and the Bulls and that last minute try by Saints' Chris Joynt, a truly great sporting moment. Watching that particular game made me realise that this was definitely now my favourite sport and I had also found a team.

Since that first season I have been to Knowsley Road, home of the Saints, as well as several other Super League grounds. I visited the Millennium Stadium for the 2000 World Cup games staged there, and was at the second 2001 Ashes Test to unfortunately see the Aussies beat Great Britain. I had the privilege to watch Bradford win the 2002 World Club Challenge, and had a marvellous day out in Wigan to see the Saints beat Leeds in the 2002 semi-final of the Challenge Cup.

At time of writing I am eagerly awaiting my ticket to the Challenge Cup Final, where as always, my good friend Steve, who is also a Saints fan, will accompany me to the game. I still watch the odd game of Rugby Union, but only England and Leicester Tigers games. For me there is now no contest, Rugby League is the far superior code and there will be no going back.

Gloucester drop out

Phil Cole, a west country true League convert, continues the theme:

"'Rugby League – a game played by pot-bellied miners so unfit they have to stop every two minutes to play the ball. Anyway, it doesn't flow like Union, and as for that padding…'

I never actually uttered those exact words, but it's still hard to believe that I'm now writing of my devotion to the game of Rugby League. This time 10 years ago, the only thing we'd have had in common would be a dislike of Stephen Jones. So what happened?

A long time ago, in a galaxy far, far away (well, Bristol actually) there lived a little boy brought up in middle-class suburban Union country. His father was a Gloucester fan who lived for the Five Nations; football was in a bad way, dragged down by violence and Bristol Rugby Union's Memorial Ground offered a safe, local alternative to the killing terraces of Ashton Gate and Eastville. He went to a private school that pushed Union and talked down League. Although Bristol City was his first love, Union played an important role in his youth.

Sure, I'd seen League on television and I couldn't share the OTT hatred of the real Union die-hards, but I still had a stereotyped image of the game. A world of amateur clubs was unheard of, the events of Vichy were unknown and League was only played to make money by a handful of clubs in England and Australia. When Cliff Morgan, former Union player said 'no current Union international was as good as the Great Britain Rugby League side', we scratched our heads in bemusement.

Then the wall came down. The events of 1995 opened a lot of eyes. The dream of cross-code matches became a serious possibility and Wigan decided the argument once and for all. Watching the League challenge was an incredible experience, even though a one-sided game was expected because of the differences in experience and training time, the difference in technique wasn't anticipated. Any doubts were soon expelled in the Middlesex Sevens as Wigan swept all before them and it became apparent that Victor Ubogu's dream of a summer League stint wasn't the most realistic of ideas.

The growing interest in League inevitably meant watching more games on television and in 1997 I finally took the plunge and went to a game. Whatever is said about the Super League World Club Challenge, it brought me fully into the fold as a friend and I took a package with the Bulls to go to Odsal for the Auckland game. I've two overriding memories of the day - the first was Odsal itself; the sense of going through those gates unable to see anything beyond and then staring down into the vast bowl like no ground I'd ever seen. The second was the audience; we passed an Asian family on the way in and there were young kids there without their parents; yet there was atmosphere and passion, not the middle-class polite applause of the Memorial Ground; no, this was my dream of what football should be.

My next game was London's historic win over Canberra and then I was well and truly hooked. Having a job that involves travelling, and having friends living on the edges of the heartland became a springboard for immersing myself in the game. Last year in 2001 I travelled to over 50 matches from Gateshead to Agen (my employers joked that I was the only person who wanted meetings a long way from home on a Friday, so I could catch a match!). Previous destinations have included Brisbane, Auckland, Edinburgh, Swansea and now every professional ground in England. A League addict? Guilty as charged m'lud.

While I may be a trifle more zealous than some, however, I can't accept that I'm the only person who would be so bowled over by the game, but it's giving people the chance. Perhaps that's why our enemies twist the knife. Perhaps those who think there isn't an audience for League just cannot grasp the concept. To them, I ask then to consider the Scottish press. On the eve of the 2000 Rugby League World Cup, *The Scotsman* newspaper launched a truly disgraceful assault on the game that signalled the open season on League that blighted a wonderful month of matches ('a feast of football' as Eddie of Sky TV would no doubt say). Such was the ferocity of the attack that I feared for the 2002 Challenge Cup final, so imagine my surprise when the same paper lavished the sport with praise for players, spectacle and fans alike. Progress?

Rugby League is a simply astonishing game. Its physical nature is such that I would never have the courage to play it. Its values of inclusion, community and decency offer hope for the future of our society. Long may that continue."

Part of the (Norwich) Union

Turkey or mustard? Rugby League awareness has spread to Norfolk. Here is Martin Alcock's contribution, received in April.

"Rugby League, so what's that then? Well, I don't think I was ever meant to find out. You see I didn't have a privileged upbringing, I wasn't born in a Rugby League heartland to be able to enjoy the sport's warmth, passion, aggression and speed, along with of course a thousand other positive attributes! I was indeed denied the right to be part of the family. Instead I was sheltered from the brutality, the vermin which some journalists would have you believe is Rugby League.

Instead I had a much more peaceful upbringing, born in Norwich I was fed a football-only diet until an exiled Yorkshireman introduced me to the

'Greatest Game' at the age of 15 via Rugby Union. This is not anti-Rugby Union. It is about receiving a fair crack of the whip. In fact in a way which I am privileged is my inside knowledge of grass-root Rugby Union circles, look away now anyone from certain national newspapers, or other media outlets but there are a lot of Union players eagerly interested in the goings on of the other code.

You see, Rugby League, like it or not, *is* a national sport – it is a sport with national interest and you are doing a disservice to your readers, listeners, or viewers throughout Britain and anywhere else shielded from our great sport by protecting potential fans from finding out about this glorious game.

Back to my introduction: while on a Rugby Union tour (under-17) to South Yorkshire we ventured to the Don Valley stadium to watch Sheffield Eagles take on St Helens in the old Stones Bitter Championship. I can't remember it as a classic game but it certainly made an impression on us, of the 16 lads that toured about 10 went to my school and we talked of this game (the 'other' game) for weeks. I remember one lad, still a close friend, buying the Saints jersey by mail order.

Soon, however, and this is the negative side of my story, we lost interest; why, you may ask? Well, not because any of us had lost any interest in the game, not because we didn't want to keep an interest in the game, but because we weren't allowed to!

Before the age of the internet the only access we had with Rugby League was the scores each Sunday on Teletext, not enough for boys to maintain enthusiasm I'm afraid.

So how come I'm here now then? Well via university in Preston and in a round about way I ended up moving to, living and working in Manchester. Myself and a friend of mine (also with a Rugby Union background I might add) were left at a loose end one Saturday in October and we were lucky enough to learn that the inaugural Grand Final was at Old Trafford that night. Ironically enough it was by one of the morning broadsheets, but I put that down to a misprint or at least dangerous information that must have just slipped passed the editor. We scurried down in the day to buy tickets and after a few beers were not disappointed with what we witnessed - even the driving rain as I remember it wasn't enough to put us off.

Well the door was now open once more and moving to Salford turned into the necessary push to open my eyes and make me fully aware. And people do seem to need that push - my word - the Rugby League introduction is never an easy one. Let's face it, we don't get a great deal of publicity now do we?

A half-hour's walk from The Willows was unfortunately not the biggest beacon for Rugby League viewing. I had to practically drag myself down by the scruff of the neck. We mustn't blame everything on adverse media; too often the Greatest Game is its' own greatest enemy. Press releases are important and so is local advertising, this is a fault that in some quarters is being addressed but still needs to be addressed much more vigorously! Just imagine the amount of money that I would have spent over The Willows turnstiles if they had brought the game to me sooner, rather than myself to the game. And it isn't just my cash either, I dragged my girlfriend along, my mates, they have dragged their mates and we keep going back.

I went home to Norwich last Christmas and I faced my biggest challenge yet; now I'm not sure whether the Rugby Union propaganda machine had been swinging a few handbags but my talk of the Greatest Game was causing a few ripples within my old club's members. Crusaders on the west of the city are not the stereo-typical Union club, born out of a class divide you would have thought that if the Northern Union had been the Northern and East-Anglian Union things may have been or so different.

A lot of the players do watch the game, but there were some typical arguments and counter-arguments which I'm not going to give a great deal of time to because we've heard them all before, but one about certain aspects of forward play really does stick out. An old warrior of the club, not actually that old as it happens, but game hardened after several stampings and rakings and cheeky rabbit-punches tried to talk up his argument that this was what the game was about, the funny thing is he wasn't convincing any of us. We didn't entertain the argument for long.

My next task is to try and get them to visit me in my northern home and show them the delights of our game, - the modern game. The Greatest Game, without the screen of the television, or the blurred vision of certain journalists shielding some of the raw action and atmosphere which is such an integral part of Rugby League. They are still Rugby League unaware - for how long?

Now it's not an easy progression from being Rugby League unaware to Rugby League aware. My opinion is that everyone should be a fan of this game, to me it is a breathtaking spectacle. If they are not a fan, well they are therefore just unaware - as I was. Beware! The game will spread."

No doubt there are many more people around the country who have yet to sample the game of rugby league for the first time. How many other Chairman M's, Phil Cole's and Martin Alcock's are there who would join the Rugby League family were they able to get a taste of the sport, underlining again how important is it for the game to have some decent newspaper and national terrestrial television coverage?

Wasps, hornets and butterflies

When the Rugby League bug bites, it can get in your blood, here Tim Hardcastle (alias Sergei on the internet) demonstrates where Rugby League fanpower can lead a bloke from Halifax, and what it can achieve.

"We all know the old saying about a butterfly in Brazil beating its wings and causing a tidal wave that engulfs the USA (or is that jumping Chinamen?) Anyway, in the great animal kingdom of Rugby League, populated as it is, by Rhinos, Bulls, Wolves and any number of vicious, dangerous animals, it is perhaps not macho enough to think of yourself as a butterfly, but butterfly I am, and my offering is about the many and varied ways in which I've tried to start a few tidal waves by flapping my little wings.

I've been involved in this greatest of games long enough to remember three point tries (and score a few, I might add), contested scrums, and the *real* chance of Great Britain beating the Aussies in a test series. Yes, I am that old. At first, the only concern I had was my own team, Illingworth, winning and my professional team Halifax, (Thrum Hallers, not Blue S*x) getting off the bottom of the old Second Division. As I got older and wiser, my love of the game got wider and deeper, if possible my every waking moment would be taken up with watching, playing, coaching, reading about or writing about this fantastic, breathtaking sport that we are privileged to be part of. I like to think of myself as a fan of the whole game, from the lowliest under-8s up to the all conquering Kangaroos, I love 'em all.

Once I had realised that my own playing career had passed its peak, and the only way was down, I began to give serious thought as to how I could carry on making a contribution to Rugby League.

Junior coaching

The first flap of my wings came in the junior section of Illingworth. My two sons, Matty and Tom, had started to run around with the under-8s, and rather than just stand watching, and criticising (as all dads do, without fail) I got involved as assistant coach with the under-16s, helping out my friend and inspiration Kenny Giles.

As time passed, and with the usual political ups and downs that go hand in hand with running a junior sports club, I eventually reached the dizzy heights of head coach of the juniors. Amongst other things, I wanted us to get into the junior schools in our catchment area, and enthuse the local kids with the Rugby League bug, and hopefully pick up a few recruits into the bargain.

I put together a presentation to be delivered to the kids. Nothing too flash, just a few action photos, and slides. We managed to get several invitations, and the show was delivered very ably by Richard Turner, who is now involved with the West Riding League. The presentation ended with an open invitation to a taster session we had set up at our club's base.

Even the most optimistic of us only thought we'd get 30 or 40 turn up, and everything was geared around those sorts of numbers. On the night we were swamped, as kid after kid turned up. The car park looked like the M25 at rush hour, and how the bar staff coped with the parents is anyone's guess. The six of us who were qualified coaches struggled manfully to get the message across, and I reckon no-one knows what junior coaching is about until they've tried to explain and demonstrate tackling to 150 kids, all wanting to be turned into Robbie Paul in an hour. At the end of it all, we were totally drained, but elated that so many boys and girls of all ages had made the effort to visit us.

I have no idea how many of those kids are still involved in the game, and of course not all 150 signed on with Illingworth, but I hope that when they see the game on television, or read about it, they will remember that hectic, anarchic evening at Illingworth.

Parlez vous League?

I had been working on a plan to take the clubs under-16s to the USSR to help the game over there, and also to give our lads something they would remember all their lives. The plan was well under way, but in late 1994, with the collapse of the Soviet state, and the relatively dangerous state of affairs in Moscow, we decided to change the destination to Avignon, in the Rugby League heartland of France. We had two games arranged against Morieres XIII, who despite being a small club at open age level, were always very strong at the junior levels. They treated us fantastically, arranging meals, visits to their sponsors (a vineyard, luckily) and sorting out some great training facilities for us.

On the pitch was a different story, and I think whenever a French Rugby League team gets chance, they seek revenge for Agincourt, Crecy, and Waterloo all at the same time.

There may not be many of them, but the 'triezists' are like Rugby League people the world over, down to earth, friendly and very passionate about their game. At the presentation on our last evening the pastis and red wine flowed like the river Rhone. Despite having a very basic grasp of schoolboy French (its amazing how all languages sound the same after a bit of alcoholic lubrication), a diplomatic incident was narrowly avoided when one of our party - ok it was me if you insist on knowing - overdid the French custom of kissing people of the opposite sex when you are introduced to them.

Apparently in Provence, it is '*de rigeur*' to kiss three times on the cheeks. Well, on being introduced to the rather attractive daughter of a Morieres official the wine took over and I 'over stepped the mark', not too far, you understand, but far enough to incur the wrath of her boyfriend, a first teamer with S. O. Avignon. A retreat to rival Dunkirk ensued, and a cross-channel war was prevented, just.

Twelve months on, and it was Morieres' turn to pay a visit to that tourist mecca of Halifax-sur-Hebble. We had arranged to meet them at Ainley Top, and I think they were excited about staying in the Pennine Hilton there. Sadly we had to inform them that they where actually staying at the youth hostel in Todmorden. Still, the chippy at Luddenden Foot saw some action, as fish and chips, 35 times with bits and salt and vinegar were ordered.

We had been in touch with *Boots 'n All* as the BSkyB magazine programme was called then, about this visit from the French junior champions, and they got in touch to arrange a rendezvous. We decided on a trip to the Oulton Lodge, the unofficial Rugby League museum at Oulton, Leeds. The French party had a great time looking at all the displays of old photos, cups, medals etc, but finally the moment of truth dawned, and it was time to do the interviews. I went first, and it felt like I was being grilled by a particularly sadistic Gestapo officer. The camera and 'furry caterpillar' mike were right in my face, and the sweat was pouring like a wet day in Salford.

Somehow I managed to blag my way through it without descending into fluent gibberish, and beat a hasty retreat to the bar to watch the next victims get a seeing to. Serge, one of the French coaches was next up, and he coped quite well, considering his English was comparable to Bernard Manning's Urdu. The third and final interviewee was a young lad who went on to make quite a name for himself with the Huddersfield Giants, Yaccine Dekkiche. He also starred for the French national side until he retired from sport to play Rugby Union. The actual match was a great event for Illingworth as we had Sky TV cameras there, about 300 people thronged the touchlines and there were three soon-to-be internationals on the pitch. Stuart Fielden was in our under-16s, and Morieres had Yaccine Dekkiche and the current French full-back, Renaud Guigue playing in the centres.

To Russia with love

In the early 1990s, as a antidote to my growing obsession with all things Rugby League, I decided to try and learn a foreign language. My ex-wife, Karen, is virtually fluent in French, very good at German, and also learnt British Sign Language. So I was used to having language books around, and fancied a go myself.

I chose Russian. Everyone learns French, or Spanish, so they can chat up the waiters or waitresses on holiday, but I wanted to be different, so Russki it was. It pretty soon became apparent that this cure wasn't going to work as those damn Soviets had taken up the Greatest Game. As I needed to practice my new linguistic skills on a native, who better than the recently formed Russian Rugby League? I made contact with a guy called Dmitri (Dima) Komar. At first it was just 'penfriend' type stuff, but soon he was sending me news, views and info from the game over there, and I was translating them and passing them to Harry Edgar at *Open Rugby* for publication.

Dima was their top referee, and had been a Rugby Union international for the USSR at junior level. Our friendship developed to the point that I invited him to stay with me and my family for the final week of the 1995 World Cup. He arrived in time to watch the classic semi-final between New Zealand and Australia at the McLego in Huddersfield. A decent house and that breathtaking comeback by the Kiwis... erm... took his breath away. Like most citizens of the old USSR, Dima had never been abroad unaccompanied, and there were several strange moments as he realised he was in the 'decadent west'.

Illingworth's club secretary, Paul Bonner, had reason to call at my house with some forms to fill in, and it was quite a while before Dima realised that

he wasn't from MI5, and about to bribe him into defecting or spying. We went to the Emerging Nations Final at Bury in midweek and it was at that time that Yorkshire Water were having all the problems with their supply, and were tankering water in from all over the country. As we were driving the rain was absolute stair rods and there was I trying to explain the drought in pigeon Russian and pigeon English as the M62 was more like the Manchester Ship Canal.

In 1996 it was my turn to visit Dima in Moscow. By this time the USSR had imploded, and sport was a very minor consideration in the minds of most Russian people, just day to day living was hard enough.

Even the well established sports, like football and ice hockey were struggling, so a 'new' sport like Rugby League was on the verge of disappearing. A small group of enthusiastic people were hanging on, with little or no contact or help from the outside world, and it sometimes felt that I was the only person in touch with them. I took several coaching videos and books with me to help them in a small way, and instructions to write an article for *Open Rugby.* I played 'touch and pass' at the Dinamo Stadium, and trained with the Russian national team as they prepared to compete in the Student World Cup.

Like any big city Moscow has its positives and its negatives. The architecture can be stunning, stunningly good, or stunningly bad, and the beginnings of its 'westernisation' were showing. At the MacDonalds on

85

Tverskaya Street, I just had a burger, thank you. I sat terrified at Dima's work place, as a very drunken ex-KGB hit man played with his loaded shotgun, and was woken in the middle of the night by a mafia gun battle near Dima's flat. To top it all off, I had the dubious pleasure of flying Aeroflot, fortunately the pilot hadn't brought his son to work that day. A truly exhausting, fascinating, exciting week, and one I'll never forget. If you ever get chance, go. Moscow could be a beautiful city, and I'm sure since my visit, the developments I saw starting will be bearing fruit now.

At the tender age of 38 I finally got the message, or thought I had, and decided to hang up the boots. After 23 years of running into brick walls on a Saturday afternoon, my body was starting to moan. As there are no social Rugby League teams, like the Union vets, I decided to start my own.

Using a variety of threats, bribery and blackmail I managed to persuade 13 other lads from the telecoms company where I work to come and have a run around and a few beers afterwards. In the 18 months that we kept the team going we managed to play six games. We actually won one and drew two others. Sadly, redundancies took their toll on our team and eventually we wrapped it up. We can still be seen having a game of 'touch and pass' on summer Thursday evenings.

I've always been a relatively small butterfly. I've never set up an expansion club in virgin territory. I've never brought a multi-million pound sponsorship into the game, I've never negotiated a television deal with Sky TV, but I hope I have passed on some of my enthusiasm for Rugby League to as many people as possible. Kids in the Illingworth area, Russians, French, 30-somethings from all over West Yorkshire, they've all had a dose of my infatuation, and I hope some of them now think differently about the game because of me.

There remains one area of the game yet to feel my zeal, but that will soon be put right. In June 2002, I'm doing the referees course, so if any of you dear readers play in the lower reaches of the Pennine League, you'll soon be having the pleasure of my company as the illegitimate, blind, biased-against-your-club git in the yellow and black striped shirt. After the game, don't leave me on my own at the bar, come and say hello, referees are human too you know, although this one has some butterfly DNA."

Excellent evidence from Sergei that Rugby League can span not only borders but language and culture, a fact often forgotten by 'M62 heartlanders.'

The *Aye of the Tigers*

A 'fanzine', an independently written and published magazine written by fans and aimed at other fans, is a direct method of mobilising and organising support for fans' issues, having a laugh and maybe earning a few quid for a chosen good cause. Often thought provoking and forthright and not always welcomed by the 'parent' club, fanzines are a dedication of hard work and enthusiasm, and a welcome contribution to the Rugby League scene.

Among the likes of the *Scarlet Turkey* (Salford), *Split, Fish and Curry* (St Helens), *In any Kind of Weather* (Hull F.C.) and many others, one of the more prominent publications (although with a website as well, maybe 'operation' is a better word) is *Aye of the Tigers*, the independent Castleford fanzine.

Issue 14 of the *Aye* published in May 2002 included a good summary of the Media Petition and ongoing Fair Media campaign so far. Thanks, men.

Here's a piece written by Nigel 'Delboy' Bennett one of the main men in the *Aye* empire.

"It was in the year 2000 that four Castleford Tigers fans, with no connections to each other except for a love of the Tigers, got together and decided to create a fanzine, a small magazine made by the fans for the fans.

Disco Stu, Stone Cold, JR and myself, Delboy, were fed up with standing on the terracing at Wheldon Road (aka The Jungle) listening to fans saying they had no voice. We were frustrated that there was no way of letting the people who matter know how they felt without actually writing to the club, which most fans are loathe to do.

We decided that this had to change and the *Aye of the Tigers* was born. From day one that it would be the fans that count and the main aim of the *Aye* would be to give the fans a chance to air their views on the game of Rugby League, whether it be in a light-hearted way or something more serious. We promise no censorship and we do encourage the fans to 'say it how it sounds'. This may seem crude but we feel that once you start to alter the way people put things down on paper then you run the risk of losing the honesty and genuine feeling of the true grass root fan.

For many years Tiger fans, and Rugby League fans in general, have had to go along with whatever authority has told them but we at the *Aye* hope we can in some way contribute to changing that view. Why should fans not have the chance to speak out and vent their true feeling about the game after all we all pay through the turnstiles to watch our heroes perform.

We started with a run of 75 copies, run off on Disco's works printer, and took them to the first game of the 2000 season, Wigan at home. When these were sold within one hour of hitting the streets we knew we had something that Tiger fans wanted. In fact we received so much positive feedback from that initial issue that we decided to go bigger and better.

This meant a glossy cover, proper graphics and text you could read! We now have 350-500 printed (depending on how much money we have left) at an established printers in Castleford.

The *Aye* sends copies to Wales, the Netherlands and even to an ex-pat in Australia. We never thought that things would go as well as they have but it just shows how passionate about our sport the fans are.

As could be expected, we received a cautious welcome from the Castleford Tigers. I think initially they thought the fanzine was a flash in the pan and we would not last. However, two-and-a-half years later we are still here and have managed to get the *Aye of the Tigers* sold in the club shop.

Last season we even donated the sum of £500 from the *Aye* sales to the Tigers so they could buy gym equipment. We decided to do this as we thought it's not really our money but it belongs to the fans who have bought the *Aye* and it is their way of putting something back into the club, a sense of belonging maybe. As with most ventures of this type, we have had our fair share of ups and downs. Perhaps the biggest down was the loss of JR who decided he could not continue due to work commitments, but this was countered by the arrival of Batman who now runs our website (www.ayberspace.com) and a fine job he does for us.

We seem to have come a long way in the last two and a half years and we believe we have achieved some of our aims and, whilst everything in the garden may not be rosy as far as the game goes, we hope we have put a little bit of laughter back into fans lives.

If we get in people's faces and cause a stir in the corridors of power then so be it, it's what the fans want.

Aye of the Tigers Editorial team: is Nigel 'Delboy' Bennett, Stuart 'Disco Stu' Lake, Neil 'Stone Cold' Harvey and Michael 'Batman' Battye."

Real purpose

A 'feelgood' atmosphere surrounded the game in May. John Whalley wrote in the *Daily Telegraph* on 8 May 2002 an article headed: "Real purpose of Super League showing through". He said: "There's been much for the Rugby Football League to crow about at the start of the Super League season. Increased attendances, a Challenge Cup final at Murrayfield between Wigan and St Helens which proved worthy of the occasion, and even rumours about massed raids from rugby union for more leading players drying up."

However, just as one area of the media was warming to Rugby League, another area imploded.

Merger - but not clubs

13 May 2002 saw the last issue of the *Rugby Leaguer*, first published in 1949, the title being sold to League Publications Limited and merged with *League Express*. Somewhat out of the blue, the first combined issue was published on 20 May.

Thwarting LPL's monopoly, a new venture *New League Weekly* appeared in July, featuring the basis of the former *Rugby Leaguer* staff.

Here Phil Stockton examines the pros and cons.

All for the good of the game?

"The *Rugby Leaguer* is dead. Long live *League Express*. Or rather, long live the *Rugby Leaguer and League Express*, because in May of this year the *Leaguer* was bought and subsumed by its sole rival weekly Rugby League newspaper. In fact, apparently the *Leaguer* is not dead but is purported as being merged with the *League Express*.

I was disappointed to hear of the *Leaguer*'s demise and was sceptical over the idea of a merged publication; my experience in the oil industry in which 'mergers' of large oil companies effectively resulted in takeovers by the more dominant partner, as the influence, culture and eventually the name of the lesser player gradually, but inevitably, disappeared.

I should point out that in no way do I think the *League Express* proprietors acted improperly in acquiring their rival publication or that this wasn't a perfectly legitimate course of action. It presumably makes sound business sense from their point of view to eliminate the competition and increase their circulation by attracting readers of the erstwhile *Leaguer*.

A rival paper, *New League Weekly*, has risen from the ashes of the *Leaguer*, employing the majority of the old *Leaguer*'s journalists. Having looked at a couple of the early copies it appears a good publication and importantly provides an alternative weekly paper for League fans. Though I may continue with the *League Express* for the foreseeable future, should I

89

become dissatisfied, then I know that a rival is out there snapping at their heels ready to take my business. It is a possibility that I could subscribe to the *New League Weekly*. So perhaps on reflection, as events have unfolded, the demise of the *Leaguer* may not have been so bad for the game after all."

Northern stars top of the Union

During the course of the 2001 Media Petition, and during the heavy media artillery bombardment against Rugby League, the *Daily Mirror* ran an headline on 4 of September that said: "*Northern stars are top of the Union*". It referred to Sale being top of Union's Zurich Premiership table, newly promoted Leeds Tykes being in fifth place, having just beaten the mighty Bath, while Newcastle were sixth. The article also referred to Leeds being ready to offer a contract to Jonah Lomu. The proposed signing could be part of northern England's 'rugby' revolution.

The problem was that the article and league table were published after only one match played in the Union season. Without wishing to sound too cynical, it did look like a swipe at Rugby League's heartlands. So how did events turn out? Leeds finished bottom of the Zurich Premiership. Again, no Union bashing intended, talk up one sport, but not at the expense of another.

Chestnuts

Two familiar old chestnuts to end this month, the first from TotalRL.com: "I listen to Radio 5 on a regular basis and get wound up at their anti League stuff or just sheer indifference. Yesterday I heard the lead into a report 'Now that the domestic rugby season is nearing its end....' Pardon me. What they meant was now the Union season was finishing. Some things never change - unless we keep reminding them."

Also, an article in the *Mirror* on 28 May 2002 about a crime verdict: "Former Rugby League star Ian Thomas" was interviewed about the character of the guilty person. The paper was in no doubt as to the specific code when it suited, not referring to a 'rugby' player, but Rugby League.

Maybe a little paranoid, but these are just a couple of examples found in the papers daily. For those who notice it is a constant irritation, for those who do not, it just adds to the brainwashing.

8. June 2002

No news is good news in June, as far as slanted or disparaging media coverage goes, sport having the chance to speak for itself. The start of the football World Cup from Japan and Korea swamped every other media story, but alongside that event test Cricket, with England playing Sri Lanka, Formula One, Lewis boxing Tyson, Wimbledon and the Rugby League season continued in full flow.

The World Cup has been hyped for months, reaching saturation point during May, and June with the event, personalities and surrounding speculation and trivia featuring on front and back pages and every single news bulletin. FIFA's event is one that has the luxury of having its marketing done for it, with seemingly every company, product and celebrity known to man wanting their name associated with it.

How does Rugby League fare in comparison? There is a long tradition of League in the Valleys. Compare the once 'game that dare not speak its name' to the present position of Welsh Rugby League.

Then let's look at the spread of the game down south, and to all points of the country as the burgeoning Rugby League Conference gets into full swing in June.

And there is also a personal experience of things across the Channel.

Sell, sell, sell

Selling the game is a subject close to Ray's heart. "Get your apples ladies, nice n' rosy," cried the fruit seller in the old cobbled market square. Likewise one could now hear the cry of "double value, ladies, two juicy steaks for the price of one, just right for the sizzling Bar-B-Que." These cries and others like it added value to the old markets, giving them unique atmosphere. Even in modern times these places can still be found, with many a stall seller being gifted with the gab. In fact many customers are attracted to this type of selling and one can witness some stalls being surrounded by many excited folk, eager to open up their purse or wallet for a bargain or two.

Taking marketing further, it has to be the way forward for any business or entertainment. Gone are the days of the 1950s when sports fans would turn up in their thousands to see a game of football, or in our case a game of Rugby League. The early period just after the Second World War witnessed huge attendances of sports starved fans in the two sports. For one it was a way to try and get back to normality, as well as the fact that there wasn't much competition as there is today.

Foreign holidays always appeared to be for the rich and affluent in my small world in St Helens during the 1950s. Now computers, car travel, golf and many more leisure activities we take for granted. The old scenario of 'they will just turn up' was quite common then. Marketing just didn't seem to be at the top of the pile and probably wasn't needed.

Yet even today some still live in this world of expecting fans to turn up at games, while others go out and 'market' their wares. Unfortunately people now have many more choices and it is folly to expect loyalty. Clubs will always have a hard core of support, yet this may not be enough to sustain the viability of the club.

Now what of our game of Rugby League? It all appears to be a mixed bag in that some clubs have taken marketing by the horns, so to speak, whilst others have lagged behind. Bradford Bulls have moved forward quite dramatically in terms of marketing and seen a steady rise in attendances, whilst success on the field as also helped the club.

Speaking to Andrew Whitelam of Super League (Europe) he quoted that female spectators now accounted for 35 per cent of attendances, yet the Bulls have got this up to 42 per cent. Marketing lean, athletic players to the ladies has gone a long way to reaching this position.

Castleford Tigers, despite their lack of trophies of late, as well as being only a small town of less than 40,000 inhabitants have done enormously well in terms of marketing. This effort gave them the title of 'Club of the Year' a few seasons ago. Likewise St Helens has jumped on the bandwagon of late and now find attendances up some 20 per cent. Brian Kelly, the new chief executive and the Saints' marketing team have brought in the 'Saints Experience' in making match days a place to be. The latter makes a nice change in fortunes, as the Saints of the past were poor at selling the club.

Now what of two other top clubs in Leeds and Wigan? Leeds, despite having only won one major trophy in over twenty years still hold up well in terms of support and are in fact there at the top. Leeds does some excellent marketing and has a very good match day experience. On the other hand Wigan seem to have lost their way according to the fans. Many blame the move to the somewhat soulless JJB stadium, while others suggest the club is focussed more towards getting Orrell RUFC into the big time. This is indeed a strange one as a conversation with Paul Cunliffe of the RLSA suggests that Wigan do excel in press releases. Maybe at the end of the season Wigan's crowd figures will be comparable to the top of the pile. It will indeed be interesting to see if the Saints can pip them, as Wigan have held court over their near rivals in terms of crowds.

According to many fans Warrington RLFC has one of the best community development schemes in the game and in fact do have a very loyal band of support even without much success on the playing field.

All in all every club has a degree of marketing with some having it finely tuned, whilst others seem to wallow around with no sense of direction. Marketing is important and vital if our sport is to rise to its ambition of a truly national sport.

A welcome surprise was a rather nice glossy brochure sent by the RFL at the end of May to those on their database advertising the main events scheduled for 2002-3 and detailing how to get tickets.

Let Stuart Duffy of the Bradford Bulls and Simon Dawson of the Saints take you on a trip to the market, with pieces submitted in June.

Bull Market

Stuart Duffy was born in Leeds and supported the Rhinos for many years. At 15 he ran away to join Billy Smart's Circus before beginning a career as a guitarist. He has worked with a host of top stars including Olivia Newton-John, Waylon Jennings and Don Everly and still plays guitar in the Castleford based Collier Dixon Line country rock band.

His introduction to Rugby League came in 1989 when he was approached by Leeds to be their video commentator. In 1994 he became media & PR manager and was responsible for the launch and running of *Radio Headingley*. In 1998 he left Leeds and has worked as media manager and latterly football manager at the Bradford Bulls since then.

"There is no doubt Rugby League has certainly lagged behind other sports when it comes to media coverage and to a large extent that can be put down to a 'southern bias' from the pro-Rugby Union editors of the popular press. But we should not be lulled into an 'us and them' attitude and put the blame squarely on the peoples shoulders. There is a lot that the game and individual clubs can do to push the game forward.

Marketing has come fairly recently to sport. For many years we were happy with the crowds we got in what was a mainly 'male' environment. 'Dads and lads' was a popular expression used by both our game and football when it came to describing the audience profile, but all that changed with the event of summer rugby and Super League. Smart clubs, and I like to think that Bradford Bulls were the smartest, quickly realised that the game had to appeal to a family audience. In the modern society that is Britain today, women no longer stay at home, do the cooking and cleaning and the ironing and such like, they work, and as such they now have a big say in the leisure activities of their families at weekends, particularly in summer.

At the Bulls we do not consider our competitors to be Leeds Rhinos, Halifax Blue Sox or St Helens, after all who would want to go and watch Leeds if they were a Bradford fan? We consider our competitors to be IKEA, Alton Towers, trips to the Yorkshire Dales, days out in Blackpool, in fact any area that competes for family leisure time. That thinking was the root of the work Bradford did when Super League was born and it is a theory that we have subscribed to ever since.

How we achieved success could fill this book alone, but the simple theory behind it all was that if we targeted the children and made them want to come to Odsal then the parents would be happy. There was a lot of work and thought by people like Chris Caisley, Brian Smith, Peter Deakin and Gary Tasker to bring it all together, each one having their own individual responsibilities. As I said, it would take a book to detail all the things that were instituted but at the root of it all was the Bull commitment to its success. Nothing was 'unachievable' and hard work would bring the rewards. Pre-match entertainment, Outer Bowl 'fun area' gameday compere, music and dancing girls were all used to make gameday 'the place to be' on a Sunday.

Off the field the Bulls Community Programme was developed into the best in British sport. Schools coaching and 'healthy lifestyle' messages became a daily occurrence but more important was the commitment to the community. The Bulls literally linked themselves to everything good in the local area. Whether it was a road safety campaign, safe fireworks, anti-drugs or cancer awareness, you could bet your life the Bulls would be involved. Not only would they be involved, they would be shouting it from the rooftops in every media outlet open to them. In Peter Deakin they had an ideal catalyst to drive things along, something that all clubs can do and it is something the Bulls excel in.

It is no good having all these good ideas and not telling anyone, and to this end local media partners are a must. The Bulls formed good relationships with both the local newspaper, the *Telegraph & Argus* and the local radio station, the Pulse. All sports fans read their local paper for news of 'their team'. They probably start from the back page and work inwards and when they reach the Births, Deaths and Marriages they put it down, but there is a larger majority, and those were the people the Bulls were looking to attract, who read the paper from the front and put it down at the Births etc section. In other words 'get on the news pages'. That way it keeps the club in the public eye and raises both the profile and the brand awareness. That in turn creates a feel good factor that makes people want to come and see, and it also makes companies take notice and realise the potential for themselves in securing a high profile team, such as the Bulls and use it as a vehicle for them to link to.

It is the same with the local radio. We know we will get a mention when Robbie Paul is unfit, but it is much better to get a mention in the news part of the bulletins. It is much better still to have an agreement whereby the presenters 'talk up' a game. That is what people listen to and is much better than 100 adverts.

When looking at the profile of our sport and where it sits in the sporting portfolio of this country, we should never underestimate the investment of BSkyB into our game. I am not talking about the News Corporation investment that enabled us to go full time professional in 1996. What I am talking about is the substantial work done by Neville Smith and his team at Sky Sports in raising the profile of our sport to a level we could not have dreamed about 10 years ago. We are exceptionally lucky in that Neville Smith is without doubt the finest producer of rugby in the world. You only have to look at the quality of pictures coming into our homes from across the world to see that Australia's loss is very much our gain

BSkyB, through Neville, has elevated our sport to a new level. Whereas we used to fit in between the horse racing and the football results and was seen as an alternative to wrestling it now stands alone as a major sport that comes over well on television. It is not unusual to see a Rugby League game follow a football programme featuring the best teams in Europe. That it now holds its own and sits alongside other great sporting events is a tribute not only to the players and coaches but also to the way it is presented on television.

High profile clubs such as Bradford, Wigan, St Helens and Leeds are the flagships of the sport. Their profile nationwide is one of the main reasons why people take up the game, either as players or supporters, and the fact that all clubs now have spectators across the globe is a tribute to BSkyB and its investment in Rugby League Football.

So we have the product and we have, in many areas, a high profile. We must keep knocking on doors to make people aware of what we are. As Brian Noble is fond of saying, 'I have never brought anyone to a Rugby League game for the first time that hasn't gone away hooked.' That is what we must do to editors, journalists and broadcasters throughout the country. What we mustn't do is attempt to make those inroads into areas that are traditionally not ours by focusing on and knocking Rugby Union. To do that would undermine all the sterling efforts of the fans Media Petition and people like John Huxley at the RFL and Andrew Whitelam at Super League who work so hard centrally to promote the game to a less than interested media. Worse still it would bring us down to the level of Stuart Barnes and Rugby League and Rugby League people are much, much better than that."

Experiencing the 'Saints Experience'

If fans now expect more than 80 minutes rugby for their money, Simon Dawson, St Helens marketing manager explains what has been happening this season at Knowsley Road.

Simon Dawson attended Cowley High School in St Helens. He has a first-class honours degree in Business Studies from Liverpool John Moores University and a distinction as a Master of Business Administration (Football Industries) from the University of Liverpool. Simon is also a member of the Chartered Institute of Marketing and has a Postgraduate Diploma in Marketing.

"'People turn up because they want to watch Rugby League' was the old philosophy at Saints and is, indeed, the current philosophy at many British sports clubs. This, however, is based on the observations of a time when men used to finish manufacturing work at midday on a Saturday, have a drink with their friends and then head to the match in the afternoon before spending Sunday with their family. As everyone will have noticed, this social pattern is at least 40 years old but is still assumed to continue by sports clubs across the UK. In the 21st century, people only go to a match if they want to.

The great American sports marketer, Bill Veeck, based his marketing strategies on the principle that people attending a sports game want to have fun. Many sports managers believe that fun equals winning but this simply is not true and Saints have, perhaps, been the world's best case study to prove that. Even though Saints won seven trophies in six years in the Super

League era, they found it very difficult to attract the crowds that were expected.

In 2002, the first year of the Saints marketing-focused strategy, we transformed the Saints matchday - named the 'Saints Experience' - into a family-focussed event based on fun and excitement... oh, and then there's the game as well.

We realise that we cannot influence the result of the match (after all an injury, a bad refereeing decision or purely bad luck is out of our control) but we can influence everything else and we can concentrate on those areas that provide fans with enjoyment.

Therefore, we focused on improving the facilities inside Knowsley Road, including the introduction of alcohol inside the stadium and improvements to the stadium toilets, the addition of a giant neon red-V (the club's brand) and a hugely improved pre-match entertainment climaxing with the best team entrance in Super League complete with smoke, lights and fireworks. It excites our fans and that is what professional sport should be all about - from the second they arrive at the stadium until the second they leave, not just during the game.

But while the entertainment value is fantastic, we have not ignored the other elements of marketing. We have great value packages making family attendance affordable (although not free and lacking value) and innovative advertising including award-winning adverts, starring Johnny Vegas, on our local radio station, WISH FM, and our aeroplane pulling an advertising banner.

We have built excellent relationships with our local media to improve consumer perception of the Saints, and Rugby League in general, throughout Merseyside and also with national media via our players. Sean Long appeared on Children's BBC during his injury, using our hugely popular St Helens Cineworld Angels (who have appeared on the *Big Breakfast* and in the *News of the Word*) and our unique telephone answering service featuring Johnny Vegas (which has been aired on Radio 1, Radio 2, Radio 3, Radio 4, Radio 5 Live, BBC Radio Merseyside, BBC GMR, Century Radio and Capital Radio.) How many sports clubs have made five appearances in *Marketing Week* this year?

Merseyside, as a whole, has been a target market for extending our fan base in 2002 and we have worked hard at opening doors that have always remained shut due to the cultural preference for football in Liverpool. The Saints have developed an excellent relationship with Merseyside

Community Police to encourage them to spread the Saints 'gospel' throughout their local neighbourhoods and we recently placed promotional leaflets in the Liverpool Tourist Information Centres. Entering Liverpool will not be an overnight success but will be essential for the Saints in the medium- to long-term.

We have worked hard, as a club, to create an image of the Saints, provide affordable and high quality entertainment and encourage fans, and indeed people just interested in the game, to experience the Saints Experience.

Looking to the future, it is important that we all realise that this is simply the beginning of the Saints Experience and we must continue to push back the boundaries of sports entertainment to ensure that our success continues.

But game day is not, contrary to popular belief, the sole activity of the marketing department in an innovative sports club - we must join our other commercial departments in providing a seven day a week revenue source. A prime example of this is Saints Energy and Saints Talk - our own branded electricity/gas and telephone businesses. We believe that this will soon become as important to the Saints as gate receipts and sponsorship. But, even in this area, we have maintained our Saints Experience belief to provide excellent value at an affordable price as fans can help their club by providing revenue while saving money from their household bills (for example, if fans converted to Saints Energy and Saints Talk they would make savings equivalent to watching Saints for free and having money left over to purchase two replica shirts) – we were the first sports club to offer this concept.

Saints' off-the-field facilities also include hospitality and entertainment areas and this is also an important area for the club. While Saints' fans are a very important market for the club, it would be foolish to ignore other markets. Saints can now host conferences, weddings, funerals and birthdays while the newly refurbished Touchlines Bar provides entertainment at least four nights a week including singles' nights and live acts. These activities may not appeal to Saints' fans but they are facilities that are available for other areas of the town's population.

What I have described in the previous 922 words is the change in philosophy, at Saints, from a club that concentrated on solely winning to a club that now concentrates on entertaining and providing the great, affordable value that our fans want to experience and we tell them in the most imaginative ways we can. By attracting a larger and more supportive fan base and adding additional revenue sources, the Saints will be able to build a more competitive team on-the-field for our fans for the future."

Another paper round

To keep the plight of fair media coverage for Rugby League in the journalists' field of view, especially given the swamping of all media outlets by the football World Cup, another round of letters was sent to our friends in Fleet Street. Ray sent a letter:

"Dear Sir,

The Super League season in Rugby League is well under way with some fantastic matches so far. I would defy anyone to say that the recent Bradford versus Wigan match was not of the highest quality in entertainment and drama. It was indeed pure theatre in sport. The closeness of the league table suggests that we may be in for some tense struggles as teams jockey for final league positions in readiness for the Grand Final play- offs.

Now what of the media relations with the sport? Since the Media Petition was handed over to the All-Parliamentary Group of Rugby League MPs much of the venom of 2001 and beginning of 2002 has subsided. This is indeed a welcome change and thanks is given to the media.

Likewise Rugby League fans have witnessed some excellent articles on the game that have been well researched, as well as received. Not getting too carried away, information can still at times be patchy, as well as fans away from the heartlands saying that coverage is still poor in some media outlets.

Very recently there was a message posted on various Rugby League internet message boards asking fans to submit ideas for improving the games image and marketing. These ideas will be forwarded onto the RFL, which it is hoped some can be used to compliment their own marketing. With this in mind, are there ways in which our sport can help your media outlet improve matters further? It would be nice to remain positive and feel that matters could be improved another notch.

At the end of the day Rugby League fans are not asking for the earth but just some respect and fair coverage of the sport commensurate with its widespread and growing support nationally.

It has been rare to receive constructive replies in the past, so I hope you can take this letter on board and give it some thought and hopefully a reply. I look forward to hearing from you.

Yours sincerely."

Four replies.

More support in Wales than you think

Jack Whittaker on the past, present and future of Rugby League in Wales:

"Born in Levenshulme, South Manchester and heavily influenced by my father, I supported Belle Vue [formerly Broughton] Rangers in the late 1940s and early 1950s. From 1957 until 1970 I lived in Liverpool, first as a medical student and later as a doctor at the Liverpool Royal Infirmary. With the folding of Belle Vue Rangers [1955] I watched St Helens whenever I could, especially during my spell at nearby Whiston Hospital. I still regard myself as a Saints fan even though attending games is now only an occasional pleasure. I am now a consultant at the University Hospital of Wales, Cardiff.

If I have two regrets, they are that my school discouraged Rugby League and that I can't write like Dave Hadfield.

I can trace it back to 1947, for that is when I first realised the connection between Wales and Rugby League. The Saturday 'football' match was my father's passion, a bastion of male privilege from which women and very small boys were excluded, but that year it all changed.

Very few will remember Broughton Rangers now, even then their glory days had long since vanished and a change of name to Belle Vue Rangers in 1946 hardly helped to prevent their subsequent demise. But in the austere times that followed the war even mediocre teams could expect a good level of support, and it was the crowd atmosphere at the games, which gripped me long before I was able to fully appreciate the sport.

That is until Ray Price arrived, a young stand-off half from Abertillery who, playing his first game of Rugby League, thrilled the crowd with an exhibition of attacking halfback play that few had seen the like of. Many years later the Rugby League writer T. A. Owen said of him: 'He was a straight plunger of lightning, gliding speed and artistry quite unequalled'.

Although Ray spent several seasons with Rangers, and was capped by Wales in 1948, it was not until he moved to Warrington in 1953 that he was really recognised. Great Britain caps quickly followed with perhaps his finest season in 1956 when he played in all three Ashes winning Tests. Surely he would have received many more international caps had his career not almost exactly overlapped with that other great Welsh stand off, Dickie Williams. The next year I met the great Clive Churchill and the legendary Jimmy Lomas who had captained the first touring team to Australia, but my most treasured memory will always be Ray Price's first game.

In those days I had no idea that Wales had produced many great players. Of course, I knew that Ray Price was Welsh, but it was years later before I realised that like the Salford Red Devils from across the other side of the city, half of the Rangers side was from Wales. Indeed, sometimes when Salford and Rangers met there were more Welshmen than Englishmen on the field.

The Welsh 'fly-half' factory, beloved of comedian Max Boyce, has stopped production long ago. You can no longer shout down the pit and bring up yet another undiscovered little master of the stand-off half position, but there is no doubt that in the past Wales has produced a stream of talented players, in this more than any other position.

More than a dozen have played in British Rugby League teams with nine touring Australasia. Literally hundreds of Welshmen have 'gone north' since the split from Rugby Union in 1895, including over 150 who had played Union for Wales. In the years before and immediately after the Second World War jobs in the economically depressed South Wales valleys were scarce and poorly paid, so that almost all these players went north to secure their futures. The majority, but by no means all, succeeded at the new game and generated interest in the rugby mad South Wales population who wanted to retain contact with their heroes.

In the past Wales has come close to embracing Rugby League several times, and the history of these failed attempts to establish the game is eloquently documented in the book *Tries in the Valleys* (London League Publications Ltd) an outstanding contribution to the literature of the sport.

Recent news of the bid by Bridgend RUFC to enter a club in Super League in the 2004 season has been welcomed generally by fans, though some feel that the team should start in the NFP. That could happen, as Bridgend may face competition from more prestigious clubs in South Wales. Writing in the May 2002 edition of *Rugby League World*, 'Insider' wrote, "Look out for some exciting news soon regarding Wales, Rugby League and the summer of 2003. It won't quite be 1895 stuff, but not far off either."

Why then should there be this interest from an area where the fan's affections have always been for Rugby Union, a game recognised throughout the World as the national sport of Wales? Space here does not permit a detailed description of the woes of Rugby Union in Wales, but the governing body, the Welsh Rugby Union, has failed totally to understand the nature of their professionalised game. They have behaved rather like a closed club for Corinthian gentleman amateurs in their refusal to embrace

101

change and the result has been a national side whose performances have become an embarrassment, leading to a failure to sell-out some home games for the first time in living memory.

The soil in which to sow the seed of Rugby League has never looked so fertile, not simply because of Union's problems but also due to the pioneering work to successfully establish the amateur game over the past two decades or more. The foundations of student Rugby League are particularly strong, with roots that go back to 1978 when Phil Melling founded the first club at Swansea University. Phil worked tirelessly to develop the game in Swansea and success came with a UAU final, losing to Liverpool in 1983. Currently there are teams at Swansea, Cardiff and the University of Glamorgan competing successfully with student teams throughout Britain. Recently, the University of Wales Institute Cardiff [UWIC] won the Student Cup and also came close to winning the Premiership final, only to be denied when Leeds Metropolitan University scored in the last minute.

In the 1980s, almost in parallel to the development in the universities, Phil Melling helped to form a Welsh student team, which regularly beat England students following a first victory in 1984. With the arrival of Clive Griffiths in the late 1980s the team had a top quality coach whose talents later led to his coaching Warrington and the full Wales international team. With enthusiastic management and first class coaching success seemed assured. In 1989 the Welsh students beat the French students in Paris, the first time France had lost at home in 20 years. They followed this by taking the European Championship for five years on the run and came close to success in the World Championship losing to Australia students in a keenly contested semi-final in 1992.

In 1992 Danny Sheehy became coach when Clive Griffiths went to Warrington. Danny and his brother Kerry played a leading role in the development of amateur Rugby League in Wales, and at that time Kerry was appointed to the newly created post of Welsh development officer. Their efforts allowed the student game to consolidate its strong base and in recent years under the current development officer, Stuart Singleton and manager Gareth Jones the students have continued to flourish.

Developments in amateur club rugby are equally encouraging with Cardiff Demons competing strongly in the Rugby League Conference last year. The 2002 season saw them in a very tough group with Hemel, Oxford and Gloucestershire, but away wins against Oxford, Gloucestershire and

102

Worcester have been encouraging. They prepared for the season with a keenly contested game against the newly created Swansea Bulls who showed that they have the potential to develop into a quality side. At the junior level possibly the development which promises most for the future is at Aberdare where Cynon Valley Cougars are running teams at under-13, under-14 and under-16 level while also taking Rugby League into the schools.

In North Wales, where rugby often competes unsuccessfully for the public's attention with the major football clubs across the border, Rugby League has had an embryonic development for many years. This has crystallised with the formation of the North Wales Coasters who, this season, have played games against teams from the Widnes area. Along with Cardiff Demons they represented Wales in the York Nines competition in June 2002, acquitting themselves well in a strong tournament. Hopefully they will be accepted for the Rugby League Conference in 2003.

Amateur Rugby League in Wales now has strong teams both on and off the field, and with the possible inclusion of Cardiff Demons in the new RFL league structure the future should be assured. The fan base for professional Rugby League in South Wales is as yet untapped, but pointers suggest that it is considerable. Coverage of Super League on Sky TV is said to get its largest regional audience in South Wales and recent support at international games has been good. More than 17,000 watched the Wales versus New Zealand game in 2000 and the attendance of 30,042 against England (at Old Trafford) in 1995 was a record for a Wales fixture.

But we must be careful not to let euphoria obscure the problems that lie ahead. In spite of the declining fortunes of the national team, Wales remains a Rugby Union fortress, and while much of the open antagonism to Rugby League has evaporated with the coming of professional Union, there are still those with power and influence who want us about as much as they would welcome an outbreak of Anthrax.

Although some time has elapsed since Phil Melling described, in *Tries in the Valleys*, his attempt to run a 10-a-side competition in August 1991, I'll quote him here: 'We sent out circulars, put an advert in the *Western Mail*, and got around 50 responses, mainly from Rugby Union teams, including Ammanford, Amman Valley and Pontypridd. A few Rugby League clubs came, like Eccles. The Welsh Rugby Union responded by saying that anyone who played in the tournament would be 'professionalised', because former professionals were playing. As a result we lost a lot of entries.

Correspondence from Dennis Evans, the Welsh RU Secretary, was also sent to every Rugby Union club in Wales about this competition. One circular had us as the first item, a higher priority than the Welsh tour of South Africa. That is how much they regarded Rugby League as a threat. Swansea Uplands (the hosts) were threatened by the WRU that funding for new floodlights would not be approved if the tournament went ahead. To their eternal credit they did not back down. We bought a trophy for the tournament and called it the Jonathan Davies Trophy. The WRU then sent out another circular that said that anyone who even 'touched' the Trophy would be 'professionalised' and automatically banned from Rugby Union. We changed the name of the trophy to the Dennis Evans Trophy but he never got the joke. The tournament went well and we had a great weekend. The whole affair proved to me that major organisations like the WRU, with their reputation for being tough and inscrutable, were brittle and neurotic.'

We in Rugby League need not be scared of them."

The 'London Eye'

Chris Gallagher again, this time about the state of the game in the growing Rugby League stronghold of London.

"So, what exactly is going on down south? Sure, the Broncos have had a few fantastic wins this season, but what about the grass roots Rugby League scene? What are the numbers? What are the plans? What exactly is going on down south?

Southern based broadcasters have often cited 'demand' as a reason for not including more Rugby League content in their (mostly national) television shows and newspaper articles, saying that there aren't sufficient levels in the south. I'm taking that to mean that there aren't enough people interested in Rugby League. I won't go into the argument as to why Rugby Union *is* given coverage nationwide when a large portion of the population (especially in the north of Britain) is in love with Rugby League. That's for another day, another page, another book, perhaps.

Until recently, the London Broncos were based at Charlton Football Club's ground (south east London), and did lots of work in the community around the Southwark region. This local community work impressed the Metropolitan Police so much, that they approached the Broncos with a partnership in mind, and have since funded a full time development officer to work with the community."

Join the Caro-van

What is demand for Rugby League like in the south, though? To answer some questions about the health of the game in the south of Britain, Chris spoke to Caro Wild, London and south development manager for the Rugby Football League.

Caro is responsible for the development areas in and around London, which is split into 6 different areas - North, West, South and South East London, plus the Thames Valley and Hertfordshire & Bedfordshire regions. He is also responsible for the development officers in each of these areas.

Schools

"In the south east as a whole, there are over 100 schools who currently benefit from professional coaching, around 50 that play in organised festivals and about 15 to 20 schools regularly competing off their own backs. Multiply that by the number of kids in each school, and you are looking at quite a number of children with regular exposure to Rugby League in the capital.

Moving up a step, every year the number of teams and players involved in junior representative Rugby League teams in the south of England and Wales is increasing.

At the RFL, they are already fairly taken aback by the sheer size of it all, and he hasn't even started adding the under-11 fixtures - the most popular age group. The current list is for all age groups from under-12 up to the under-16 and academy levels, and includes representative teams from West, North, South East and South London, the Thames Valley, the Cynon Valley, Cardiff, Hertfordshire & Bedfordshire, and Gloucester.

With the number of people coming in to the game, the current structure needs to be changed to increase its capacity, and that's one area on which Caro and his team are working. They hope to encourage local area teams to start up, to add another step in a youngster's progress.

Think of it as a pyramid. They have a large base level (the schools), and at the top, the service areas teams such as Thames Valley. To cope with the increasing number of kids playing the game, they are trying to insert a new middle layer to this pyramid, namely, local area clubs.

The best children would graduate from their school to a local 'town' team (i.e. Croydon, Lambeth etc). The best players from those teams would then graduate to service area squads (i.e. South London, Herts & Beds, etc).

The fact that these sorts of measures are being attempted is testament to the ever-increasing number of people playing the game outside the 'heartlands'.

In addition to the school teams, the local teams and the regular representative schedule, there are talent camps, regional camps, tournaments and the London youth games to include. Cap it all off with two England versus Wales test matches, and you're running a pretty big, and rapidly expanding schedule.

The RFL are keen to increase capacity, and they are soon to receive a grant of £100,000 per year (from Active Sports) for Rugby League in London alone. In addition, further funding has recently been granted for the Reading and Slough areas through Sport England.

Where do the kids go after that? Well, the very best players will be picked to go to a training camp, and will play against equivalent teams of the likes of Bradford Bulls, St Helens and Wigan Warriors. That's up until age 16, anyway.

Juniors to academy

At academy age, the system changes. The idea is that the very best players will go into the Broncos academy team. Some of the others will go to the academy teams of the Rugby League Conference sides (i.e. South London Storm), and the remaining players would go to the academy section of teams in the London League (second teams from the Rugby League Conference and other London League first teams e.g. Greenwich Admirals). The game is already seeing players from these structures playing open age rugby in the Rugby League Conference and other competitions.

Conference round London

One of the teams currently in the Rugby League Conference is the North London Skolars (sic). They have been steadily growing over the years and are at a stage now where they would like to increase their standing within the game. They have been accepted into the Northern Ford Premiership, the 'professional' standard. Another few years, and we may even see another London based Super League club.

To me, this suggests that the clubs themselves and the administration are both doing a good job in promoting and supporting Rugby League in the south. One of the latest big success stories of southern Rugby League is

Desi Williams. He started his career with the London Skolars and had been playing in the London area for a few years now. His performances had caught the eye of scouts from the big clubs, as he has recently signed for Wigan Warriors.

Taking a step back, I asked Caro what was main obstacle he faced. Was it resources? Was it the number of kids? Was it a lack of coaches? Not really. The main obstacle he faced was the game's profile. "Ask any kid who Andy Farrell is, and most won't have a clue. Only slightly more will know who Jason Robinson is."

At club level, even with - or should that be despite? - the present profile, there are more kids getting involved all the time. The South London Storm club is a great example of this. They started the senior team in 1995, and after a few seasons, and cup final appearances, South London successfully applied to join the Rugby League Conference, changing its name to include the moniker Storm. In the same year, 1999, they launched their junior section, initially called the Sharks.

In the years since then, the youth sides have developed much further. In addition to their senior team, the club now runs teams at every age from under-10, right through to under-16 and the academy teams. This strength in their youth development programme, and the enormous potential for Rugby League in the south of the capital make the Storm believe that they will soon be challenging for honours.

They have forged very good links with the London Broncos, even now that the Broncos have changed their home ground again. More often than not, if you attend a London game, especially at Griffin Park, you'll probably see one or two Storm shirts in the crowd.

Some of those wearing the shirts play in the Storm first team, and therefore in the Rugby League Conference, as I've already mentioned, and this particular competition is increasing in popularity year on year.

Crawley Jets, based near Gatwick, have featured in three of the last four finals, and won two of them. Add in Kingston Warriors, North London Skolars, West London Sharks and South London Storm, and you have an entire division of London based Conference clubs.

Conference all over

For those who think that the game is stagnating in the northern counties, I have one thing to say to those readers - League's just a northern game? My eye. Allow me, if you will, to list the last four winners of the Rugby League

Conference:

1998 Crawley Jets
1999 Chester Wolves

2000 Crawley Jets
2001 Teeside Steelers.

Of the 30 teams playing in the Conference in 2002, just five came from the traditional Rugby League areas. The other teams are spread far and wide in England, with the notable addition of the Cardiff Demons from South Wales. Last year, the Conference teams were strengthened to such an extent that the powers that be had to change from four to six divisions – North East, North, Midlands, East, South and South Central.

After 2002, this system is going to be changed somewhat. Instead of a completely separate competition, the Conference teams will form the new National League Division 3, Northern and Southern sections. This provides a clear progression path for teams on the up, a change that can only encourage more involvement from new clubs.

The game's development in the south is mostly based around senior teams playing what was the Rugby League Conference. Almost every club finds that once a senior team starts, there are younger players interested in taking up the great game.

There are senior teams popping up all over the country now. In 2001, a whole division of new teams was incorporated into the Conference. Five teams from the north east made up one of the six divisions covering the whole of England (and South Wales in the form of the Cardiff Demons). These north eastern teams are Bridlington Bulls, Durham Phoenix, Newcastle, Sunderland City and the winners of the Conference in 2001, the Teeside Steelers.

The RFL are taking the southern development seriously, and the grants from Sport England and Active Sports organisations are certainly greatly appreciated, although more resources are always welcome, says Caro. More coaches and more players will surely follow if the main issue - getting the kids interested in the first place - can be overcome, if the profile of the game is raised. (Cue discussions on media coverage on television, newspapers, radio, internet sites, etc)

I think that the south is a vital area for Rugby League in the next few years. If a good foothold could be maintained and strengthened with regards to both the quantity and quality of players, more media organisations will be looking to cover our growing sport. This increased media coverage will prompt more people to get involved, and so the circle continues.

Overall, I'm very positive for the present and the future. Southern teams are getting stronger every year, more and more kids are playing Rugby League, and after a brilliant cup final, along with some meaty media coverage, I think that the outlook for the South is very good.

There's just one question remaining to my mind. How many years until we get a three-way County of Origin competition?"

Rugby a treize, *en croute*

Manchester-born and Swinton-raised, John Marchant, Rugby League fan for over 40 years now lives in France. In between earning a living and renovating the pile of rubble he calls home, John and his wife Dorothy manage to sample the delights of the French arm of the Greatest Game.

France is a foreign country: they do things differently there.

"OK I admit it. I am not ashamed. I am a Wigan fan. You have no choice if your wife's family is from there, going back to at least 1780. But I digress. What you really want to know about is the Rugby League experience in France.

Pas de tourte à la viande

Most important thing first. Pies. Quelle surprise. Pies. Not any old pies, but real pies. Pies a million miles removed from your insipid and stodgy north of England pie. Close your eyes, imagine this and salivate: new potatoes, cooked to perfection, sliced and set in crème fraich, dusted with a blend of aromatic herbs, the secret known only to the maker of these delightful creations, the whole thing wrapped in golden brown and light flaky pastry. And when we venture forth to watch the Greatest Game, we take a couple of 'pâté de pomme de terre' with us. Not forgetting a bottle of red Saint Pourçain. Just like at the JJB, really.

Mixing with the élite

And that is how the experience begins. However, you have to bear in mind that the game in France is much smaller than in Britain. As shown in recent Challenge Cup outings, the top French Elite One clubs can hold their own with clubs in the upper reaches of the NFP. But at the lower end of Elite One it is a struggle, sometimes unsuccessfully, for survival. And Elite One is the top competition. The best comparison is imagining Rugby League in

Britain without Super League, without the Rugby League Conference, and without BARLA. I know, I know. Don't say a word. In fact, it is a testament to Gallic pride that the game is as strong as it is and that has such an enthusiastic following in the south and south west. It seems to me that if some of this enthusiasm were transplanted to Britain, the game there would be much healthier than it is.

What ever happened to wozzisname?

So let me tell you about my first ever experience of Rugby League in France, at the Charlety Stadium to watch Paris St Germain versus Wigan. Most memorable thing about that trip? Beer (well lager actually... yeaarrgghh) at three times the price in England. Enough to keep you sober, I can tell you. Second most memorable thing? Terry O'Connor getting in the lift at the hotel and it instantly going dark 'cos he blotted out the light. Oh, all right, the third most memorable thing was getting Jason Robinson and Inga 't winger to be photographed with 'er indoors in the hotel restaurant. By the way, whatever happened to them? No, not the wife. I know where she is, don't I just... no, I meant the other two. I hear they have been put out to grass. Is that true?

Second... out of two

Now, about my second experience of Rugby League in France. In the heart of the fertile plains of Comtat Venaissin in the Vaucluse, Carpentras offers a real treasure to all lovers of history and architecture (it says in the tourist guide) not to mention Rugby League (which it does not mention in the tourist guide). Castleford this is not. Carpentras versus Roanne in the Elite Two competition. I found out about the game from a shop poster, even though I was staying over 50 miles away at the time, in Peter Mayle country. So armed with the date time and location of the game, off we set to Carpentras.

Arrived in the town centre half-an-hour before kick-off. What a crowd, what an atmosphere. The town centre was buzzing with people and jammed with cars. Nose to tail. Never going to make the kick-off at this rate. If only it was like this in Britain. Can you imagine people queuing like this to watch, say, Oldham? No? Well not in Carpentras either.

No one told us that the town would be virtually at a standstill, not because the mighty Roanne were in town but because it was fête weekend, with a fair and a flea-market and all the stuff. It was the St. Siffrein fair. It begins on 27 November and coincides with the equally famous black truffle market. Excellent candied fruit, strawberries, melon, bonbons 'berlingots' and grapes (used for the Cotes de Ventoux wines) are Carpentras specialities.

However, when we actually arrived at the ground, things were back to normal with a crowd of around 500 and a referee of questionable parentage, at least according to some of the crowd. Still, a good game, if a little raw at the edges. No shortage of commitment and a degree of personal animosity between some of the players to keep the interest up. For the record, Roanne came second. Out of two.

How many Wigans?

So with that happy experience under our belt we decided that we would have to have more. But rather than arriving just half and hour before the game we would in future make a day of it, so that we could take in the delights of places such as Carpentras before the game. And that is how we found Viilefranche. One of the things you have to bear in mind about France is the geography. The 'Hexagone', with roughly the same population as the United Kingdom, covers two-and-a-half times the area. And since the big cities are spread right across France, rather than confined as they are in Britain to the bottom two-thirds of the country, everywhere is a long way from everywhere else. And when you live in the centre of the country as we do, don't you know it? Off we go. First off, make sure we are going to the right place. There are at least 16 Villefranches in France. The one we were after was Villefranche-de-Rouergue. There are also over 70 Villeneuves in France (the Rugby League one is Villeneuve-sur-Lot). Imagine if you will, 70 Wigans in Britain. Now wouldn't that be something?

Only the bars were open

Oh, it's ever such a long way to Villefranche. Five hours of driving to be precise. But not your 220 British miles of clogged motorways and Sunday drivers. Just a long stretch of A75 toll-free motorway with hardly any traffic, a motorway sweeping majestically through the hills of the Massif Central, a motorway rising at times to 4,000 ft above sea level. After the motorway come the normal roads, still traffic-free on a quiet and sunny Sunday morning. Trolling along at 50 mph. Lunch? A picnic (pique-nique) of pâté de pomme de terre and tarte au myrtles in the beautiful city of Rodez with its traffic-free centre around its cathedral perched high above the surrounding plain. Onwards then, on roads more or less devoid of traffic, diving down the hillside into the small and sleepy country town of Villfranche-de-Rouergue. A quick drive round, find the stadium, park and then wander round. Believe me, this is the life. If you have not experienced a warm sleepy spring Sunday in southern France you have not lived. Supermarkets, DIY centres, lots and lots of small shops, and bars. And all of them closed except the bars.

Grin and bear it

Come on now, you have to admit it - it sure beats Batley. In fact, this could be a way of life. Well, certainly a holiday. Why not persuade your family to take a late holiday this year and take in some of the superb towns, villages, food and wine and scenery of south west France, out of season when it is quiet and when the prices are lower? Only later do you need to say that, purely by coincidence there happens to be some great Rugby League to be had at the same time and that it is the ideal way for the whole family to spend a Sunday afternoon. Go on, try it. See where it gets you. Well, for us it got us a weekend in Saint-Gaudens, close to the Pyrenees.

The Bears versus the Blue Sox in the Kelloggs Nutri-Grain Challenge Cup. A mere 340 mile, six-hour drive each way. But worth it, well worth it. Why? For just one thing. The programme. For there at number seven was…G. Muttley Clinch. And there at number eleven was… D. Tess Tickle! Try explaining that to bemused French fans.

However, I will say something for the Saint-Gaudens Bears: they sure know how to welcome their guests. Since we were on holiday we bought VIP tickets, heavily promoted on the club website. £25 each, mind you, but well worth it. A champagne reception on arrival at the ground, a named seat in the centre of the stand (Steve Linnane just behind me screaming into his walkie-talkie, 'Just complete a set of six for once.!') Do you know what the French for 'walkie-talkie' is? No, wrong. It is in fact 'talkie-walkie'. Look it up if you don't believe me.

A Ferré tale ending

The town was awash with posters for the game. I know, I helped relieve them of some. There was a real buzz about the place. And the after-match reception was even better than the pre-match reception. For as well as lots of food and wine (this is France, for heaven's sake) you got to meet the Halifax team, the Saint-Gaudens team, Mr referee Kirkpatrick and many other famous personalities. Even the infamous M. Ferré, in charge of the French Federation, was there. And they all took the time to talk to you, too.

So replete with salmon and of course wine and even more importantly, Rugby League, staggered back to the hotel, determined to do it again. And we did - UTC versus Wigan, Perpignan - more food, more wine, more posters. And we did - Villeneuve versus Pia, Carcassonne, in the final of the Lord Derby Cup, more food, more wine, no posters. You should give it a go too: you'll love it. Because France is a foreign country, and yes, we do things differently here."

Coincidence for June

On 15 June 2002, the day before Father's Day, Ray attended a *The Petition - Enough is Enough* book signing session at W. H. Smith in St Helens. It was decided to take one of the five hefty books that each contains 6,000 petition signatures. Once at the shop the book was partly opened to display some names of fans that had signed.

During the afternoon a lady purchased a book whilst also glancing at the signatures. To her amazement there on the open page was her dad's name (Mr Lamb) and signature. We were both took back at such an amazing coincidence. What are the odds for one name in 30,000 to be on display and catch her eye at that moment in time?

The actual day was shared with Geoff Lee, author of *One Winter* and *One Spring*. He too was signing his books. At first we were apprehensive, as the day coincided with the England versus Denmark football World Cup match. However, our fears of a meltdown were unfounded as we sold 65 books between us. Our pre-event negative thoughts proved to be unfounded.

There was also an interesting point in that those people that purchased the books may not have done so, only for the fact that Geoff and I were on hand to sell them.

Selling or marketing, you can call it what you like, but it does work. We simply focused people's attention that the books were available. No doubt a nice little profit to show for the shop.

Trust the fans - The rise and rise of supporters' trusts

Cliff Spracklen, Chair of the Rugby League Supporters Association submitted this thought provoking piece during June:

"One week in November 1999 shattered any illusions that I had about the relationship between the so-called leaders in the game, and the fans. In one week Gateshead were moved to Hull, and Sheffield Eagles, fairy tale winners of the Challenge Cup at Wembley, over mighty Wigan, were on their way to Huddersfield. Technically they were 'mergers', but supporters of all four clubs knew the score. Hull F.C. fans were still drinking in the nightmare of oblivion, following the David Lloyd period, and were probably just grateful to have their club back from the brink. But Gateshead and Sheffield fans saw it as the end of their club, even though there were some nominal attempts made by the 'Shuddersfield' Giants to play some games in Sheffield.

Defenders of the mergers blamed the Association of Premiership Clubs for rejecting the proposals for the merged clubs to run NFP teams, as well. Either way the Super League ambitions of Sheffield and Gateshead fans were crushed.

Even worse they believed that the new entities were eventually going to be simply Huddersfield and Hull. At very short notice new independent bids were made to the NFP, from new Sheffield and Gateshead clubs.

Whilst these were not supporters' trusts, the supporters' clubs of both Gateshead and Sheffield were very active in their support and involvement, and indeed took some small shareholding. The new Eagles club has a clause in its articles, limiting individual ownership to 15 per cent of the authorised share capital.

At the same Bramley's directors announced at very short notice the club's resignation from the Northern Ford Premiership. No obvious reasons were given. The club had been nomadic since leaving McLaren Field, now sadly a housing estate, and had been playing at Headingley.

There were no apparent financial problems at the club, which was due to receive the highest revenue levels in its history, for the forthcoming season.

Bramley fans were mortified, and at a supporters' meeting it was decided to ask the club's directors to reconsider. Unknowingly the fans were talking to the wrong people. The directors were not the majority shareholder. The detail is another story, but Bramley did resign from the League, and the fans were shattered.

However, the supporters then formed the Bramley Action Group, had already told the directors that they would form a new club, and this they did. The new club was to be very different from the old, being owned by the supporters themselves, with no one individual being allowed any control. Democratically modelled on the Barcelona Football Club, the new club has a unique constitution, and in legal-speak is an *Industrial and Provident Society.* In other words a 'mutual' or 'co-operative'. The club's aims are stated and the directors cannot deviate from them. They certainly cannot sell the club.

At the same time the Football Task Force had recommended greater fan involvement in the running of clubs, and set up, and funded, Supporters Direct.

This organisation is funded to help football fans set up supporters' trusts at football clubs. These trusts should have a democratic constitution, and the IPS model, similar to the new Bramley Rugby League Community Club Limited is recommended.

In football this has taken off with over 50 per cent of English league clubs having a supporters' trust, even at Arsenal and Manchester United, and the movement is also growing rapidly in Scotland, with Celtic fans' supporters' trust the biggest. In most cases the aim is to work with the club, raise funds, take out a shareholding, and hopefully gain a seat on the board. The trusts are separate legal entities, and not necessarily set up to take over the parent club. However, in one or two dire financial situations this has happened, notably at Lincoln City and Chesterfield football cubs.

The Bramley story is now well known. The fan-run club put in a bid to be accepted into the NFP in 2000, but was rejected solely on the grounds that Farsley Celtic AFC, the chosen venue did not meet the RFL's criteria.

But the club has not given up, and this year has again submitted a five-year business plan, with a view to initially playing at nearby Morley RFC, before returning to the Bramley area. By the time this article goes to print we should know if that bid has been successful or not, but the interesting thing is that this time the club was encouraged by the RFL to apply, in the light of the need for new clubs to make the proposed new National League structure viable.

That represents an amazing 'about turn' in the attitude of the Rugby League authorities towards supporters' trusts. At the same time that Bramley RLCC was being formed the RLSA was trying to interest the Rugby League authorities in the new 'trust' concept. Having a policy of encouraging the creation of independent supporters' associations at every club, the RLSA saw this as a further step forward to giving fans a say. The then RFL chief executive Neil Tunnicliffe was encouraging, but clearly it was the clubs that needed to embrace the idea. Unfortunately, many fans groups were having difficulty in getting independent supporters associations set up. Many clubs saw them as a nuisance at best, and subversive at worst. So a supporters trust was to many 'beyond the pale'. What particularly rankled the RLSA at this time was the lack of interest or support in the 'trade press' at the time, although the old *Rugby Leaguer*, did become convinced, perhaps influenced by events at Bramley, and now *League Express* has now also given public support. But supporters' trusts still smacked of 'reds under the beds' to many. Indeed some fans criticised the RLSA for becoming 'too political' in getting behind this development.

But whatever caused it I am not too sure, but there was a conversion by the new head of operations, at the RFL, Nigel Wood, sometime last year, that makes Paul and the 'Road to Damascus' fade into insignificance.

At a historic RLSA meeting at Drighlington ARLFC, Nigel admitted that the trust concept could play a key role at smaller NFP clubs in difficulty.

A few weeks later at a packed meeting of Bramley fans, at their now famous operations centre, The Old Vic, Bramley, Nigel warmed to the enthusiasm of shareholders/supporters by encouraging Bramley to apply for a place in the new National League structure. Perhaps it was the wide range of 'real ales' available, but more seriously, with the 'in danger' flags flying over a number of NFP clubs, there appeared now to be a rather more sober view at HQ that the fans needed to be mobilised if some NFP clubs were to have any future at all.

Ironically, when the Bury F.C. fiasco came out, with the consequent knock-on effects for the Swinton Lions, the RFL itself recommended to Swinton officials, that they look at the Bramley model as a way forward. Prior to that, however, the Lions' fans, under the leadership of Steve Wild, had already decided to act quickly, and arranged a public meeting, at which they resolved to form a supporters trust. This was officially launched at a meeting at the Folly Club, on Station Road itself, on 1 June 2002, with revered former stalwart Albert Blan as guest of honour. He was also enrolled as a new member. In fact former Lions players have been allocated the first 200 membership numbers, a determination that there is also a role for past players in the future of the club.

The 'shambles' at York where the Wasps went into receivership mid-season, again saw a galvanising of fans. Led by lifelong Wasps fan Gary Hall, a supporters' trust has been set up, to help bring a semi-professional team back to the Minster city.

As with the Swinton Trust, the York Wasps Trust will not seek to run the club, but to raise funds, and take a share in the club, with other investors, and York will enter the League, as a new club, in 2003.

So 'it's all right for NFP clubs, but won't work at Super League level' is a view that has been put to the RLSA. Sorry you cynics, but the ambitious Warrington Wolves, who are thinking long-term, bit the bullet, and finance manager, Neil Dowson, has applauded and encouraged the Wolves fans, who have now set up a supporters' trust, which fits nicely into the consultation that Wolves have initiated on the proposed new stadium. Perhaps it was the recognition of the need to have the fans on board, through the difficult period of planning enquiries hat swung it. Or maybe it was having Lord Doug Hoyle on board at the club, a member of the All-Party Parliamentary Rugby League Group, who have backed the RLSA demand for supporters' trusts in Rugby League. But I believe that shrewd finance manager, Dowson, as well as being only a title removed from the terraces, recognises that trusts and supporters, especially at bigger, well-supported clubs are going to be the major investors and sponsors of the future.

Yes, at the time the Wolves were at the bottom, you might say, but it won't work at the very top clubs. But the signs are that a supporters' trust will be set up at arguably our most successful club of recent years. With the largest membership of any ISA, numbering thousands rather than hundreds, the relationship with the parent club was not close. While the fans were expected to turn up in their thousands, which Saints fans do, they were as in the dark as anyone about St Helens' impending problems. It took a new chairman, chief executive and board to open up, and now the relationship seems excellent, to the point where all parties appear to see the potential. If it works at Saints, then the idea must surely be relevant for every club.

Bramley, Swinton, York, Warrington and Saints are putting their trust in the fans. Such developments will give supporters' groups the chance to influence the direction their clubs are taking, but it is not one-sided of course. By setting up trusts the fans are also committed to 'rolling up their sleeves' and working for the clubs. The role of the trust member is to make a contribution to the well-being of the club, in terms of fund-raising, but also in being prepared to put their own skills at the disposal of the club, and working for well-being of the club. This means more than just turning out

117

on a Sunday. But it does banish the stereotyped view of 'the supporter.'

Trusts have members with skills in areas that the parent clubs may lack: marketing, PR, event management, IT, fund-raising, personnel and others that can save thousands. Time for the game to wake up, and trust the fans."

Rugby League 'ere again

Ay oop, me old muckers, Rugby League 'ere again. End of June and the 2002 season is 'alf ower and what entertainment I've given thee. Some grand games, some surprise results and a champion Challenge Cup Final among me new mates north of t' border. I seem popular when I visit there. 'Appen there's a promise of a visit from New Zealand cousins in October. (Best watch those lads, some of 'em think that one day they can do that fierce Maori Haka, the next they can become an English toff.)

Also bin practising me Belgian stilt walking for th' Grand Final day. Rumour has it that old Jonesy is thinkin' of takin' t' match in and I wouldn't want to disappoint 'im. I've also started up another business, just in case matters go astray. T' was Barnesy that give me th' idea and it's goin' well, sellin' them empty stadium seats, for a shilling or two. I've heard that they're doing the same at Headingley when the Tykes play.

I see th' honourable members down south were happy to receive me petition, an thanks is given to all me family that signed and the rest that would have, given the chance. It does seem like me enemies have piped down a bit, so well done everyone. It makes me proud of th' effort put in by one an all, a reet good do. Still, can't rest on't laurels an must make sure th' effort goes on, so shoulders to the wheel, lads.

I've got a new gaffer tha knows, seems to know what he wants, but I wonder if all his deputys want same? Need t'get sorted if I'm to spread me wings a little more. Nivver knows where I'll be performin' next. I'm in five continents already but I wouldn't mind goin' to a few more Pacific Islands, or sum other exotic places. Would need to take me Union Jack boxers for a bit of a swim and sunbathe. What about our Claire at the BBC? Ney mind th' horsey stuff, she's certainly fell for me charms. Had me old legs bucklin wi pride wi'er comments. I say 'let's 'ave more', what dust tha say?

9. July 2002

In this world of spin and scrutiny of every current issue, in July let's look at some differing views on our favourite subject from the worlds of media and academia. Perhaps using different depths of analysis, articles include media man Dave Swanton who submitted his thoughts in July.

Skooternik revisits the clubs, lukewarm about the petition as it was happening in 2001, to see if its aftermath made any sort of impression in our 30 or so 'sleepy hollows'.

July featured the dreaded one-off test from Sydney, Australia. Some found it newsworthy, others didn't, given the result, maybe just as well.

On to a new venture in Eggchasing. But let's start with Swansea Jack, from the Totalrl site, who spotted this in the *South Wales Evening Post*. Is it a coincidence that Rugby League is back on the agenda in the Principality?

One sport in danger of turning into a rumour

Mark Orders in the *South Wales Evening Post* on 4 July launched into Rugby League, claiming that the news that League is a summer game arrived by pigeon post. Outlining all the other sporting attractions to come in the summer, he concluded that we should be "sparing a thought for Rugby League - a sport in danger of turning into a rumour".

It appears the 'pot is calling the kettle', especially when the Welsh RFU is in a financial mess with another rumour that they will have to sell the Millennium Stadium. With all that is going on in sport, surely he has better reporting to consider. Might make the nationals eventually…

Futtocks, from the Totalrl website responded: "Spare a thought for Rugby Union - a sport which is apparently played in the winter. With the FA Premier League, UEFA & Champions' League, the Rugby League Challenge Cup and the Ashes tests in cricket vying for space in the media spotlight, the 15-a-side code did not exactly monopolise the public's interest over the past season, despite the BBC's best efforts.

Never mind. Between football, cricket and Rugby League, Rugby Union can then stake a claim for public attention. When the Zurich Premiership comes to a climax, it will probably engage some, but Rugby Union seems to expect all rival sports to vacate the scene. My advice to Rugby Union fans, players and officials is to get over it.

Rugby League's Great Britain versus New Zealand series starts after

119

their Grand Final. The following months will feature the qualifying rounds of football's European Championships, horse racing's Prix de l'Arc de Triomphe and the aforementioned Ashes which will in turn give way to the UK Snooker Championships from York.

We are then into early 2003 - the start of the Australian Open Tennis and the Challenge Cup. Which is where we came in, sparing a thought for Rugby Union - a sport in danger of turning into an irrelevance."

Touché.

Research is no Holliday

Michelle is a student who recently in 2002 decided to look at the professional game of Rugby League as part of her studies, and in particular, the problems with expansion.

Now that rugby players of both codes have a free gangway to play either sport without discrimination the grassroots appear to be flourishing, especially in the armed forces, student game and the Rugby League Conference. Likewise, other grassroots areas are also on the up. Yet out of balance some amateur areas appear to be struggling like other sports. Below Michelle Holliday gives her views as a young Rugby League supporter:

"A question that has long been present within the sport of Rugby League is if the game will ever grow into new areas, and why it has struggled to expand?

A research paper was produced and aimed to identify how far the game of Rugby League has been able to spread throughout Britain on a professional basis, to assess what the reasons are for possible non-expansion, and to look at what the future holds for the game.

In order to reach these aims methods included questionnaires, interviews and data collection. To discover the degree to which the sport has been able to spread, maps were created showing the location of all professional teams every 10th year since 1895. The maps showed that from the very beginning teams were mainly within Yorkshire and Lancashire, and through the years despite attempts to take the game into new areas it has been largely restricted to these northern counties. Attempts have included taking the game to Paris, London, Gateshead, Whitehaven, and Workington and South Wales. From these only Workington is really classed as being a success in trophy terms, as they won both the league and cup within six years. It was also noticed that quite a few teams in new areas did not survive for many years, as many were not found on consecutive maps. But what are the reasons for the lack of spread, why has it not followed the sports of football and cricket with world-wide expansion?

To help address this question over 100 Rugby League fans participated in a survey. Within the sample population every Super League club was represented. To gain a more detailed view interviews were carried out of key personnel within the game. These included representatives from the Rugby League headquarters, professional clubs, and media personnel.

From the research it became apparent that the majority of fans are of the opinion that Super League's attempts to expand the game have not been successful, and that the teams in new areas have struggled to survive. There was the view that the expansion did not have a good strategy; that it was taken to the wrong places and was destined to fail. A strong opinion was also expressed that giving automatic promotion to certain clubs into Super League is unfair and is degrading the game, that it reduces the competition for teams, as they do not get rewarded for winning their divisions. And that it is the smaller teams who are suffering and being denied the chance to move up to the higher divisions. However there is the strong view that further attempts should be made to expand the game, but in different ways to those tried.

To look at the histories of sports such as football and cricket, differences can be seen if these are compared to that of Rugby League. These games developed much earlier, when little organised sport was played across the world and within communities, so they had less competition. Rugby League developed at a much later date, when many other sports had already established themselves. This was seen in other sports, when football tried to expand into the US it too met stiff competition from the American games of baseball and American football. The populations have strong holds to their traditional sports, and are reluctant to adopt others over their own. This has been the case with Rugby League; its late development in 1895 meant that it had football to compete with. Also the split of the game meant it would always have difficulties spreading in the southern counties, with both forms of rugby trying to dominate throughout England.

As Rugby League is taken into large cities such as London, it is questioned whether this aids or harms the game. Largely due to Rugby Union's presence and the media coverage, it is felt that the game is not given any chance to grow in these areas on a professional basis. The game is not made attractive to local people who are likely to know little about the sport. London is still an important area where the game has existed professionally for over 20 years, starting at Fulham in 1980. Yet for all the hard work being carried out the game does need another professional club down in the capital to complement the ever growing grassroots game.

The questionnaires highlighted the opinion that the attempts to expand in other areas have not been carried out in a successful way. That rather than trying to take the game into the larger cities which are often far from the heartlands, the game should attempt to grow out from its core into surrounding regions. Why this has never really been done with more thought perhaps needs to be looked at, as this would hit areas that have had some degree exposure to the game. It was also said that when the game is taken to these new areas it is thrown in at the deep end, in the respect that the game has never really been played there but it is introduced at the highest possible level. Maybe it should be introduced gradually, at amateur and school levels, so that the roots are then laid for the future of the game to develop through the levels. This would allow for more local players to develop and so hopefully larger fan bases as they would then be supporting their local team, not a team full of overseas players. After all, is this not how rugby successfully grew in its early years."

Rugby League and the media: Power without responsibility

Mark Falcous, Sociology of Sport lecturer at Chester City College, writes:

"Any Rugby League fan will be aware that national media coverage of the two codes of rugby is hugely disproportionate. This imbalance is present across all forms of media. For example, on Teletext, Rugby Union always appears above Rugby League. Likewise, click on to *The Guardian* website for 'rugby' and you will automatically come to Rugby Union coverage. On BBC Radio 5 Live, Rugby Union reports usually precede League reports. Similarly, the BBC extensively promotes its Rugby Union coverage, but does very little to promote League in a similar way.

This sporting hierarchy is not 'natural', or the result of chance, but the consequence of the workings of the media. The media do not simply reflect issues and 'news' within society in a neutral way. Alternatively, they actively construct what constitutes news, making selections of what counts, what doesn't count, and establishing agendas. In actively shaping 'news', they largely align with their own interests and subsequently, work to reproduce relations of dominance within society.

Media ownership and personnel in Britain are largely white, male, middle-class and southern *based*, and it is no surprise that in consequence they are also white, male, middle-class and southern *biased*. This bias rarely takes an overt form, but is subtly reflected in editors and journalists selections of what constitutes news, what is given relative importance, what is relegated to the margins, and the 'slant' within which issues are represented. Subsequently, the media are exceptionally powerful in shaping our very perceptions of the society within which we live, in marginalising certain 'voices' and promoting others. This power, however, comes with minimal responsibility or accountability.

The way in which media output is created and engineered, frequently reflecting relations of dominance, is reflected in sports coverage, which is characterised by hierarchies of dominance. Within Britain, the London-based national media dominate.

Subsequently, coverage of the two codes on the basis of class and regional bias is massively different. Rugby League is subsumed to Rugby Union, reflected in less national television and radio exposure and less attention within the print media, notably national daily newspapers. The media actively works to marginalise Rugby League. Yet it must be understood that this is not the result of any crude conspiracy, but the consequence of the backgrounds, in-built biases and pre-dispositions of media owners, editors, and journalists. A good example of the background and pre-dispositions/biases of journalists shaping coverage is the way in which the Oxford-Cambridge 'varsity' Rugby League game gains coverage that is out of proportion to its stature as a Rugby League game.

In 1994 I carried out preliminary, yet systematic research exploring the media coverage of the two rugby codes within broadsheet newspapers (*The Times, Daily Telegraph* and *Guardian*) over a three-month period. The results confirmed the magnitude of the imbalance between coverage of the two codes. A summary of the research, at the time, read as follows, 'in all three newspapers Rugby Union was represented with more frequency, in larger articles, with larger headlines and a greater number of photographs than Rugby League.' Across the three papers, Rugby Union coverage appeared 3:1 over League.

Additionally, I discovered overt bias toward League on several occasions with journalists taking the opportunity to 'snipe' at Rugby League, and qualitative differences in the nature of coverage - Union featuring 'personality' features, and commentary/analysis pieces rather than simply match reports. Additionally coverage of Rugby Union extended to the women's game, junior levels, student and schools matches.

123

Since this research, the sport-media relationship, in both codes, has shifted in significant ways. Rugby Union has turned professional and undergone accelerated commercialisation in the same way Rugby League has, yet the imbalances in coverage remain. Indeed, in a series of ways, they have been increased. One only has to look at the levels of coverage devoted to Jason Robinson since he changed codes. Was it that he suddenly became a more media worthy commodity in terms of his sporting abilities since his move to Union? Clearly not, he was as equally brilliant during his League career. The only difference is that he plays Union now, not League. Consequently he has been judged differently on that basis, and subject to a great deal more attention. The message is clear; Rugby Union is afforded higher media status than Rugby League. The basis of this imbalance is the media's bias, not any objective criteria.

Of course, media groups and personnel may argue that League, at the professional level, is solely a regional sport, and does not deserve national coverage. Yet, the media marginalisation of Rugby League is self-perpetuating. Other than long term institutional change, there is little reason to suspect the representation of Rugby League will be altered in any significant way, thus perpetuating the regionalisation and stereotyped image of the game.

Reading *The Petition - Enough is Enough* book confirmed my concerns regarding the failure of leadership figures and decision makers within Rugby League to *understand* the importance of mobilising the media. Take for example, what I consider to be the naiveté of Maurice Lindsay, demonstrated in his correspondence within the first volume. To think that the media are somehow a neutral institution and will respond to Rugby League according to its sporting 'worth' and spectacle is naiveté *par excellence*. As noted above, the sports media bring with them their own biases and pre-dispositions - contingent to which is the marginalisation of Rugby League in comparison to Rugby Union.

The lack of foresight of the leaders and owners of Rugby League clubs, in this regard, is perhaps the results of their own intransigence as they seek to align themselves with shifting commercial sport structures. Central to this is the new opportunities for cross-code ventures including alignment with Rugby Union clubs and authorities. Yet, in doing so, they betray the heritage and dignity of the game, which has never yet received an apology from the RFU despite 100 years of overt discrimination. The failure of the Rugby League leadership in this regard is reprehensible and irresponsible - and is borne of a naiveté and lack of insight into the wider social forces which shape the game.

Rugby League itself is shaped in an even more direct manner by the relationship with the media. In fact, it is no longer possible to separate the two. The Super League itself was created and premised upon media priorities. Indeed, Super League is characteristic of the fusion of media, sport and commerce, which are global in scope. Within this sport-media relationship, the media are dominant, dictating League formats, kick-off times and scheduling. Thus, in the quest for improved viewing figures, and hence more advertising revenue, the traditional live fan base is neglected. Hence, 8pm Friday kick-offs, or Saturday 6.05pm kick-offs which are often the least popular times, and most difficult for travelling support. Thus alignment with the media can alienate traditional fans.

Yet, in aligning themselves with BSkyB, the elite clubs (in the guise of Super League) has done little to improve the national visibility of the game. In fact, the game has suffered reduced prominence, and even geographical retraction within Britain, with the loss of professional clubs in Sheffield, York, Gateshead and South Wales. Within British sporting culture, Rugby League has become *more* peripheral during the Super League era. Specifically, the shift to a summer season saw terrestrial coverage of League reduced by at least half. Where the Regal Trophy, test matches, the Challenge Cup and Premiership used to be shown on terrestrial, only the Challenge Cup remains within terrestrial broadcast schedules. In turn, the failure to secure nation-wide terrestrial highlights, with the *Super League Show* confined to northern regions, merely reinforces the regional, and marginal image of the game. In contrast, coverage of Rugby Union has been cemented and expanded with the continued appearance of the Six Nations championships, on both BBC and ITV, the Zurich play-offs, and a European clubs competition broadcast and promoted extensively by the BBC.

The irony is that in securing a lucrative deal with BSkyB, Rugby League decreased the breadth of its exposure due to the UK satellite market, to which far fewer people have access than terrestrial channels. Alternatively, both football and Rugby Union enjoyed the large revenues from BSkyB, but crucially maintained a terrestrial presence, thereby securing and extending their prominent cultural status. Thus in summary, aligning with certain satellite media, a move apparently 'good for the game', has done extremely little. Indeed, it may have harmed the game in actively marginalising it from the widest possible audience. In the age of the quest for global markets, wider audiences, and merchandise sales; mobilising the media is pivotal to the success of commercial sports. This key battleground however, is one in which Rugby League possesses an extremely weak footing in Britain, and the games promoters seem scarcely aware."

Swanning along

Dave Swanton is aged 45 and is the media and PR manager for Sale Sharks Rugby Union club. Dave saw his first game of Rugby League at Borough Park, Blackpool back in 1970. After working for many radio stations Dave joined Warrington RLFC in 1996 and stayed there until 1998 when he joined Wigan RLFC. After Maurice Lindsay returned to Wigan, Dave moved back to Warrington before joining Sale Sharks in 2000. Dave has been voted the Best Media in both Super League and the Zurich Premiership. Dave also co-hosts *League 2002* on BBC Radio Lancashire with Mike Latham.

"I read the *Petition* book with a lot of interest but feel that many of the contributors were shooting the wrong man so to speak. Peter Jackson of the *Daily Mail* came in for some flak but since joining Rugby Union I have got to know Peter well. Peter openly tells everyone that the best try he has ever seen on a rugby field was scored by Chris Joynt for St Helens against Bradford Bulls in the play-offs a couple of years ago. Peter said that Jason Robinson would be a huge success in Union after his move to Sale Sharks.

Rugby League is in a lot of ways its own enemy. Clubs employ people as media executives and they have not got a clue on how to send a press release out, how to court the press, how to hustle for column inches.

Since joining Sale Sharks I have kept in touch with the majority of Rugby League press men and even present a show on BBC Radio Lancashire which covers just about everything positive in the game. Many journalists tell me their frustration regarding the lack of news from clubs.

The hierarchy at Rugby League is wrong too, Andy Whitelam and John Huxley are good at their jobs as are Stuart Cummings and Gary Tasker but on the top table, only Gary Hetherington has any idea on what is good for the game. The board is a closed shop and before you shout rubbish just remember that the people at Red Hall are looking after your game.

The Sky deal is another issue, without it, the game is bust. There is no way terrestrial television will give the same amount of money for the game. Just look at ITV Digital's deal. Many clubs took advances on money during my time in the game because they could not balance the books. Players are paid too much. How do I know? When I joined Warrington in 1996, players had become full-time, some saw their pay increase from £400 for a win to £40,000 a year with a car. It doesn't stack up and the game is suffering now.

That's what is wrong with the game. The answer is go back to part-time players, pay them accordingly and look after teams in the NFP. Furthermore, appoint people who can do the job at the RFL, Gary Hetherington, David Howes, Eammon McManus, Phil Clarke, Chris Caisley and John Wilkinson. Give the rest of the board a P45 each.

This may push the game back a bit, but will protect its existence for many years to come. The alternative is to carry on as you are and you will have a four team Super League in three years, everyone else will be amateur. Again before you say rubbish look at the Rugby League Conference, it is growing all the time and what input have the RFL board got in this competition, very little. I will do anything I can to get the game column inches - I have actually kept the flow of information going since I joined the Sharks in 2000. You as fans should apply pressure to get the game run by people who care and have a knowledge of what is needed to make the game great again. In doing this you will be protecting the sport for your children and grandchildren to watch.

Before you say 'Get lost, Swanny, you left us to join Union.' Of course I did, to protect my mortgage payments and I was fed up with how badly the game was run. I have had invitations to return to Rugby League and while you never say never, I am not putting my family's income at risk rejoining a game that is so badly run. I couldn't work for the governing body so I will just sit and wait, but I am not holding my breath. I rest my case."

Footnote

Thanks is given to Dave for being forthright, whether the reader agrees or not. However here are a few comments: Not disputing that Peter Jackson of the *Daily Mail* is a nice guy or not but some of his media articles have, we feel, been unduly biased against Rugby League. There is also the point that he never once replied to any letters. One can only judge as one finds.

Interesting point about going back to part-time in that it would be difficult from a media point of view. I'm sure some journalists would get the bunting out. Similar opinion to Maurice Bamford in that the game needs to go back to the drawing board.

Skooternik investigates

"When Ray asked me to write a piece for his second book, that he was co-writing with Tim Wilkinson, I was mildly surprised to say the least. On first coming across *The Petition* cynicism was to the fore. In my past life, as they say, a history of protest and petition was not new to me and it can be of little use if handled badly. There was great talk of 'The Rebellion' as it became known, and storming Fleet Street. The point that most major culprits against whom the campaign was being aimed had decamped to Wapping was overlooked - marching on Wapping doesn't really have the same ring.

I felt it prudent to point out that people make rash promises in the heat of the moment, but rarely follow them through. I could see disaster looming. Although some viewed it as pouring cold water on the whole concept, nothing could be further from the truth. It was more that I could see the problem they were attacking, but just knew from experience that those involved would in all likelihood end up with egg on their face if they continued along this road. I was very glad (to put it mildly) when this talk fizzled out and the book was pushed as the main factor. I was delighted to accept when Ray asked me to take part in the follow up. So here I am.

A follower of Leigh since I was perhaps 10, my father used to bring me up from North Wales where I then lived to watch them play on an increasingly regular basis, and have - in my mind anyway - followed their fortunes with a passion common to most, if not all, Rugby League fans and their teams. Further to that though is the love of the game itself, of the aggression and passion rarely found in professional sport these days. There is an increasingly commonly heard concept on Rugby League bulletin boards that the one is a fan of the game as much as his team. That is my view, but is it the view of those in power at the clubs? I decided to find out.

In Ray's first book, *The Petition - Enough is Enough*, a contributor, Tim Wilkinson, said: "Surely the people with the greatest interest in the game (those in the club boardrooms) and those with the greatest physical commitment to the game (the coaches and the players) would want fair representation in the papers, and on television for their endeavours? Funnily enough, it seemed not."

As well as capturing a sample of the volume of public feeling about media neglect, expressions of support from a few senior figures in the game would add a bit of gravity to the campaign.

He then went on to explain how, despite sending out around 50 letters to the professional clubs' management and coaches he received a meagre 15 replies. No wonder the game seems to have a self-publicity problem.

With this in mind, and it having been a fairly major plank of the petition, Ray asked me to follow up Tim's work and re-contact the clubs' chairmen and coaches to try and elicit some views on the petition itself, the strongly held view of Rugby League fans that the game is held back by in-fighting and the lack of respect apparently given to a club's biggest asset, its fans.

With this in mind, the following letter (with a stamped addressed envelope at my own expense to boot) went out to around a dozen representatives at both chairman and coach levels to gauge a response:

'No doubt you are aware of the petition about media bias against Rugby League organised by Ray Gent, and the subsequent book *The Petition*. In the process of writing the book Ray has highlighted many problems within the game. One main area of concern is why certain elements of the press attack Rugby League at the slightest excuse. There is also evidence that, as a sport, we are not promoting Rugby League as well as we might, both on a club and a national basis. It is on this subject that Ray has asked me to write a piece for the follow up book (own agenda) about the impact of the petition and the general state of the game's self publicity, and I am writing to you, and other people for their views.

There is some considerable evidence that 'in-house' politics has held the games self-promotion back over the years, which always makes for good Rugby League bashing press. Do you feel that this has harmed the game in the past, and in your opinion, is there still an element of this today?

Finally do you think the game's fans are given enough say, at club or national level? As the largest group of sponsors in the game, many fans feel that their views on the sport are frequently ignored. Is this right?

I look forward to receiving your views on this, and please feel free to add any other comments that you feel relevant.'

I expected a slightly better response than that which I got: **None.** Not one person in the most important roles at any of the clubs contacted could be bothered to put pen to paper to reply to someone who made it clear that the information gained would be used to enlighten the game's followers as to how they saw the state of the game. Thanks guys.

Post Haste

With this in mind, the next task was to do the only thing I could, which was to find the details of every club chairman and coach, and write to them all.

While I didn't manage to find the details of all clubs, I managed most and so 60 or so letters, and an amount of research that I don't think I ever did in school, it was time to sit back and wait for replies to flood in.

To my surprise, less than a week after my letters went out I actually had a reply. With trembling hands the letter was opened to find a reply from Barrow chairman Alan Tucker for which I am still grateful, as it proved to be one of only nine replies that I received.

Let me repeat that. Out of approximately 60 requests posted for an opinion there were less than 10 replies.

Each morning, until disillusionment set in, I eagerly checked the post for a sign of an envelope with my writing on. Every morning I was at best buoyed up by a reply or depressed by the lack of one. It wasn't until I received a brief note from one of the game's leading coaches explaining that he was bound not to talk to the media (apparently that includes me). It was in the middle of this waiting, incidentally, that one of Super League's chairmen complained to all and sundry because his opponents didn't field a full side against his. One rule for chairmen and one for the coaches it seems. Not that any fan of the game would be surprised to hear this.

It was now time to correlate the information received. Unsurprisingly in view of the aforementioned reply from the coach, most, although not all, replies were from boardroom level, the only other reply from a coach supported the views of the chairmen. It is reasonable to assume, therefore, that these are the main problems faced by the game as seen by those in the game. They are fairly agreed on the main points, although one did make a surprising point, which I shall finish on.

The main topic of agreement is that there is too much internal squabbling in the game. It appears that every club considers itself above the game, but holds the strange view that it's everyone else's fault. One chairman drew particular attention to the ongoing (at the time) squabble mentioned above.

The issue perceived from this was that the problem was always seen to be someone else's fault. It seems that from where I stand, as a fan, that there are clubs out there that consider themselves more important than the game, and some of those aren't afraid to promote themselves as such. The sad truth is, however, that Rugby League is a very small sport that has more than its fair share of detractors and that any in-house squabbling does nothing to promote the image of the sport to outsiders, who are those to whom we should be pushing our game. There are no worse detractors from our game; it seems, than those whom we entrust to run the clubs within it.

It is my opinion that the people in charge of the game are those who should be silenced, if anyone is, and that it should be within the powers of the RFL to punish those clubs that bring the game into disrepute. This is not a criticism of any one chairman in particular; it is my belief that there isn't a club out there in the professional game that can claim to be entirely free of neglecting the interests of the sport.

It is also widely felt, from the narrow input received, that the attacks are both made and received by the same few people at the same few clubs. As these tend to be clubs that are successful within the sport it is arguable as to whether this is 'sour grapes' from the losers, or bad sportsmanship from the successful teams. Whichever it is, with the game finally beginning to establish a global foothold, now is the time to stop, take a look at ourselves and concentrate on promoting the game.

It was also commented on that there seem, at times, to be concerted attacks on individuals within the game from the 'high and mighty' in the sport. Again, whether there is any substance to this is debatable, but in talking to other Rugby League fans that I know there is again a feeling from the fans that this is true to an extent.

A second widely held view seems to be that in the past we have suffered too much from part time management. This is actually something that personally I believe has historically been the case, but with the introduction of a professional, full time chairman of the RFL in Richard Lewis, perhaps this will change.

What is certain though is this: 'How many times have we seen what seem like excellent ideas for expanding our game slip into abeyance due to the lack of a concerted drive?' The ideas are there, but the willpower always seems to be lacking. We have seen big reviews of the game, proposals for new structures, we've even tried one or two of the ideas, but no one seems to have the willpower to say 'we've done this, now let's give it a chance.' A great example of this is the current debate over whether we should split the Northern Ford Premiership in two.

As a fan of a perpetually second-rated but always striving to improve team, I have for many years held that there isn't enough money in the game to promote the amount of fully professional teams we have, that clubs that have no money and, in some cases, apparently no ambition. They seem to be holding back those that do by stopping them from making their own way and their own success or failure. We are currently in a situation where, with the proposed launch of NFP2 in 2003, this is finally going to happen, but with the weaker and poorer clubs now realising their gravy train has been stopped all hell is starting to break loose.

With stronger leadership this would not be allowed to happen. A suggestion was made, it was voted on, and the majority line was taken. What we need now is for leadership to ensure that the policy was followed through. We shall see if Mr Lewis can make it happen. I have my doubts!

But I digress; Richard Lewis is the only man now who can make policy stick. From my feedback from the clubs it seems his appointment is widely, and warmly, welcomed. As long as he has support it seems that the game may finally drag itself into the 21st century and into the limelight held by the other code and by football where it belongs.

The final criticism that I mentioned earlier that was brought up by only one chairman was that of the Rugby League's own media. It seems that certain personalities delight in criticising and highlighting every dubious decision by referees, making up their own interpretation of rules to suit the moment, which are immediately contradicted at the next play, and making general attacks on the game in general. They are seen to offer nothing but complaint to the game. I appreciate we all do this when we are at games, but I would have thought that it would be unprofessional for those whose livelihoods, and whose employers' livelihoods depend on the good of the game to be denigrating it all the time. It is another of those regularly heard moans of the Rugby League fan that even those promoting the game can't help knock it. This certainly seems to be the case in our own media. Why pour scorn on something you profess to love? Take a lead from the Rugby Union commentators on the BBC, and the daily and weekly newspapers on the same subject. If there is praise to pour, shout it from the rooftops. If there is fair and consistent criticism to be made, make it. Otherwise shut up and sit down.

On the subject of media, I was disappointed by the difficulty I had actually getting details of who to write to from what is supposed to be the media of tomorrow, the internet. The RFL's own site is rarely updated, it doesn't seem to have links to club sites, there is no press release section and its overall appearance does nothing to give the impression of a thriving sport. Sadly this attitude seems to be widespread throughout the game, as many clubs don't host their own websites or makes them difficult to find. They don't seem to be aware that for many people (certainly within the media) the internet is the first place to look for information.

I was told in one reply that every club is supposed to have a PR officer.

Do none of these own computers? As a Leyther I'm lucky that my club has several good sites supporting the club, but most clubs only seem to have supporter sites hosted by the Rugby League Supporters Association (RLSA). In this age of information technology is it too much to ask that clubs can represent themselves properly, or is it another case of 'if we can't make money out of it, we don't want to know'? If it weren't for the good folks on Totalrl.com forum I would have struggled to find the addresses of many clubs, including several major ones.

It isn't just on the internet that I had problems in getting the exact details of whom, and sometimes where, I was needed to write. There doesn't seem to be available, to the best of my research, any standard volume in print giving details of how to contact teams. More PR problems there, from a researcher's point of view. Would it not be possible for one of our periodicals to put out an overview of the game with contacts and addresses, or is that too much to ask - free publicity for the teams that keep the magazines selling? Something to consider there, perhaps?

A further, and infinitely more pressing problem is that of getting the good news out to the media. I cannot comment for certain, as I couldn't find out from the RFL site, but I have read that the RFL does not have a press officer in London, the home of the national media. How this oversight has been allowed to happen is entirely beyond my understanding, but that has to be a major problem for the RFL to correct. If the press cannot collar a Rugby League representative when stories break, than they are going to ignore the stories as journalists, in my experience, have more important things to do than to go chasing around after what are, in their opinion, filler stories to begin with.

Sometimes I just despair

But its not all doom and gloom, attendances are up, nationally the game is as strong as it has ever been, and we even have a halfway decent Lions squad - providing they can all be fit at the same time - and clubs in general seem to accept that the game needs its fans as much as they need corporate sponsorship.

To this end there seems to be a rash of independent supporters' associations (ISAs) and supporters' trusts springing up, the majority of whom seem to have their relevant clubs, if not at their beck and call, then certainly sitting down at the table with them to discuss the running of the club. This shows that there is forward thinking at least some clubs, and that

133

the future of the game is perhaps in the hands of those for whom the game is an important part of their life. The fans. Now let's get it right!"

Good times at last ?

Richard Rae in the *Sunday Times* on 7 July had a positive article on the Australia versus Great Britain test. Headed "Lions out to spring ambush", he outlined that: "Keiron Cunningham, the world-class British hooker, believes the tourists can win Friday's one-off Test with Australia... The theory that the world is becoming a smaller place will be tested to its fullest by the Great Britain Rugby League team this week... Having arrived in Australia yesterday, the Lions have just five days to prepare for a single Test against the world champions in Sydney before immediately returning home to resume their club campaigns. It underlines the sport's determination to maintain regular international competition after the interest generated by last year's Ashes series." Positive coverage.

Put to the Test

The message seems to be that the media will take an interest in international events, this 'big stage' we hear so much about, and surely Britain versus Australia at virtually anything ranks up there.

A surprise therefore that the BBC declined to feature its coverage of the first test match between Great Britain versus Australia from Sydney in 10 years nationally.

Grandstand would have seemed the Test's obvious home among that weekend's coverage of British superbikes, athletics, Scottish Open golf and horse racing, but no, it was shunted off to the minority interest Sunday morning 'opt out', our friend the *Super League Show*.

An interesting contrast was in Australia with a highly respectable 32,000 crowd and a TV audience in Sydney alone of 735,000, proportionately massive.

Let's have another look at the *BBC*'s logic on this subject, with a few selected e-mail exchanges between BBC staff and disgruntled fans over the last year, collated by John Thomason.

Super League Show: Peter Salmon - 7 August 2001: "Our current feeling on the Super League highlights show is that it is hitting its core audience by being scheduled across the whole of the north of England and it is doing pretty good business for us each Sunday morning. I appreciate that there are many fans of the game outside of the core group and we will keep the matter under review."

Peter Salmon - 31 October 2001: "...We can't at present expand our output. BSkyB are the exclusive rights holders for this competition and consequently we can't show any action on terrestrial television. We can show the Super League Show as an opt out in the two northern regions thanks to a sub-licensing agreement with Sky, but again that agreement precludes national coverage. I can assure you the BBC is... trying to expand our Rugby League portfolio."

Pat Younge - December 2001: "As regards your point about the Super League Show, I should let you know this is a Sky programme which they allow our northern regions to broadcast. Our Rugby Union matches and Rugby League matches all rate well, with the latter rounds of the Challenge Cup and the Heineken Cup delivering very similar ratings. We'd like more live Rugby League, but Sky has a near complete stranglehold on the sport."

Peter Salmon - January 2002: "Rugby League is a great game, but its governing bodies have sold the major rights to Sky guaranteeing its invisibility so it's really an issue you should take up with them."

Peter Salmon - February 2002: "There are currently no plans for all 11 English regions to licence and carry opt-outs from Sky. These English regions allocate sports priorities on a local basis, dependent on the scale of interest in their own area... if both Sky and Super League are now willing to offer further rights, you can always make contact with your regional BBC sports department to see if they'd like to take the offer further. BBC Sport looks after network rights and production only and offers advice and support locally to our different stations."

Naomi Cooper, BBC Information - 27 February 2002: "The reason behind it not being shown nationally is that the programme is aimed at fans in the areas where the interest is the highest and [those] are in the north."

Naomi Cooper, BBC Information - March 2002: "May I explain that the reason that the Super League Show is broadcast in the north is because just about every team is based in the north - the notable exception being the London Broncos."

Pat Younge - 14 March 2002: "In Rugby League there's only two significant television properties, the Super League and the Challenge Cup. We have the Challenge Cup, and promote it accordingly. But although we cover Super League on radio and online, there's no terrestrial highlights requirement and so there are no network TV rights. That's why the competition, and the sport, has vanished from the public eye.

At the end of the day it's an issue for the rights holders. They can have large cash sums and limited exposure on pay-TV, or less money and greater exposure on terrestrial. It's their choice and one prominent Rugby League chairman said he thought they'd made the right choice. So, in the circumstances, I believe I'm justified in saying they've sold your sport to Sky and the rights holders have to live with the consequences."

Nigel Walker, BBC Wales - 25 March 2002: At present we have no plans to show Super League highlights on BBC Wales. However, the breadth of our sporting coverage is constantly under review…"

Pat Younge - 10 April 2002: "There is no network contract between BBC Sport and Sky for Super League. There's clearly a contract between BBC North and Sky or Super League, but no contract with us. It may be possible for other BBC regions to get access to that material if there's demand, but I

136

repeat there's no network contract. All our substantial contracts are with the rights holders, not Sky. When the new rights are available we'll consider what's on offer and at what price, and take a view."

And also in another email the same day: "Why don't you encourage them to talk to us... they should be talking to us if they have something to offer. Because of our existing commitments it's unlikely anything will happen before the new Super League rights are offered, but I await their correspondence with interest."

Super League Europe - 15 April 2002 (telephone call): "There are no regional restrictions on the broadcast of Super League clips."

Rugby Special: Pat Younge - January 2002: "As regards *Rugby Special* having little to interest fans of League, all I can say is watch this space. The fact that the man in charge of our Rugby Union policy is an avid Widnes fan, born and bred. If anyone is going to make it a good watch for League followers then he's the man."

The BBC's stance

That explains the BBC's stance. Clear as mud, whichever way they dress it up, either as a stand alone programme or incorporated into *Grandstand*, they don't want Super League Rugby League.

Their management's attitude is supported by your licence fee. However, the BBC's website 'Sport Academy' Rugby League section tells a different tale. To quote: "If you ever thought Rugby League was an exclusive sport played only in the north of England, hand your head in shame now, for Rugby League is growing at an amazing rate of knots across the country.

More and more schools in the south are discovering the fast, physical and hugely enjoyable game which has been played for years in its traditional home of Cumbria, Lancashire and Yorkshire. Times are changing. The sport has been shown on the BBC for donkey's years, but kids in the south never got the chance to play League at school or club level. But thanks to the Rugby Football League (RFL), the sport's governing body, this is all changing. And fast. The RFL want as many children as possible play the game no matter where they live."

Although there are some discrepancies and confusion between the two codes, overall a very good site, and a contrasting message to the characters above and their excuses. Now, what about the *Super League Show*?

"The best Rugby League magazine on earth"
(as voted by me and my mum)

July also saw the birth, or should that be hatching, of another august Rugby League publication courtesy of Phil Griffiths, *The Egg Chaser*:

"Rugby League fans seem to be such a strange breed of people. Among the most colourful, humorous, knowledgeable and passionate fans in any 21st century sport, it seems sad that no area of the media seems willing to reflect that in any of its writing. This can be seen when the national tabloids concentrate on the premature 'death' of the game because a high-profile star has been tempted by the filthy lucre of another sport (usually Rugby Union, occasionally beach volleyball) rather than concentrating on the fact that the likes of Wigan and Bradford have performed better than in their final seasons with Messrs Robinson and Paul.

Depressingly, it can also be seen in Rugby League's own press, which seems pre-occupied with the lack of money in the game, refereeing controversies, the 'yobbish' elements of Rugby League crowds and the ineptitude of those in charge at Red Hall. Sure, Rugby League has many problems - both on and off the field, but that should not detract from the fact that we are watching the most exciting team sport on Earth and the second most watched team sport in our own country (second only behind football).

Don't get me wrong, I like reading the Rugby League press at the moment but at times it just gets a little too self-important and 'holier-than-thou' in its attitude.

So, a few months ago, I was getting annoyed at all the melancholy that shrouded the media's attempts to cover Rugby League. Then, I had a dream. (Not the one about the Corr sisters, the bubble bath and the milking stool, which is covered in a different book.) No, I had the dream to start my own magazine, which would concentrate on covering the game with a light-hearted perspective. It seemed like a perfectly reasonable idea considering I have no previous journalistic or publishing experience.

Taking my inspiration from *When Saturday Comes* (which continues to entertain and amuse me long after I've lost faith in its subject matter: football) I started writing articles in an attempt to reflect the humour that exists in Rugby League fans. I tried to enlist the help of members of the Totalrl.com forum and was pleasantly surprised by the volume of respondents - there seemed to be a market for this. All of a sudden, I had a product in the making.

With articles coming in thick and fast, I suddenly realised that I didn't have the means to print the magazine - or a title. Hastily, the credit card was ordered to pay for the printing costs; a printer was found across the road from my workplace and it was decided that the magazine should be called *The Egg Chaser*.

Not that it was all plain sailing, though. Some people would find obstacles in producing a magazine with contributors e-mailing articles to them when they don't have access to the internet at work or home. One of the articles was an interview with Steve McCormack, the head coach of the Salford City Reds. Since meeting with such a great Rugby League brain as myself, the Reds went on to lose every game for two months and Steve ended up getting fired. Thankfully, this kind of luck was not to curse the entire production of *The Egg Chaser*.

Eventually, all the articles and illustrations were gathered. The finished article was picked up from the printers on the afternoon of the first Origin game and then it was time to meet the public and do the hard part - actually sell the thing.

Yes, it meant travelling the north to such glamorous locations as Headingley and St Helens in a battered old Nissan Sunny purchased especially for this purpose. Standing on street corners trying to persuade people to buy something they'd never heard of (with the exception of a few from the forum). So far, though, there does indeed seem to be a market for *The Egg Chaser*. On top of that, it seems quite an impressed audience after the first issue - which makes it likely there'll be another issue.

Many have questioned my sanity in undertaking such a project when I'm not reaping any financial rewards. There are two answers I can think of for this. The first is that it will give me a magazine that I actually *want* to read. The second is that, if it can raise any profits when costs have been covered, these will then be donated to any cash-strapped Rugby League clubs.

If, in hundreds of years time, I'm wandering past a Rugby ground watching a game that involves a club that wouldn't be there if it wasn't for *The Egg Chaser*, that would be my little way of giving something back to the game that has given me so much. And money couldn't buy satisfaction like that."

Contact Phil at 330 Manchester Rd, West Timperley, Altringham, Cheshire, WA14 5NH

Pies, northern ale and a few cartoons

Darren Broadhurst (Daza XIII on the Totalrl.com message board) has kindly drawn a few cartoons for this book. Darren tells his story:

"Born on 17 December 1967 in Birmingham and been here ever since. Used to watch a bit of all sports on *Grandstand* when I was a kid, including Rugby League, but didn't grow to love it until much later.

About age 12 or 13 we had a new kid come to our school called Colin who hailed from Wigan. (KOL on the Totalrl message board) We became best mates then and still are now. Talking to him, and his dad Norman I started to get into Rugby League a bit more but it wasn't until I saw my first game live that I realised what I'd been missing. Kol took me up north to see a Wigan versus Australia game and I've never looked back since.

Don't get to see many live games unfortunately, half a dozen a year, but I'm an avid armchair fan and big fan of the Australian NRL competition. I follow Wigan as the first team I ever watched live, and also Melbourne Storm in Australia and I'd be hard pushed to say which one I like more.

Personal heroes would have to be Glen Lazarus from the past and Terry O'Connor from the present day as I love the big blokes. In fact my favourite quote would probably be from Tony Mestrov when asked about halfbacks: 'Backs! No mate, that's much too complicated.'

I'm also a big lover of pies (Wigan version) and northern bitter and both Kol and his dad think I was born in the wrong part of the country. In fact I'd loved to have been born in the north and exposed to League at school because they've told me that I have the physical size, attitude and intelligence to possibly have made a career out of the game. Ended up as a health and safety manager for an asbestos removal firm instead.

I am a regular poster on the Totalrl message board and am sadly proud of asking stupid questions. I love the fact that that there are some similar people on the forum whom I would call friends, yet I've never met them.

Other than that I play a bit of golf (badly) and have been drawing for most of my life, be it cartoons or proper art.

Never really tried to sell, or get anything published but a few of my Rugby League drawings have appeared in Griff's '*Egg Chaser*' and also in the Wigan independent magazine. I am always available for anyone who wants some drawings done and can be contacted at darrenbroadhurst@hotmail.com."

Stevo and Sergei

Allan McKeown is responsible for the caricatures of Stevo and Sergei and is an ardent Liverpool F.C. fan. He confesses to only having been to one live Rugby League game between Halifax and Wigan and thought the atmosphere was brilliant. While in Australia he saw the Aussies defeating the British Lions at Rugby League and made Allan as 'sick as a pig'. He does confess he could be converted, so go on Allan give it a go. In any event, thanks is given for the drawings: allanroymckeown@hotmail.com.

Happy Families

Sam 'Bullseye' Grundy is the media spokesman for the Bradford Independent Supporters Association. Ray and Tim were guest speakers at the BISA meeting on 24 July.

At the time of writing BISA were up to their necks in their 'Try for Odsal' direct action and busy countering talk of a 'blackout' of Bradford Bulls matches from Sky mooted by Bradford's chairman, Chris Caisley, accompanied by his criticism of 'stay-away' fans. Sam found time at the end of July to add his personal experiences.

"In over 16 years of watching Rugby League I've seen many examples of 'fan power' at work. This manifests itself in many different situations and it is there to see at any Rugby League ground in the country. Only at Rugby League for instance do you see the power of fans at work to help the referee. The cries of 'Forward.' and 'gerremonside' from the terraces have been ringing around the grounds for years. Can you imagine that at football? The sound of fans shouting 'throw in' just doesn't have the same ring to it.

Now some things that fans shout at referees have changed over time. No longer does the crowd shout 'feeding' whenever a scrum half chucks the ball into the second row at a scrum. Also the chance to put off a player under a high ball by shouting 'mine' at the point he catches the ball has decreased as tight little grounds like Thrum Hall become just memories.

However fan power is still with us and I am in no doubt that the greatest sports fans in the world are Rugby League fans. Picture the scene. It was 1996 and my family were on our way home from a thriller of a Cup Final. Our beloved Bradford lost but we were happy nonetheless. Or at least we were until we stopped at Leicester Forest Services.

Now my Dad's car wasn't the meanest of machines and was prone to breaking down at the most inopportune of moments. I don't know whether the 400 mile round trip was too much for it, but it wasn't cut out for motorway driving. When we got back in the car to resume our journey north it wouldn't respond. It was up to us to push it in the hope of getting it going.

We gave it a good go, but it was quite a large estate car and we weren't doing very well. However it was this moment when we were joined in our efforts by two Leeds fans and two Saints fans who really put their backs into it and got us on our merry way again.

Now in what other sport would you see the fans of your bitterest rivals and the team that beat you in the cup final come and help so willingly? I can't think of many examples and this makes me proud to call myself a Rugby League fan. We can be the loudest and most partisan fans in the world but we can also be there to help out others in a spot of bother. With fan power like this Rugby League's future is assured."

New faces / old friends

At a Rugby League Council meeting in Halifax on 30 July 2002 the fanpower demonstrated by the individuals behind the meteoric rise of the North London Skolars and the reborn York City Knights Rugby League club came to the fore as both clubs were provisionally accepted into the third division of the new set up for 2003.

A new obstacle was placed in both clubs paths, late in the day, being the RFL's insistence on a £75,000 bond. This caused a bit of a scramble, especially for York's supporters. Once again, fanpower came to the fore and the money was mustered with the assistance of the *York Evening Press* and a local company of solicitors, following a series of social events, collections, individual donations and a generous 'eleventh hour' donation of £5,000 by John Smiths brewery.

Sadly, Bramley were again declined despite presenting a robust and much applauded business case. No doubt the Bramley Rugby League Community Club will fight on for a place in the new structure.

10. August 2002

A long month, August.

It was mentioned earlier in the book about trying to keep a balance for you, the reader. *RL Fanpower* is predominately about the fans of the game. These fans can consist of turnstile fans, as well as those elsewhere within the structure and administration of the game. However, it is still important for this book to highlight a few main issues facing our sport in 2002. Pieces received in August highlight a couple of areas of concern.

Fanpower takes Ray into the corridors of power again, this time to Red Hall. Tim investigates the 'leisure pound' and Rugby League's attempts, or otherwise, to seize it.

Also from within the game, Trish Goldsmith puts into words her labour of love as managing director at Hull F.C. and Jason Smith speaks as a senior player. Peter Smith tells of the struggle that is writing about Rugby League in the *Yorkshire Evening Post* and Phil Hodgson, from *New League Weekly* admires a French legend and the context of the times in which he played.

More 'Rugby (*sic*) Sevens,' this time from Twickenham, and what was perceived as by many as a media blackout following Bradford Bulls triumphant gatecrashing of the party.

A view from one of our colleagues 'Down Under' and Dave Dooley outlines what St Helens Independent Supporters Association is up to.

To start August though, the nation's attention, and that of many millions around the globe was focussed on the magnificent spectacle of the Commonwealth Games which took place in Manchester, under our noses. But where was Rugby League? Tim sums up his frustrations.

All the world's a stage

"The Manchester Commonwealth Games proved a success beyond its wildest dreams, and left many of the doubters dumfounded, especially those in the national media who sought to belittle the event before it had started.

Seeing the fantastic City of Manchester Stadium, full to its 38,000 capacity prompted the tide to turn and for its 10 day duration Manchester basked in the glory of a successful and well organised games, the biggest sporting event yet staged on these shores.

'London, the joke's on you' headlined the *Daily Telegraph* on 3 August 2002, 'Games success leaves capital red faced and raises Manchester's profile for Olympics.'

The 'Rugby Sevens' event played to an aggregate of 100,000 or so spectators over three days, a tremendous 'shop window' for that game and ensuring its presence at the 2006 games scheduled for Melbourne.

In fact, the Rugby Union's IRB, seeing the opportunity and acting positively, held informal talks with the International Olympic Committee's President, Jacques Rogge, towards seeking inclusion in the 2008 Olympic Games in Beijing.

Rugby League did have a presence in the 'Rugby Sevens' in that former and current League players such as Henry Paul and Marcus St Hillaire, Lesley Vainikolo and Tevita Vaikona turned out for England and Tonga respectively and the England set up was coached by former Wigan great Joe Lydon. There the presence, and any reference to Rugby League, ended.

While the 2000 Rugby League World Cup drew widespread media criticism (including from within the game) for fielding teams from fledgling nations such as Lebanon and Russia, not an eyebrow was raised about the presence in Manchester of such as Malaysia, Trinidad & Tobago and Sri Lanka, despite those teams featuring non rugby playing athletes to make up the numbers.

The Manchester games took place in Rugby League's traditional 'heartlands', Melbourne is home to one of Australia's exclusive elite of 15 NRL clubs and Rugby League is played among many of the Commonwealth nations. Yet unless some serious agitation happens to convince the 72 delegates to the Commonwealth Games committee without delay, it looks like Rugby League will miss the boat again.

Yet who will do this? In my view, the Rugby League International Board seems to be an occasional luncheon club rather than a full time professional organisation dedicated to furthering the games international profile.

Maybe the game can't afford such an operation, maybe there is insufficient will. Either way, if the game is serious about its international status, this needs to change."

A Red Hall day

Tuesday, 2 August and off to Red Hall, headquarters of the RFL, to meet Richard Lewis, the game's newly appointed executive chairman. Ray had written to Richard enquiring about some fans' issues and he wrote back volunteering to meet him.

Armed with Tim's 'easy' guide to travel it was on the road at 6.30 am. A constant drizzle certainly wasn't on the weather menu, and murky conditions prevailed. In particular, the M62 traffic grudgingly created a constant spray of water. Anyhow, arriving at Leeds without mishap, it was now over to Tim's guide to avoiding the city centre. I arrived at Wellington Hill, shot straight past Red Hall Lane and ended up at the Wellington pub.

Back at Red Hall, the reception from Richard Lewis was warm, encouraging and a breath of fresh air. For over an hour we discussed several issues including the BBC *Super League Show* being shown nationally, international fixtures, better communication between the various groups within the game, looking at the possibility of a Rugby League fans' conference some time late in 2003, a 'Gold Card' scheme and issuing more positive stories.

One particular potentially national story seemed to have missed the boat. During the York Nines Rugby League tournament played in May 2002 there was an Asian team competing, which consisted of mixed nationality players. This was at the same time as India and Pakistan were potentially close to war. The mixed Asian team would have provided a great Rugby League story for national media, yet somehow sailed on by. Richard Lewis agreed that this is the type of story we should be portraying.

The 'Gold Card' scheme was an idea from one of the Rugby League message boards. It would envisage fans contributing a sum of money each month in return for various discounts on Rugby League merchandise and main match tickets. It could in principle raise much needed money for the sport. However, it would need much input and energy to make sure the monies were spent wisely.

At the time of writing this article it is hoped that further meetings could take place and that some of the ideas could bear fruit. As they say: 'watch this space.'

Two's company, 12,000's a crowd

Frank Machin from the Totalrl.com message board takes a look back (unusual for Frank) to see if indeed our game has moved forward since the advent of Super League and summer Rugby League.

"I kept my mouth shut because I knew these guys weren't going to listen. We were in the bar at Featherstone Rovers after a game and two blokes, both of whom are now directors of the club were taking me to task about something positive I'd said about Rugby League crowds. It's not just me, I believe all Rugby League lovers take note of and interpret crowd figures. They are a (though not the) barometer of the sport's popularity. We want our sport to do well and so check out the crowd figures. We nearly always use the best ones to reinforce our opinions about how popular the game was in the past.

That's what these two blokes were doing. They were citing the championship finals of the early 1960s. Although I'd bet my mortgage that they'd be against this way of deciding the championship itself if you asked them, but that's another can of opinions. "Do you realise that 60 odd thousand people used to turn up at Odsal for the Championship Final? You wouldn't get that now. Crowds are nothing to what they were." Then they started to give me a load of Maurice Lindsay stuff. This was the year before the current play off system, and the 60,000 crowds at Old Trafford that were to prove them wrong. I didn't argue, there was no point.

If I'd been in the mood I'd have told them that while they were trooping up in their thousands to Odsal for those finals, Bradford Northern were rapidly going bust with crowds of a couple of hundred at an increasingly desolate Odsal. Bradford Northern one of the big names, a city club, a club with one of the proudest of histories and the hosts to the biggest, at the time, crowd in Rugby League history. Going broke and nobody caring, smack in the middle of the good old days.

First then let's try to clear things up about these so called 'good old days.' As far as I can see, they fall into two distinct periods; the post-war period to the early, mid-1960s, and the late 1980s to early 1990s. It is easy to deal with the first one. People had endured the worst war in history and all that it entailed, people had come back home and re-started their lives and the country after initial austerity was starting to become prosperous. People wanted to enjoy themselves and there weren't that many televisions around just yet (the first live full game broadcast of a cup final was the 1952 Featherstone versus Workington game). So all sports enjoyed a massive boom in attendances.

Then gradually it tailed off and it tailed off for a long time. By the 1970s clubs could win the championship with crowds of 3,000 or so (Featherstone and Dewsbury) and even Leeds could be champions on the back of an average of about 7,000. Can you imagine what the 'our game is dying' brigade would say if the Rhinos polled attendances like that these days? In this period a club could have a reasonable season by its standards go on to win the Challenge Cup and still have an average crowd of less than 3,000.

As the 1980s progressed, things changed. Unlike the post-war era, the causes of this are a little harder to pin down. But here goes. The game became more exciting and athletic, due to the way that Australian teams had changed their coaching and playing methods. People became aware of how big the game was in Australia because communications had improved. This was the period when fans wore Australian jumpers to games as much as they wore their own club colours. There were some classic games... Hull versus Wigan, Wigan versus Manly, the 1988 Sydney test (broadcast live remember). The last game is important because it introduces another factor into the equation: international football.

Great Britain had become competitive against the Australians. By the end of the 1980s we could fill Old Trafford, nearly fill Wembley (I'll never forget Jonathan Davies' try and Sir Cliff doing a load of Jerry Lee Lewis and Little Richard numbers and telling us that Rugby League was the new Rock n' Roll). We had stars that people all over the country had heard of, Jonathan, Ellery and Martin for instance. On the back of this, club crowds increased as well. The game seemed vibrant.

However, the media profile of the game was under represented and badly represented as well. The BBC gave the impression that it didn't care about a sport that had given it so much. On top of this, despite the increase in crowds, clubs were bankrupting themselves. The result: the Sky deal and the Super League war, along with the loosely connected change to summer.

So, relative to the superficial boom preceding it, the upheaval of the change was bound to see crowds at the top level fall. People walked away. Only some clubs had any kind of handle on how to make the changes work. For instance, we are now in Super League VII and St Helens have only now got hold of the idea of promoting the most exciting and successful club of the Super League era. So after an initial drop, crowds started to rise again. Leeds Rhinos' crowds dropped alarmingly in the first years of Super League. The club were openly opposed to the changes and pointedly refused to get into the spirit of things. Once they woke up to what you are supposed to do, they became the best attended club of any code of rugby in the country by the end of the century.

Now crowds are down again and the game (yawn) is supposed to be dying. Rugby League must have had more death bed scenes than Greta Garbo. The Northern Ford clubs are going back to summer, after failing to make a success of playing again in winter... the time of year when apparently they used to be hanging from the rafters at every home game.

They, or some of them still think that all you have to do to attract people is stage the game at a certain time of year, when there is more to it than that. It doesn't bode well if the reaction of the chairman of my home town club, Featherstone Rovers is anything to go by. In a programme article he said that he and the entire board were opposed to summer football. How inspiring is that? How are they going to make it work when they don't believe in it?

I was at the Featherstone Rovers versus St Helens game in 1959 that posted the record Rovers crowd, at the end of the post-war boom. I'll never forget it. Nobody will who was there. The trouble is most people forget the vast majority of games, and I'm not just referring to Rovers here, some of which were the fabled passionate local derbies we hear so much about, that had grounds less than a third full.

So back to the dip in crowds. What's going on? I'm tempted to say: 'search me chief.' But I'll have a go. Nobody wants to be associated with failure. Other sports such as football, Union, Formula One have a patina of success and wealth and people want some of that. We probably don't mess things up more than other sports, but when we do people take more notice. Failure breeds failure as much as success breeds success.

The media does have some responsibility here, but so does the game and its culture: one of curmudgeonly parochialism which it is unwilling or unable to shake off. People have built a career on it.

Next there's particular problems at individual clubs. Wigan's fans seem to be at war with the JJB Stadium and Dave Whelan simultaneously and the received wisdom is that fans are staying away because of this, thus depriving themselves of some great entertainment. Also the crowds this year are down on previous years at the self-same stadium.

Bradford. Well it's Valley Parade isn't it? Manningham on a Friday night is a not a family friendly place to be. I speak as an ex-resident. Many fans feel that some stewards are totalitarian and the stadium doesn't lend itself to the kind of event that Bulls' fans had become accustomed to.

The Blue Sox recently complained that their crowd for a game against Saints was down because of the local holidays. There could be something in this, but it is hardly a trend. On the same weekend on 2001, they had just under 6,000 for the Bulls' visit. You would have expected more wouldn't you? There are other individual problems I'm sure, but you get the idea.

What about summer footy? Don't think so. Remember that the crowds are down on previous summer seasons. Let's look at the promotion of the game. This is an ever-changing thing, it demands energy and creativity.

Have clubs who took promotion of the game on board now become stale and stereotyped? The biggie in many peoples' eyes seems to be Sky. We now have a Friday night game and a Saturday tea-time game. This means that kick-off times are all over the place It also means that we now have had seven years of two televised games a week.

There was this sociologist called Durkheim. He had one of the classic theories on why people committed suicide (nothing to do with watching Chorley Borough), but everything to do with a phenomenon called 'anomie'. He described this as 'normlesness'. People need norms... when they can expect things to happen. We no longer know when to expect Rugby League games to happen. I'm not saying this is enough for people to top themselves, but it can't help you to connect with your local Rugby League club. You'd drift off and do something else wouldn't you? Maybe people are sated with all this Rugby League over the past seven years. I haven't because I'm obsessed, but I can see other people getting Rugby League indigestion.

That Saturday game is a killer as well. People are not interested in going to sporting events on a Saturday tea-time. We even had one on a Tuesday night recently. Wigan versus Saints... 1,000 down on the previous year on the box and played in a monsoon. I was grateful that it was only 1,000 down. On a Saturday tea-time you are busy having your tea. This might not be a deterrent if all games were being played at this time and people could expect it and change their habits (difficult, but not impossible), but its that normlessness.

And the BBC? Well that's a whole separate issue. Apart from test football, they now broadcast as much Rugby League as they have ever done. The quality has improved marginally. But you have to ask yourself what responsibility they bear over the years spanning 'the good old days' for the way the game has been perceived nationally and the effect that this would have on interest and thus crowds at games...it's that 'failure thing' again. People find it cheaper to go to a comfy boozer and watch a televised game. Which brings me to pricing.

'Lerrin-em-in-fer-nowt', as my compadres in the Rovers clubhouse say doesn't work. It devalues your product. 'It must be crap, otherwise they wouldn't be giving the stuff away' kind of thing. Lots of clubs do good deals on tickets but maybe the admission fees to game are too high. Crowds are down and it's a worry. But it isn't a death throe or the spasmodic twitch of a corpse. It needs seeing to, by the game's gaffers and by those running the clubs. It doesn't exactly inspire confidence does it? But you never know.

149

Lastly, I hope that whenever some reactionary starts going on about how great crowds were in the 'good old days', you'll be ready for them on the back of reading this and some casual research through the year books. Now then I remember when local derbies were local derbies. Fev packed 4,134 people into Post Office Road in 1983. Those were the days."

Footnote

Statistics issued by the RFL after the 28 regular Super League matches, before the play-offs and internationals, stated that Super League attendances had improved on average for the 2002 season. Each of the 168 games averaged 7,087 (2001 season) to 7,220, an aggregate of around 1.2 million, with the largest attendance of 18,789 at Wigan for the visit of St. Helens.

Add in the five-figure Northern Ford Premiership weekly turnout to the weekly Super League average of 43,323, plus amateur games and the regular interest in Rugby League starts looking like a pretty big 'minority' and justifying Richard Lewis' description of Rugby League as the 'number one summer sporting competition in Britain.'

League and the 'leisure pound'

Whether Rugby League attendances are up or down depends on which statistics you see and how you interpret them, and in any case there are lots of issues other than price that affect the weekly turnouts positively or negatively and price may be merely one factor.

So, is entertainment price sensitive? It's worth a quick comparison to other attractions which tempt fans and their families elsewhere. Prompted by a government announcement, Tim's quick 'snapshot' survey looked at the lay of the land over one weekend in August.

On 9 August the Culture Secretary Tessa Jowell, reported that in the seven months since 1 December 2001, when all public museums were made free of admission charges, an extra 2.7 million visits had been made. This represented an increase of 62 per cent. The Victoria & Albert Museum attendance had increased by 157 per cent.

By all accounts a recent reduction in admission prices at NRL games in Australia have led to a significant increase in crowds. (The weekend's seven games' aggregate was 101,938, average 14,562), bringing with them increased revenue from peripheral matchday activities, such as programmes, merchandising, catering, bar takings etc.

As a quick comparison, the cheapest adult admission to the Parramatta Stadium was Aus $15 (by my reckoning about £5.25), to Newcastle Knights Aus $17 (around £5.96) and Ericsson Stadium for the NZ Warriors NZ $10 (£3.) I'll repeat that, £3 to see the team laying third in the NRL.

As a pretty unscientific ready reckoner, applying the cheapest adult admission of £5.96 to the NRL aggregate gives a rough total admission income of £607,000 for the weekend.

Typically, Super League grounds charge around £11 and upwards per adult for standing, perhaps on an uncovered terrace at a traditional ground, and a minimum of £12 for the cheapest seat at the all seater Valley Parade and JJB stadia.

The same weekends Super League aggregate, admittedly among the poorest of the season, was 35,094 (from 6 games, average 5,849.) Using comparable logic of the cheapest adult admission, say £11, roughly equates to an income from admission charges of £386,000 for the weekend.

Of course, the equation is far more complicated than that but the principle would seem to be that less, it appears, can be more.

Again, over the same weekend, and mindful of the debate prompted by Bradford's Mr Caisley regarding television's effect on attendances and given the fact that August is high season for holidays, the two matches televised by Sky were Halifax versus Bradford from the Shay and Leeds versus Wigan from Headingley.

The respective games, the highest profile games over the weekend, drew 4,170 and 10,049, disappointing to say the least.

Neither stadium is a glamorous venue for a night out. The Shay still resembles a building site with one stand unfinished and Headingley, although loved as a 'traditional' rugby ground, looking increasingly tired with its uncovered ends, obstructed views and distorted PA system. More so when compared to the sparkling recent developments in its cricket facilities. What were the options to a wet Friday night in Halifax or a Saturday evening at Headingley?

Watching on telly at home saves £11. Take this to W. H. Smith and you can secure a CD or, better still, a rather good book on Rugby League, which will provide hours of pleasure for years to come.

Ten films were available at the 16 screen Showcase cinema in Birstall, a short trip from The Shay. With the £11 needed at the Blue Sox's cheapest turnstile, not one, but two people could have had an evening's warm and dry entertainment from the latest Hollywood blockbuster with 50 pence left

151

towards popcorn. The game can wait on video until later.

The Headingley Taps pub, within a stone's throw of the ground and a favourite of Rugby League fans and students, had a large screen showing the game. Rather than paying £11 to get into Headingley a fan could have a seat, watch the game and spend his money on six pints of beer.

Of course another option is to watch the game unfold in a comfy chair at home for free, perhaps with a take-away curry for two to placate the wife, which my local Indian restaurant will provide for £11.

Across the city from Headingley, the same night the magnificent Grand Theatre staged Agatha Christie's classic thriller, *A Murder is Announced*. (Not inappropriate given Barry Mac's four match ban for punching Stuart Fielden that week.) At £8.50 for the best seat in the house the ticket price left £2.50, enough for a genteel drink in the theatre bar during the interval (and more than enough for those who prefer to leg it across New Briggate to the Wrens for a pint of Tetley's.)

By this I am not suggesting that Rugby League fans will 'switch codes' defecting in droves to high opera or ballet, but the point remains that the leisure market has never been so accessible and diverse, and the battle for our 'leisure pound' so competitive.

Of course a hard core of fans will always go to the ground for the 'live experience' come what may, but clubs need to be aware of the myriad counter attractions available to the potential Rugby League customer, especially those with partners or families for whom Friday and Saturday nights are at a premium.

In Britain at least, Rugby League is no longer a cheap entertainment.

As seen by the failure to sell out two of the three unprecedentedly expensive Ashes Test matches in 2001, spectators are increasingly exercising their right to choose, and will no longer just turn up to fixtures on command. Rugby League fans will not be ripped off."

Wot I did on my holidays

August is the height of the holiday season, with around 20 per cent of the population off work. Need this have a proportionate downward effect on crowd sizes? Tim again (aged 37 and a half) does his 'back to school' essay.

"Rugby League clubs tend to market themselves, such as they do at all, towards their local population and those in areas surrounding or adjacent (remember the spat between Halifax and Bradford last year as the Bulls advertised in the *Halifax Evening Courier*?)

Well what about the other section of society, the visitor? Maybe business, maybe tourist, either way probably untapped.

The Lake District: In July this year I took a trip up to Bouth in the Lake District for a long weekend. I like mountains and lakes scenery and all the tranquility that that brings, but would I starve of Rugby League? No fear, Cumbria is a hotbed, and is the primary sport there, I've heard as much many times.

How many Leaguies go to the lakes on their holidays each year? Probably thousands, How many visitors go there that could catch the League bug? Probably tens of thousands.

Summer visitor attractions abound, maybe a barbecue or a day on the beach, but according to one statistic I found, out of 365 days each year in Cumbria on average it rains on 200 of them and snows on another 20.

So, what's on, League-wise? Plenty on the back page of the *North West Evening Mail* I scanned in the checkout queue of Asda in Barrow, but I'd guessed that would be the first port of call for Rugby League information. That was about it.

Local tourist offices for Whitehaven, Workington and Barrow each produce a pamphlet advertising the history of their town, and its virtues in terms of visitor attractions. Of these three only Barrow's makes a fleeting reference to their town having a Rugby League club. It seems the presence of a Macdonalds take away is cause for more civic pride, as that august establishment received a better billing. Not a peep from the other two.

The wider encompassing Cumbria Tourist Board doesn't seem particularly proud - or conscious - of their primary sport and Rugby League heritage either.

Visiting their website (golakes.co.uk) and looking under 'events' in all locations the only sporting suggestion that they came up with was Grasmere Sports and Show. A marvellous one day event in itself but, as a directory of what is on offer to those seeking a sporting game to watch, a little deficient.

Searching again under 'sports ground/stadium' the only venue that came up was the Indoor Go Kart track in Carlisle. Wot? No Derwent Park?

Persevering, some success in that another site (visitcumbria.com) did list a Workington Town home fixture in their 'what's on' list. But by that point any browsing tourist looking for a sporting event to while away a few damp hours would surely have given up the ghost and headed out for the Naworth Castle Antiques Sale or the Grange-over-Sands and District Art Society Annual Exhibition, obviously the hot tickets of the Cumbrian tourist season.

Rugby League seems to figure lower in the tourist marketeers' field of vision than the Gurning competition at the Egremont Crab Festival. (On the other hand I can think of a few Rugby League forwards I've packed down with who might have a chance of winning that.)

I don't suspect there is anything Machiavellian in any of this, its probably just that no one's highlighted the presence, or local importance, of Rugby League to the bright young Leisure and Tourism graduates that abound in such organisations employ. Now is a good time to let them know.

Tried to buy a *League Express* in Ambleside? I for one have never succeeded. Maybe there's a good distribution reason for this, but if we can put a man on the moon, and I can get an *International Herald Tribune*, published in New York in the same shop...

York: Let's look at another example, the finest city in northern England. Good luck to the new regime at York City Knights RLFC, I'm sure they've got enough on their plate just getting up and running, but here's some food for thought anyway.

The Minster City is a premier attraction for 3.84 million visitors, tourists and day trippers, who arrive each year looking for something to interest them and spend their £247 million on, yet who would think of Rugby League? Since the move to Huntington there has been no reference to the club anywhere in sight within the city centre. Nothing. Not a trace.

Further, the Economic Development Units stats record that 54 per cent of visitors stay overnight. Apparently most of these are in the 35-54 age group, 67 per cent of whom arrive with a car. Prime targets. Get 1 per cent of some of this lot and you're on to something. Other attractions do: £15 each per UK visitor is spent on admittance to York's attractions alone.

There are 7,500 bedspaces in York, each room with a dossier of pamphlets for excursions and attractions. Why not give each hotel, b&b and the many other tourist info outlets a supply of fixture lists pamphlets?

Even if people don't go that time, some 'brand awareness' might just lurk in the back of some minds for next time they return, as 74 per cent of visitors to York do. I'm sure this model could just as easily translate to Cumbria, who would have far fewer business travellers and a far higher proportion of tourist visitors.

Ray tells me that on a trip to Southport he picked up a glossy leaflet for Bradford Bulls. Well done Bradford for getting their name and, dare I say it, 'product' on to the shelves where the public can see it, but Southport is barely 20 miles from St Helens - shouldn't the publicity tempt the reader

154

into a trip to Knowsley Road?

Rugby League clubs with big visitor numbers (London as well, and why not the Rugby League Conference clubs, such as Oxford, Cambridge, Chester, Durham, Bridlington etc) could print some leaflets or fixture lists for local distribution fairly cheaply. My local branch of Safeway delivers me one every week, whether I want to know their latest bargains or not!

A good place to start in these two tourist areas would be at Windermere Lake Cruises and Flamingo Land Theme Park, both of which attract in the order of 1.1 million visitors a year.

After that they could do worse than approach their relevant tourist board and have them add a link from their tourist board website to their club's own site. Or just mention that they exist.

All this costs more effort than money, although surely not a lot of that, *pro-rata* to the massive audience the material would receive. Maybe this has all been thought of before, but in the brave new expanding era the visitor pound (or Euro) it's an untapped market surely worth looking at. I'll do it!

Now, where's that barbecue set and which way is it to the beach?"

Pure Gold

While browsing through the Hull F.C. message board Ray came across a post by Trish Goldsmith, the Hull F.C. managing director. It has to go without saying that Trish is a great communicator with her club's fan base. Not only replying to questions on the message board, but also doing it with a love and warmth that generates respect. However, it was a particular post (see below) that even bowled me over. I just had to contact Trish for an article and seek out her views.

"I was approached by the board of directors to relocate to Hull after the merger with Hull Sharks as second in command to the chief executive. My role is now managing director with the responsibility of the day-to-day operation of the club. Shaun McRae, Hull F.C.'s director of rugby and myself run the operations of the club as a partnership. Shaun concentrating on all football matters and I am responsible for the business side of the Club.

I was married to my first husband for 21 years and we are still good friends. My second husband, Steve, is not just my husband, but also my best friend. I have an extended family that I try to look after the best way I can. They are friends and work colleagues who I have worked with in the past and friends and colleagues at work, business friends and the supporters. The reason I came to Hull in the first place was out of loyalty to Shaun, the

155

players and the board of directors. I felt they needed my help. Being needed is important to me. I have a great love and respect for children and the aged.

What is it like being a woman in the world of Rugby League?

As with any role of a senior manager I feel that a woman has to work harder to prove herself in a male-dominated industry. However, I do not find if frightening or daunting. I worked in the greyhound industry, which was very male-dominated and moved in those circles with ease. The same in Rugby League. If you are hardworking, do not use your sex as a weakness but a quality, treat people with respect and deliver what you promise you will be accepted in any work position. I enjoy the physical part of our sport whether it our athletes performing on the field or their sheer physical fitness - it must be admired. I also enjoy the community and family atmosphere.

What effect has Rugby League had on my life?

I am a Taurus, who are known to be obsessional. When I was asked to take on my role, I knew it would take over our lives. My social life always involves some form of Rugby League; my personal life becomes wrapped around Rugby League because my family support Hull F.C. We all work long hours at Hull F.C. and I believe in leading by example so I try to be one of the first people to arrive at work in a morning and the last to leave.

What is your favourite Rugby League moment?

The first time I heard the fans singing *Old Faithful* in the Boulevard Bar when Shaun was doing his first man-of-the-match presentation at Hull F.C.

Why did you become interested in Rugby League?

The very first time I attended a Rugby League game was in 1999: Gateshead Thunder versus Bradford Bulls. The board of directors had asked me to join the club and they asked me to a game. I was knocked out by the enthusiasm and passion of the fans and amazed at how many children were there.

What Rugby League means to me

An abstract from a message which I put on the message board to the fans dated 20 July 9.21 am. I think the message says it all: 'There is a guy I know who always says: 'the future is bright it is black and white' and I totally agree with him. We do have the best coach in Super League as well as the best fans. You all have my own personal promise that I will work my butt off for you to improve the customer care and service, the marketing of the club and to communicate to the fans news as swiftly as I can. All, without exception, the staff are motivated professionals, but also have the added qualification of being black and white mad. It hurts when we lose, but it is great when we win. Up until four years ago I had never been to a live game of Rugby League. Never supported a team with passion.

Football is the game everyone cries about in Newcastle and Sunderland and even though I would watch it with my family and husband, sometimes going to a game, it never occupied my heart and soul like Rugby League. What is it about Rugby League that I love? It is not only the physical side and the excitement of the game, it is the people. The people at the club from players to the volunteers who week after week give their services to the club for nothing just to help the club. It is the fans that give up all of their spare cash to support the club. The sponsors who also in their own way give all their companies spare cash to the club and a lot of the time their own personal cash. The kids with their black and white paint on their faces and their little faces looking up at their heroes when they ask them to sign their shirts. It is young Scott and his dad who come to every home game and every away game. Seeing Scott singing with his followers in the Boulevard Bar last night and Toa looking on with tenderness and caring at this young lad who has a lot to put up with in life. Our friends in the disabled section whom look forward to saying hello to our off-duty players on a match day.

Well I have rambled on for long enough I will just end with saying I understand your frustrations, I have them. I understand your passion because I also have it. Shaun knows what he is doing; trust him to do his job. I know what I am doing along with my fellow staff. Trust us to do our jobs. Tell us what you think but please do not think what you say has not already been thought of or actioned. Everyone has the right to their own thoughts and if they need to say them, do so but sometimes remember that other people read your thoughts and at times when motivation is essential personal attacks are better directed to a group, rather than an individual person. We need your thoughts and interaction but we cannot do it without your support.'

Hull F.C. has 20.8 per cent female season ticket holders.

Hull F.C. has 60 per cent junior season ticket holders.

Take care and best wishes always."

Our game could do with a few more Trish Goldsmiths.

Press for action

Peter Smith is the Rugby League writer for the *Yorkshire Evening Post* and reports on Leeds, Castleford and Wakefield, as well as four local NFP clubs and the West Yorkshire amateur scene. Peter submitted an article offering his insight into the frustrations of being a Rugby League journalist:

"The media isn't always to blame. It's easy to say there's a conspiracy between the press, television and radio to ensure Rugby League doesn't get the coverage it really deserves. Well if there is such a conspiracy, I've never come across it. True, many sports writers and broadcasters aren't interested in Rugby League and others, for their own personal reasons, are actively hostile.

But the fact is Rugby League is a sport watched at professional level by no more than 60,000 people on the average weekend - and the vast majority of those are confined in a small area of northern England. Bear that in mind and perhaps Rugby League does better than it has any right to expect.

Until and unless Rugby League ever puts down successful, professional roots in the south of England, it is always going to struggle to make its presence felt in the national media.

On the other hand, there's no doubt northern editions of national newspapers could give the sport a better show, but again the volume and standard of coverage isn't entirely their fault. Rugby League has to take a hard look at the way it conducts itself if it wants the situation to improve.

Meaningful international competition is the key - just think back to the mass of positive coverage in the national media following the first Test win over Australia in 2001.

London-based editors can relate to Great Britain more closely than they can to Wigan or Castleford, but Rugby League rarely takes the international game - which is the rival code's great strength - seriously enough.

And, worryingly, over the last couple of years the Great Britain team management has become increasingly unhelpful to the media. The first Test at Huddersfield in 2001 did not sell out, yet in the build-up the Great Britain management, in my experience anyway, were at best indifferent to the needs of press and broadcasters - who were offering in effect free advertising for the game - and at worst actively obstructive.

On one occasion I attempted to contact a Great Britain player for a feature article about the game. Failing to reach him directly, I left a message on his answer phone and then tried to get hold of him through the team management. They told me a request would be passed on and later came back to say the player did not want to speak to me. Which would have been fair enough had he not, in the meantime, returned my original message and conducted a full phone interview.

In 2002, the Great Britain team management refused all requests to announce their squad for the one-off Test in Australia in time for early editions of local newspapers, claiming they wanted to inform the players personally. The news, therefore, missed a huge audience in Rugby League heartlands such as Leeds, Bradford and Hull. Yet when this reporter approached players named in the squad for their reaction, no one from the Rugby League had bothered to inform them.

The media who travelled to Sydney for the game found there were no press conferences arranged at which all Great Britain players would be present - and there was at least one case when an interview was blocked because it hadn't been arranged in advance.

Domestically, Super League's kick-off and match day lottery is a huge stumbling block to better press coverage. If the sport wants to get its matches coverage in the national papers, then 3pm kick-offs on Sundays are the ideal time. Games that start at 8pm on a Friday finish too late for some papers' northern editions. Most Super League clubs now at least pay lip service to the needs of the press and some have media managers who do an excellent job - but there are others who could learn a lesson from amateur clubs like East Leeds, Milford Marlins or Oulton Raiders. The *Yorkshire Evening Post* carries a regular Academy round-up, yet some clubs are unable to confirm details of their junior teams' scorers, first names of players or even results - and if that sort of basic information is beyond them, there's not much hope.

One group who can be absolved of blame are the players. Over the past decade I've conducted hundreds of interviews with players in all sorts of circumstances and only twice have I been told: 'I don't want to talk to you.'

The players should get a better show in the media. People like Kevin Sinfield, Paul Sculthorpe, Danny Orr and many others deserve to be national figures. And unlike Jason Robinson, they shouldn't have to switch codes to be recognised as world-class athletes. But they also deserve better from their sport, which often remains indifferent to the quality of its star asset."

Remember you're a Womble

Tim spots fanpower in action elsewhere. Something of a departure from

Rugby League, but hats off to Wimbledon F.C.'s fans for their demonstration of fanpower on 10 August 2002.

With the news that Wimbledon F.C.'s chairman intended overseeing the clubs relocation to Milton Keynes, 50 miles distant, their first match of the new football season kicked off at their shared home stadium, Selhurst Park, with Gillingham the visitors.

Less than 700 Wimbledon spectators were inside the ground while over 2,000 were peacefully venting their feelings outside. Television, radio and newspaper coverage of the proceedings abounded. The official Wimbledon F.C. website did not refer to the incident, nor comment on the sparse attendance of 2,476 mainly visiting supporters.

Whatever the ins and outs of the respective arguments, and no doubt both sides have a case, the fact that so many fans stood up for what they believed in speaks volumes for those fans commitment to their club.

Rugby League out of puff

Phil Hodgson currently has his hands full working for the fledgling *New League Weekly*, the replacement weekly newspaper for *Rugby Leaguer*.

Phil found time to express his admiration as a fan for one of the legends of the game in an era when Rugby League enjoyed better success in France.

"Not to put too fine a point on it, Puig Aubert would not have fitted into the modern day game. I've spent some time recently thinking about the France and Carcassonne full back, as we ran a quiz, based on his career, in the *New League Weekly*.

Aubert was before my time, playing in the 1950s, but the tales of his antics leave an indelible impression when you read about them. He was the last - in fact, probably the only one - of a breed and his career spanned an era in which France were a match for any other side around.

It is said that the French have slipped behind the rest because of an over-casual approach to the game. If they are too laid back now, they had a fine mentor in Aubert who always wore shorts fitted with pockets. The reason? Because he needed somewhere to put his cigarettes and his matches.

There are players around now who are straight into the toilets after the game for a quick puff, but the French great took it a step further, often lighting up at the back of his defence if his side were on top.

I don't know what he did if the opposition broke through. Presumably he threw his fag to the floor - so it's just as well he didn't play in the era of

160

summer rugby as many a pitch would catch fire on these sun-baked grounds, we were all promised.

Aubert, despite, or maybe because of, his eccentricities, carved a huge reputation as one of the finest attacking full-backs of his era and shone on the tour to Australia when France carried all before them in front of huge crowds. Sadly, he died a few years ago - of, I believe, cancer - and another of Rugby League's legends was lost.

Would that the Tricolors were still as good or that we had as many characters in the game. One thing's for sure, though - no player would dare light up on the pitch in these politically correct times. Would they?"

Interview with Hull F.C.'s Jason Smith

Jason Smith is proclaimed king of Humberside for the Black and Whites. Or so it seems from the Hull F.C. faithful. I would even suspect that a few other Rugby League fans wouldn't mind Jason's talents to be on display for their club. He certainly stands the test of time with many of the great Australian players who have graced these shores in our sport.

Players have a voice seldom heard except in the context of on field matters, so to get a deeper understanding of the players input into the game Ray again made contact with Trish Goldsmith, managing director at Hull F.C, to see if a player would oblige. What transpired next was Rugby League enthusiasm at its best. Within a half hour of Ray contacting her, Jason was on the phone to give an account of his life and Rugby League in general. Once again, well-done Trish for such speed and consideration.

For Jason, life in Rugby League started at the tender age of seven, while playing for several Brisbane junior clubs. Whilst a junior, it was common to be asked to play in many positions, unlike the time period when 'specialist' positions was the order of the day. After a six-month spell with Souths in Brisbane it was off to Canterbury Bulldogs in 1990 and after six years he was then transferred to Parramatta.

Two Grand Final appearances were made 'back to back' in 1994 and 1995. These two club highlights of his career did have a mixed bag of fortune. He was to pick up a losers medal in 1994 against Canberra Raiders. Such awesome players as Mal Meninga, Laurie Daley, Bradley Clyde, Ricky Stuart and Brett Mullins were on the opposition side, so no disrespect in losing. Triumph did arrive in 1995 via a win against Manly.

Sixteen Test matches and 16 State of Origin matches is testimony to the fact that Jason is indeed a talented Rugby League player. I did ask him if any match really stood out from the rest, but he assured me that most games were hard. He certainly was party to many sporting battles in the Rugby League arena on the 'bigger' stage.

Jason was honest to say that the money was a big factor in signing for Hull F.C. as well as the chance to re-test himself on a 'new stage' and also have the chance to travel. As well as holidaying in Italy twice, he has been to Scotland, Ireland and was due to go to the Lake District. The Yorkshire Dales has been an added attraction for him and five visits to the grand city of York are on his travelling map.

We sometimes take players for granted and forget that they are human beings with all the ups and downs that we mere fans have. On 25 September 2001, his good wife Janelle gave birth to Jasper. Jason admits that the pregnancy period for his wife was certainly not easy in terms of being in a new country, as well plying your trade for a new club. We do indeed sometimes forget that there are matters outside of the game that players have to live with, while trying one's best to deliver the goods on the playing field.

Jason definitely said he would not progress to coaching. Not for him the frustration of match days and not being out on the field of play to dictate terms. More likely is a return to Australia although future ambitions after playing are not at the forefront of Jason's thoughts. As he put it: 'Dedication to diet, training and match play' are all that matters at the moment.

A question was put to Jason as to which rule he would like to see changed. To a chuckle or two it was to have a rule where one would never lose. Such is his attitude to winning. Likewise I asked which are his favourite away grounds. The McAlpine was one due to the size of pitch and Leeds for atmosphere. He was certainly impressed with the vocal support over here and especially the song *Old Faithful*.

Mention was made that all pitches in Australia had to be the same size - 100 metres long. This was in sharp contrast to Britain in that many grounds have various dimensions. In fact rumour has it that some clubs over here have deliberately altered pitch sizes to confuse certain opposition teams.

In terms of injuries Jason has been in his own words 'fortunate' with the longest spell on the sidelines being nine weeks. Referees came into the conversation but only in respect of interpretation of the rules. It has been known for him to stand confused at certain decisions by our referees.

Jason did play Union, as well as League for a couple of years during his mid teens but has never harboured the thought of playing Union full-time.

For now Jason has another two years at Hull F.C. and no doubt, all being well, we will see him ply his undoubted Rugby League talents.

Jason came over as a very articulate and helpful person, which does seem par for the course with most Rugby League players. They never let us down do they?

Jason mentioned frequenting the Hull F.C. message board and gave this comment: "It's good when the comments from fans are positive but not so when they are negative." Jason is not the first player to admit taking a look into the world of message boards and so it is important to keep comments to just about the game and not get into other matters that infringe on a player's life and personal matters.

And a few questions for Jason…

Did you hear of the Media Petition and if so did you sign it? Many from Hull did: "I did hear of it through *Rugby League World* show on Sky, but I never had the opportunity to sign it as I never saw anyone with the petition to sign and I don't know of anyone who has signed it from Hull."

Do you think the new ground is a break from tradition, or a window of opportunity? I think it is sad to see the Boulevard go, but nothing lasts forever: "It is a great window of opportunity as the facilities will be a lot better for players and supporters alike. Obviously it will be sad to leave the Boulevard, but also exciting to move into a state of the art stadium."

One idea to improve Rugby League's image to a more national audience: "I don't have any ideas on improving the image of the game, but you and I know what type of game we have got and I am sure the rest of the country will pick up on this game (eventually)."

Do you follow the press and media and understand as a player that bias against Rugby League does exist? "I don't read many papers or watch the news that much as I seem to be more interested in the news back home."

Would you change anything in the game's structure? "I have heard and spoken to a lot of players about the amount of games we play and everyone seems to agree the amount is way to high. Why we need to start playing sides three times in Super League is obviously ridiculous and if they reduce the amount of games I believe you will get a better standard of Rugby League."

As a player would you encourage more international games? "Obviously it would be great if there was a set time in the year for international games to exist, which would make it something to look forward to at that time of the year and would prepare everyone involved for these games."

Any outside interests away from the game? "Yes I do have other interests outside of Rugby League such as golf, fishing, travelling, watching other sports and doing things with my family, but as you know Rugby League takes up a lot of time so you don't get much time for these things. My elbow is getting better slowly. Any more help don't hesitate to contact me."

A sting in the tale

Chris Gallagher observes from his London standpoint:

"Something strange happened on 17 August 2002. I don't know if you felt it too, but I know some of you did. Before this date, the Middlesex Sevens were a prestigious Rugby Union showpiece event, the most famous sporting charity event in the world. It was (and I quote directly from the official website) packed with "England favourites Jonny Wilkinson, Austin Healy, Phil Greening and Mike Catt... among 40 internationals" playing in the event.

Furthermore, the clubs were looking to prove that they "mean business by naming strong squads packed with star names". London Wasps, one of the favourites for the event, named all four of their England internationals that represented England in the Commonwealth Games.

The event attracted live television coverage on BBC1 and BBC2. Then the shift happened. At roughly the same time as Bradford wiped the floor with these international packed teams, (prompting booing from the crowd, no less) the media changed its stance.

Suddenly, the Union teams were under strength, the Zurich Premiership clubs didn't really care about the competition, and the Bradford players, coming to the climax of the Super League season, were match fit, unlike the poor Union boys.

Admittedly, for the newspapers that could bring themselves to report on the event, a lot was made of Bradford's preparation for the event. (A heavy home loss to championship rivals St Helens 12 hours previously and four hours sleep following their coach breaking down and a 3am arrival in London). Most media outlets, however, stayed strangely quiet - much quieter than the equivalent Hong Kong sevens win for England at any rate.

However, this time, and after a six month absence of 'League dying / merged game' stories from the national papers, there was to be a sting in the tail. In the *Guardian* newspaper the following week, two articles appeared, both lambasting the state of Rugby League. One piece of work in particular, by Stephen Bierley, jumped onto the old 'League is dying' bandwagon, and included comments such as "for dodos and miners, read Rugby League."

In our opinion it included the usual anti-Rugby League spin, misdirection and inaccuracies (to which a long e-mail to the sports editor protested.) To quote: "it may even be that those such as Wigan, Bradford, Leeds and Hull simply cross the divide, such as it is. There is an argument that if Rugby League went back to being part-time all the best players would desert, but this is happening anyway."

Hull F.C. switching codes? Behave. 'All the best players?' - name names. The article even got the score in the one-off Australian test humiliation wrong (probably thinking of the 1998 Australia versus England Rugby Union score of 76-0, now that's research.)

The timing of these articles seems to be inspired by the Middlesex Sevens, a backlash against League's success. No new information was forthcoming from Mr Bierley in an article that could have been written, word-for-word at least a month ago. Take out mention of the Australia test, and it could have been written six months ago. The fact that Rugby League's star was shining brighter for a few days in the media circles seems to have made Fleet Street call for a dozen big brushes and a large can of tarnish. Just in time to gee up the troops and get more bums on seats for the new Union season, too.

In my view, the *Guardian's* anti-League agenda displayed once more. They do, however, appreciate feedback at reader@guardian.co.uk

Seventh heaven

Stuart Duffy gave his blessing for us to use his piece from the Bradford Bulls' programme, which was drawn to our attention by Andrew Foster.

"The Bulls' victory in the Middlesex Sevens certainly ruffled the feathers of the Rugby League press. There have been conspiracy theories, ranging from the sublime to the ridiculous, as Rugby League fans have been looking for something to justify the supposed lack of coverage of the event in the Sunday newspapers.

Much as I, for obvious reasons, would like to see more League in the media we have got to accept we can't have it both ways. Rugby League supporters would have been the first to complain if there had been no League teams involved and the tournament had been splashed all over the sports pages of the quality press the following day. What coverage there was gave fulsome praise to the Bulls for their display and it is always good to see the club's profile in areas that are not the norm for Rugby League.

Many Rugby League fans, and there were plenty of Bulls supporters in this bracket, felt the club were making a mistake in entering. They reasoned that if we had lost we would have been pilloried and our sport ridiculed. They may well have been correct and they are entitled to their opinion but we didn't lose and the plaudits received, in the national, local and Rugby League press, as well as on national television were well worth the risk.

The television coverage of the event was excellent. We could go on all day as to why the BBC would choose to devote the majority of its Saturday afternoon sports coverage to an event that many see as nothing more than a pre season tournament. Not only did they commit a large part of *Grandstand* to the Sevens but they also showed the final on a special programme on BBC2! But the BBC is not there to pamper to the needs of the Rugby League fan. It exists to show programmes that appeal to a large number of viewers and, like the Boat Race, the Derby and the Grand National, the Middlesex Sevens has become a bit of an institution. It's also, I should imagine, fairly cheap to broadcast.

So what can the game as a whole and the Bulls take out of it? Simply that the profile we received on national television was better than we have seen since the Challenge Cup Final. Rugby League came out of it with flying colours.

Anyone watching could give nothing but praise, however grudgingly, to the Bulls for the quality of their play and the way in which they put the adversity of a nightmare journey behind them to take the competition by storm. It was quite obvious that our game is streets ahead of the opposition in fitness, skill and strength. For the Bulls it was a chance to show the non Sky television audience in Britain what a quality outfit we are. It gave great profile to our sponsors, something that we will need to keep high if we are to attract sufficient support for the new venture at Odsal.

Profile is something we should never underestimate and it is vitally important to those investing their money into the club. Let's not beat about the bush here, JCT600 probably got more profile for their brand last weekend than they have received from their association with Bradford City in the last five years. That alone, at a critical time for the club, made it a worthwhile exercise and to beat the Union boys in their own back yard, and their own game, put the icing on the cake. People such as Ray Gent have worked very hard at raising the game's profile, and he has said on many occasions, something that I totally agree with, we must keep knocking on doors. Well, last week we knocked some down."

Rugby's other class war

Dave Dooley has been a fan of Rugby League and the Saints in particular for almost 50 years. He is the secretary of the Independent Saints Supporters Association and dedicates his piece 'to all those at St Helens RLFC who have opened their eyes, seen the light and turned the corner.'

"One of the most enjoyable and informative reads on the game of Rugby League must be David Hinchliffe's *Rugby's Class War* (London League Publications Ltd). Hinchliffe examines the bigotry, elitism and hypocrisy that underpinned Rugby Union's century long campaign to denigrate and outlaw the finest spectator sport in the world. It is an analysis of an establishment condoned apartheid system within British sport. However, if we are to make progress within *our* game then we must recognise that some of the very same dark forces have been evident within the professional sector of Rugby League. Every member of the Rugby League *community* is entitled to equal respect by the owners and managers of our clubs. Of course, it is in the interest of those at the top to push the boat out for generous sponsors, but I have sadly witnessed poor treatment of supporters in the offices, shops, bars and stadia all of which have conspired to undermine the culture and community that has provided the bonding for Rugby League people throughout our history.

My own club St Helens has had more than its fair share of bad publicity over the past 15 years. As I am convinced that the Saints is now being run well, under the astute and positive leadership of Eamonn McManus with true regard for its loyal supporters, perhaps the time is right to uncover some of its dark history and paint a picture of how all clubs can make social, economic and emotional progress off the field.

In the midst of the infamous Hanley (Saints' club coach at the time) suspension in 1999, the former chairman at St Helens RLFC questioned whether or not the town and its supporters 'deserved a Super League team'. At the time there was much discussion regarding the 'franchise' system and aggrieved souls made mock threats of taking the Saints to obscure midlands settlements where they would be assured of better support. In my mind such thoughts are tantamount to treason! It is interesting to note that as the team conquered all before them over the next two years, the very same managers and carers somehow managed to take the Saints to the brink of insolvency.

This financial and managerial incompetence can be forgiven. We all make mistakes. The fact that some directors at the time refused to meet with supporters to discuss positive action to improve the performance off the field is beyond belief. When the Independent Saints Supporters Association (ISSA) wrote to the then chairman in July 2000 to discuss such matters, the response amazed all concerned. ISSA, an organisation of some 1,100 members, were told that they could bring up any concerns at the Fans Focus group scheduled for October that year. It's not just the message that rankles, it is the associated lack of respect for loyal supporters that in my opinion betrays the elitism, snobbery, self righteousness and lack of vision held by such messengers. Inevitably this led to a divided club where the talents of the many were ignored and supporters were treated like sheep.

These are the dark forces and attitudes that have threatened the Rugby League community. I know fans at other clubs have faced similar problems. New stadia have been constructed without consulting the supporters who are expected to make it their new emotional place of worship. Other clubs have changed hands or lost their grounds without any reference to the supporters. It seems every time there is such an occurrence the spirit and fabric that lies at the heart of Rugby League communities is irreparably damaged.

What then can be done about these dark forces? I believe that clubs need to be organised by the way of community led forces. There are many examples within the game of excellent community initiatives - the game needs its best performing clubs to be role models in this respect. I would implore all who are in charge of our game to ensure the following is part and parcel of their very existence:

Both home and away supporters should be made most welcome at the grounds and attached social facilities: We have long prided ourselves on the fact that our crowds are not segregated and supporters of opposing teams can stand or sit shoulder to shoulder, enjoy a bit of banter and support their respective teams. However, there have been some undesirable incidents that should not be in our game.

Clubs should organise their management structures to ensure that these bodies include democratically elected match paying supporters: This has been a welcome practice at many football clubs as well as Rugby League clubs such as Halifax.

Supporters trusts should be set up at all our clubs: This would allow a wider range of supporters feel a genuine part of their club and reap dividends far beyond the monies raised for the club. Moreover, it would provide a ready-made safety net should clubs fall into any financial abyss in the future.

Directors and management should meet with supporter groups regularly: I have seen the benefits of a free exchange of ideas in communicating with supporters in various forums. There is a need for hard-nosed objective views on how supporters feel about being consumers and participants in the general life of Rugby League clubs. The best examples of this have been in well attended ISSA meetings. Some clubs however, insist only on talking to fans who give them the answers they want to hear.

Use the expertise of the supporters: The supporters have a fantastic range of talents. In a sport that is often financially challenged we need to make the most of this expertise - and more often than not supporters are more than willing to offer their services for free.

Promote our game in schools: We need to ensure that our grandchildren can watch this great game of ours. A high priority must be increase the number of children playing and watching Rugby League. Clubs have had fantastic schemes to encourage this development. We need to maintain and increase our efforts in this respect.

Maintain an overall view and love of Rugby League: Some commentators believe that this aspect of the game's spirit is not as strong as it used to be. This is down to the supporters and administrators. We need to make decisions that take the game forward while at the same time preserving our fantastic heritage. All of us need to support our teams and the game with equal passion and always remember our glorious heritage.

Treat your supporters with respect: After all they coughed up for season tickets, paid at the gates, bought programmes, erected satellite dishes, queued up in the rain for yet another new club shirt, purchased lottery tickets and had time to read the entire match programme whilst waiting for a pint in the social club. Even though this makes sense from an economic standpoint, clubs should respect fans because I believe they are *equal* members of the Rugby League club's community."

South Sea Bubble

John Camroux (known on the internet as 'Napoleon') writes in late August from Caringbah, New South Wales, Australia, with the state of play especially in the Australasia and Oceania areas.

"The traumas of the Super League war in Australia, have given way to a new found zeal for the game both locally and internationally. The expulsion of the Canterbury Bulldogs (due to salary cap breaches) from the NRL semi-finals indicated the level of passionate support for the game on Australia's eastern seaboard. Newspapers, radio and television stations were inundated with e-mails, faxes, letters and talk on this dramatic event. It also rammed home to the officialdom of the Union and AFL codes, that League is far and away the people's game.

The appointment of Richard Lewis with his forthright views, and David Gallop who impressed everyone with his leadership qualities and compassion when announcing the severe penalties to the Bulldogs, augurs well for the game in both countries. These gentlemen have stated their position as to the importance of the international side of our game.

International sport is the initiator of sponsorship from international companies and arouses the passions of a country. The support of the RFL, NRL and NZRL for the Tri series is an indicator that the message has finally hit home. It is now accepted that Rugby League is played in more countries than at any time of its existence. In the space of four months this year Serbia, New Caledonia and Lebanon have joined the League family.

The game is getting back on its feet in Australia despite the defections of a couple of wingers to Union, and the growing competition from that code and AFL. Junior playing numbers increased by 3 per cent in 2001, and I understand have held their own against other codes this year. Television ratings for State of Origin consistently out rate Union internationals, and despite the lop sided score, the Great Britain against Australia test was still a ratings winner for the television channel.

The Melbourne Storm are finding it difficult to make a big impact in the AFL mad state with a hostile press (sound familiar?). Also, live television for all their local games hits the crowd figures.

Female development officers have been introduced into Australian primary schools (where female teachers predominate) and have proven to be an outstanding success.

New Zealand numbers have dropped to 30,000, however the success of the Warriors, a newly introduced junior development programme and a more receptive press bodes well for the future. The Warriors' crowds and television ratings are both on the up.

Papua New Guinea remains the only country where League is the national sport, with fanaticism that defies belief. The country stops during State of Origin. Touring is restricted though as the country is cash strapped.

170

'The M62 Game...?'

The Pacific Islands have varying degrees of involvement in the game. Tonga has 15 clubs playing in First and Second Divisions and has the support of the King. The Cook Islands has six clubs with the competition commencing on 9 August. The Fiji competition is down to nine clubs in 2002 and junior numbers are at an all time low, due to players being paid in the past years. The FRL chairman is working on building the game up. The writer believes that the defection of the Brisbane Bronco's Lote Tuquiri to Union will not help League's cause in that country.

Samoa where the game collapsed in recent years is looking at a 20-team competition in October. The SRL are awaiting confirmation of a grant from the government in order for the competition to proceed. The introduction of a five team competition in New Caledonia, and plans to stage a 24-team sevens tournament in March 2003 is a boost for the game in that region.

One has to feel optimism for the game internationally, when we read of the work of League enthusiasts in north-eastern USA and in Japan. The pioneering work in Lebanon by Australians of Lebanese descent, and the selfless work performed by Hussain M'Barki in Morocco, has laid the platform for further expansion.

In Russia 12,000 juniors are registered and the main limitation for further growth is resources. The resources and finances can only be achieved through funding by the RLIF (now with a part-time development officer and limited finances) - further justification for tri-series and more Tests.

The writer was brought up on a diet of private school Union, his conversion coming by way of his wife and father in law. Having witnessed

171

the sheer magic of Gasnier, Raper, Murphy, Bishop, Millward, Fulton, Rogers etc. the writer has no intention of returning to the 'dark side'.

The resilience of our game, when it is supposedly down, is the foundation on which a strong future will be built."

French farce – or Greek tragedy?

At the end of August, a long awaited report was published by the enquiry set up by the French Government to investigate injustices to Rugby League during and after the Second World War.

One article that proved very popular in *Enough is Enough* was the one on French Rugby League by Roger Grime. Many fans were oblivious to the extent which the game had suffered across the English Channel and asked if another article could be penned. Roger has kindly agreed and takes you back in his 'time machine' to see for yourself.

"Just imagine if Hitler's invasion of our island had been successful in 1941. Key posts in every area, including sport, would have been filled by sympathisers and collaborators whose fascist tendencies would have laid the blame for Britain's defeat at the door of moral and physical decadence.

The 'golden age' would have to be re-created when only 'gentlemen' could afford to play sport for leisure. Everyone would know his place (usually humble). In my opinion at the centre would be officials of Rugby Union, an elite sport whose adherents enjoyed status and power - power to suppress anyone and everything they wanted, especially some upstart deviant code of rugby whose popularity had swept the country. Thankfully this never happened but...

It did happen in France where, on 19 December 1941, Marshal Pétain, puppet head of the 'French State', dancing to the FFR (French Rugby Union) tune, banned Rugby League and confiscated all its property.

The Commisioner for Sport under this Vichy government, famous Basque tennis champion, Jean Borotra, 're-established the unity of rugby' and, despite massive protests, the hugely popular Rugby League was forced back into the clutches of the envious FFR. Rugby Union, its coffers depleted by forced exile from international fixtures and the huge success of the other code, came out of the war enriched. How? And what happened to the League's bank deposits, kit, grounds, possessions etc? I think we all know.

So did the Treizistes just give up? They protested, but were told the decision was final. It was war-time and half their country was occupied by the Nazis, the other half (south) being under the control of the puppet Vichy collaborators. They tried but met closed official doors.

It seemed that the infamous wrong would be soon remedied. General de Gaulle, leader of the Free French Forces and Government in exile, issued his Algiers Decree in 1943, stating that all steps taken by Vichy would be reversed, including actions against any sporting body.

Rugby League was filled with fresh hope for it was proud to have been at the centre of resistance to the invaders and collaborators. Lyon-Villeurbanne's Charles Mathon and Réné Barnoud had founded a resistance movement in sport called 'Sport-Libre' and Mâquis (resistance) cells were a feature of the League family in those dark years. Surely it would be remembered and the ravages of the war years overturned?

Despite the sport's reputation for resistance during the war years, even De Gaulle, who had backed the efforts of Treizistes after the Liberation to seek out and bring to justice the Vichy traitors, now refused to hear their case and referred it to the CNS, that same federation of sports bodies, which had blocked their entry before the war. Dominated by the French Rugby Union and its henchmen sympathisers, it continued to refuse the Treizistes entry without which the code had no official standing.

It was laughable if it had not been so unjust - Vichy had declared Rugby Union the *only* form of rugby allowed, banned League and stolen its assets, yet after the traitors had been expelled, the 'good guys' were left without status and with their possessions stolen by the code that yet again sought to suppress them.

Luckily, they found a champion in former resistance leader, Paul Barrière, who fought to get the game reinstated. In France, a sport must gain admission to the Sports' Federation (CNS) if it is to function properly and receive anything in the way of grant assistance. Union continued to block its entry until Barrière persuaded two minor sports, archery and real tennis, to join his own first love, cycling, in seconding League's application.

Still the persecution persisted. In 1946, the Union-dominated CNS agreed with the FFR's argument that there could not be 'two rugbys' , so Rugby League must henceforth call itself 'Jeu à Treize' (13 a-side game) despite the fact that the CNS's own regulations permitted any member to call itself whatever it chose. Furthermore, as Rugby League had been banned by Vichy under the name of Rugby à Treize, it had no longer existed from that very day in 1941 and so could not reclaim the possessions stolen immediately after this date. 'How can something which does not exist own anything?' went the argument. And anyway, it was now 'Jeu à Treize' which could not have owned anything before 1946 when it was forcibly created. Catch 22 indeed. These were the tricks used against League. Can you now appreciate the lengths that Rugby Union went to before, during and after the war to destroy our brothers?

Despite all this, the Treizistes tried to reorganise and the comet that was French Rugby League flared brilliantly in 1951 when the Australians were defeated before huge crowds in their own back yards and Puig-Aubert's team returned to a massive welcome home in Marseille.

But the war years were beginning to take their toll as Union reaped the harvest of those years of their code being compulsory in schools. Threats to careers from Union-dominated committees kept League out of the French education system. Children and their teachers found almost insurmountable obstacles to a game of Treize in school or after school. Slowly, the code went into comparative decline as the British home Unions swallowed the FFR's line that, of course there was no professionalism in French Rugby Union, and recommenced lucrative international fixtures.

Constant persecution now undermined the code. Blackmail and threats restricted sponsorship. The media toed the line of their Union-leaning owners. Firms faced cancellation of contracts and the drying up of business if they were suspected of any support for or sympathy with League. Jobs mysteriously disappeared only to be recreated with a Union player or sympathiser in possession.

All efforts to recover League's stolen properties or even launch an inquiry into the crimes of the Vichy era were blocked, but frustration finally boiled over as those that should have led the fight for justice, the French Rugby League Federation, were seen to be broken reeds.

In 1993, the fight to win back the title 'Rugby' was won, but infuriatingly to the grass-roots, the Federation chose not to publicise this major victory, seeming unwilling to upset Union. Faced with such lack of action, especially with regard to the recovery of the assets stolen during the war, XIII Actif, a pressure group, was founded by physical education lecturer, Robert Fassolette, in 1997.

Sick of the lack of progress in reclaiming the game's birthright and feeling that the Federation was allowing Rugby Union to marginalise its rival, XIII Actif took on the role of agitator for League's stolen assets and sought to safeguard its future. But under the French system, only the

'The M62 Game...?'

Federation could press for restitution - and it wouldn't, merely suggesting a working party which never materialised.

Relations between the Federation and this ginger group worsened to the extent that there is now no communication. When, in 2001, a splinter group of top clubs sought to create a mechanism to move the game forward, it was met with resistance and these clubs were excluded by Federation President Jean-Paul Ferré from discussions on major issues. So the game in France is in chaos with 'loyalists' (i.e. those not making waves) receiving rewards from its President while the game shrinks and the progressive clubs, led by Guy Troupel of Villeneuve and Toulouse's Carlos Zalduendo, are blocked at every turn. At the April, 2002, meeting of XIII Actif in Carcassonne's MJC, Cliff Spracklen, of the RLSA, made an impassioned plea for dialogue between the warring parties. How else could Rugby League prosper?

In 1997, the Minister for Sport, Madame Marie-George Buffet, initiated an inquiry into the Vichy years, not at the Federation's prompting, but through sustained pressure from Jewish activists who wanted this can of worms opened. She asked how the collaborators committed their crimes while feathering their own nests. Rugby League people could tell her.

Now, in 2002, the report on sport during the occupation years has been published and what should have been a glorious moment of triumph and vindication for our game in France, has been met with an astonishing lack of enthusiasm by the Federation: 'The usual purpose of such enquiries is simply to set people's minds at rest' responded Ferré tamely, seemingly terrified of rattling the Union cage.

But the report says quite clearly that officials of the French Rugby Union took steps to get rid of their rival. It goes on to say that although the

175

Commission of Enquiry cannot, itself, force through the restitution of all that was stolen, its report could be used as a basis for such action. The Federation, as Ferré's quote above shows, is not inclined to take action.

XIII Actif thinks differently and wants action and justice, but a camp divided will achieve nothing. This is the farce of Rugby League in France: beset by Union enemies, factions bicker among themselves in a house divided. We, in Britain, must not throw up our hands in despair but use every opportunity to nurse them back to prosperity. We have to involve them in our competitions, offer international fixtures at every level and help them to recreate their golden age.

Without this, Rugby League in France may become no bigger than the sports of archery and real tennis which helped it find its proper place in the sun in the heady days of 1946. That is the tragedy."

Further Reading and Acknowledgements
La Tribune de XIII Actif (Robert Fassolette)
L'Encyclopedie de Treize Magazine (Andre Passomar)
Le Rugby à XIII, le plus français du monde (Louis Bonnery)
Rugby à XIII ou Jeu à XIII? (Robert Fassolette)
The Forbidden Game (Mike Rylance - League Publications Ltd)

Cri de couer

The *"cri de coeur"* of a French "treiziste" - Maurice Boule volunteered his thoughts on the state of play in France just prior to the beginning of the nw French season as the game pushes to get back onto television and re-enforce its numbers in Paris with new clubs there:

"Bonjour tous mes amis treizistes in Britain. Great to see the initiatives of fans in Britain, such as your Petition, RLSA, supporters' trusts, giving fans a 'say'. Most of all great to mix with English fans, at games like the Broncos versus Warrington at Carcassonne.

We need that involvement with you because we are isolated here. It gives us courage and confidence to continue to fight, to see we are part of a bigger movement, not just a forgotten minority.

Its not always been the case. In the 1950s we had our 'golden days' when we could beat you *rosbifs* in test matches. We beat the Australians in their own country. France went mad, and we had good coverage in the national press. *Treizistes* were treated with respect, because of the high standards on the field, and we were seen by many as heroes of the resistance because of the Vichy ban. In Marseille, around 100,000 people turned out to greet and cheer Puig Aubert's conquering heroes as they disembarked. Marseille XIII is still there, but just an amateur team.

Super League was to be a big step forward and we were proud to see our PSG put one over the English teams. It was a long trip, with overnight stays in Paris, for we fans from the south. But it was worth it, as we were finally back in the Rugby League family and treated with respect by our friends from across the Channel.

But then we were let down. You 'kicked us out'. We had secured our place on the field, but we were back to square one, with no Super League team, and hardly any international games.

At least we had televised games. This year it looks like the French games will not be shown but we still have Super League and NRL. Its great to watch the stars, and French kids are growing up to marvel at Andrew Johns and Paul Sculthorpe. Just a shame they won't see French stars.

We love it when the British come for games like the Test at Agen. It makes us feel part of the family. But we want more contacts. We would love to see your NFP sides playing the likes of Villeneuve and UTC down here. Inclusion in the Challenge Cup has helped, now that there is a chance of a French team being drawn at home. We still suspect that your lads would rather play in Australia or New Zealand, than here where the language and food is different. We still remember Joe Lydon, when he played for Great Britain, saying he did not like playing in France 'because of the food'.

I suppose we expect a lot from you Brits. Your game looks so strong compared to us. You moan a lot about the press, attendances, not beating Australia. Yet you have two weekly papers devoted to League, Sky and BBC coverage, and the current Great Britain team would put 50 past the French. If only we had your problems. Mind you, even you have a way to go, but we admire the way you do fight for changes, to give fans a voice and to criticise the leaders of the game. We don't see our leader, and have little means of criticising him. There is no official Federation website, little newspaper discussion, and if you send a letter criticising the Federation, to our only magazine, *XIII Magazine,* it does not get printed. This is because it is run by the Federation, who don't like criticism. It is one of the reasons we formed XIII Actif, and why we now produce a newsletter, *La Tribune de XIII Actif,* based on the wartime resistance news bulletins. At least it lets fans know what is going on.

Where I live in Provence, the south-east, we were one of the 'hot-beds' of the game. Marseille were famous in the 1950s, providing many international players. Cavaillon were a top team, but now are not even allowed to play in the stadium which once belonged to them. As a smaller team now they play on the open pitch at the side, while the Rugby Union team play in the main stadium. Le Pontet were champions 20 years ago, and very professional, but now they are gone. Its just Union there. The ambition to have an Elite club at Avignon collapsed last year, and now we only have Carpentras in the top division, and they struggle financially.

I suppose we are a bit like Cumbria. Lots of grassroots Rugby League teams, but not much exposure these days to the 'big league'.

It's better in the other main region, Languedoc-Rousillion, where there are clubs like Villeneuve, Toulouse, Carcassonne, Pia, Lezignan and UTC. Our 'big three' are doing really well, and they give your NFP sides a good game, in the Challenge Cup. Maybe they should be in the NFP? But all three would like to join Super League. I don't think Super League will let all three in, but we need a Super League team. It would be better if we had one team like the New Zealand Warriors, supported by all the clubs, or perhaps two regional teams, one in Catalonia and one in the Aude. We need Super League to raise our training and playing standards, to increase our media profile, and to make sure our best players don't go to Union. But at the moment the 'big three' are competing with each other and there appears to be no lead from the Federation.

Equally, there is little response from the Federation to the French Government report, which included official confirmation of the discrimination against our game, the banning by the Vichy Government, and the collusion of the French Rugby Union. We still face problems today. The Vichy XIII club had to fight for two years for a pitch, Cavaillon XIII can't play on the municipal ground they once owned, and discrimination continues in the schools against League.

XIII Actif was a great idea, and has achieved a great deal of publicity, but the president of the federation will not talk to us. How different from your country, where you are able to talk to your officials.

So keep us 'Frenchies' in mind every time you are arguing for changes in your game. You are so important to us, but we hope we are important to you. We want more games between British and French teams, at every level. Until we get a Super League team it will be hard for France to compete with Great Britain, but we can compete with Wales, Scotland, Ireland, Russia, England 'A', or the NFP. The progress with Russia, Morocco and Lebanon gives more opportunities.

Ironically, we have seen some steps forward in the north around Paris and it would be good to see links between London and Paris clubs at all levels, as they are close together.

It is frustrating being a French fan. Our junior set-up is good, but to see an Elite game, we sometimes have to travel hours. So just getting fans together is not easy. But at least we know how to have fun. Our '*troisieme mi-temps*' (third half), is where we like some good food and wine, while we have a go at the ref...

We may never get the 'golden days' back, but we can make a lot more progress, if you British fans and officials, keep us as involved as possible. *Que le bon temps rouler!* Let the good times roll!"

Digital revolution

At the end of August, and compensating in some part for the demise of the Rugby League friendly Teamtalk 252 radio station, with its excellent Jonathan Doidge, good news from the BBC in that the new BBC Radio 5 Live Sports Extra radio channel is now regularly covering live Rugby League games uninterrupted. Presentation is by former London Broncos star Tulsen Tollett and, among others, Dave Hadfield (i.e. knowledgeable League people.)

The station is available only to an audience limited to those with digital radio receivers, and subscribers to SKY and cable TV suppliers such as NTL and Telewest.

Of course rather than watching a blank screen and listening to the game via a radio channel on the satellite or cable set, most would prefer to flick to the Sky Sports channels and actually watch it, but, hey, any extra coverage is welcome.

The Big Issue

One could categorically say that the game of Rugby League has faced many issues during its one hundred plus years but now we seem to be a sport of 'jet setters', or so it seems from a playing point of view.

The *Big Issue* magazine is sold in many towns and cities by vendors who are trying their best to beat the homeless trap. The 'seller' receives a percentage of the money raised to hopefully help gain a foothold further up the ladder to a better life. The magazine is full of stories, comment and occasional humour. It was interesting then to find in a summer 2002 issue an article on Rugby League.

Apparently 'Aussie Rules' is here to save the working class from sporting disaster! It states that the sporting heritage of the north of England was forged in the furnaces of the Industrial Revolution and the golden age of mining, mills and steel foundries. It made comment that out of the hardship the workers wrought what are now two of the most popular games in the world: football and Rugby League.

Further it stated that both gave the working-class men an opportunity to burn off the frustrations of grinding weekly slog and bound together toil-hardened communities of working class towns and villages across the north west. (Some more research ed, as the article forgets our cousins in Yorkshire and Cumbria amongst others.)

It now appears that the times have changed with the advent of professionalism, particularly to Rugby League in the last few years. It is now suggested that both sports are well above the grass roots level. It continues with the comment that especially Rugby League has now got a vacuum (not a Dyson!) between the sport and ordinary working man. The sport features some of the fittest pro athletes with pay packets to match.

This vacuum may not remain empty for long with the arrival of a new game in the north west called 'Australian Rules Football'. First played in Victoria, New South Wales in 1858 it is to become the new 'peoples game' of the north west', and in particular the town of St Helens. The writer seems to think that the Rugby League team has gone from a bunch of local born amateurs in the sixties and seventies to a multi-national jet-set of professionals whose working week is geared solely to match days. 'It belongs as much to the town as the lollo rosso and teriyaki on sale in the local deli.' The article then continues to explain how the St Helens Miners team has enjoyed a solid, if silver-ware free, first season.

Perhaps Rugby Union and other professional sports had better watch out, as the Aussies could indeed 'rule the roost in sport' and do a complete take over! 'Banish the jet setters of sport' could be the cry of the workers.

11. September 2002

September starts with a curious admission from an old friend at the BBC, who appears to have blown his own argument out of the water, very much in public. Bradford fans' voices are heard as their campaign for a return to Odsal comes good, and the Rugby League Conference summer season draws to a close, reviewed by Phil Cole. A flurry of improbable fixtures shows how fans' persistence has spread the game recently. Stuart Cummings, RFL controller of refereeing explains what many of us have wondered - why on earth do they do it?

Pat Younge's slip of the tongue

On 1 September 2002, the top letter in the *Sunday Times* sports section was from Pat Younge, head of BBC Sport. He was responding to an article by Stephen Jones the previous week about the decision to play Six Nations games on Sundays (apparently at the request of the BBC), which Mr Jones had found abhorrent, and something that no true 'rugby' fan would accept.

Pat Younge defended the scheduling on the basis that 'in the last three years, viewing figures for Six Nations matches have decreased by 50 per cent,' and that a switch to Sunday will re-invigorate the figures. Let's just take a moment to contemplate this statement....

A 50 per cent decline in three years? Did he really mean that half of the people once viewing the tournament no longer watch?

The BBC paid £70m (with no other bidders) to show Six Nations on the basis that is was to be a jewel in their crown, but now they tell us that Rugby Union is the code millions of people no longer turn on to watch?

When the man in charge of BBC Sport admits that international Union is not quite the draw we were all lead to believe, but still, apparently, worth £70m of licence payers money, a few questions need to be asked.

The Odsal campaign

Thanks to Jacky Tranter, from Bradford Independent Supporters Association, who got some good news early in September:

"I suppose the die-hard Rugby League supporters would describe me as a glory fan, having only followed Rugby League in the Super League era. Having moved to Bradford in 1996 from Wales, and with a Rugby Union background, I was dragged grudgingly to my first game between the Bulls versus Rhinos at Odsal Stadium and from that game on I've been hooked.

The speed and ability of the players shocked me and it wasn't long before I was dragging my family to every Bulls game. I've always felt that Rugby League is overlooked somewhat with the media, so when I was approached at a match and asked to sign the petition I did so eagerly. I never for one moment realised that it would end up as huge as it did. The strength of feeling and passion in the supporters of Rugby League still astounds me.

The recent Odsal saga prompted me to join with some like-minded people and set up BISA with our aim being positive promotion of Rugby League in Bradford, while the main item on the agenda was to see the Bulls back at Odsal.

We started off campaigning towards the development but when this fell through the feeling of the majority of fans was that Valley Parade, home of the football club, would become our 'permanent home'. As supporters we didn't want this, so started to campaign for a return to Odsal with the option for the Bulls to develop it themselves. We launched the 'Try for Odsal' campaign during the Saints versus Bradford match at Knowsley Road back in June 2002. Sky Sports were there and the cameras picked up on the banners. The campaign took off with the help of BISA members and supporters of other clubs as 'Try for Odsal' banners could be seen at every Bulls game.

Earlier this month we received the news that we would return home for the 2003 season and was the best news we could have got. It just goes to show what you can achieve if you get enough people speaking with one voice. As with the Media Petition it's another success for the Rugby League family of supporters having once again proved their passion and commitment. Where else in the sporting world can you get support like it?"

Try for Odsal

Andy Clough fills out the story:

"In November 2000, Bradford Bulls announced they would be leaving Odsal, their home ground since 1934, to temporarily share Valley Parade, home of Bradford City. It finally seemed that Odsal Stadium would be re-developed into a 26,000 all-seater ground with an adjacent retail complex, including a Tescos supermarket, multiplex cinema, restaurants and an 80 bedroom hotel. It was envisaged it would create up to 1,600 jobs. Sterling Capitol were the firm chosen to develop the site (the stadium would be based on Sunderland F.C.'s Stadium of Light.) Bull's idea was to move to Valley Parade for the start of the 2001 season, and move back to a re-developed 'home' for season 2003. It wasn't the first time that re-development had been ear-marked. In 1993, the plans to turn the ground into a Superdome with sliding roof fell apart, after the council had given the planning company five years' worth of extensions. Indeed, since 1954 Odsal has been mooted as the Wembley of the north. However, as we were moving to Valley Parade to play our home games, it seemed like the dream would come true. The plans for the new stadium were submitted to the Planning Department of Bradford Council in December 2000.

February 2001 witnessed the first game at our 'temporary' home against Widnes in the Challenge Cup. This brought forth the first problems of Valley Parade. With it being all-seater, a few fans were not sure on the rules of having to sit for the majority of the time. This was to become a common event that would blight Bulls at Valley Parade throughout their two-year stay, effecting home fans and away fans alike. Problems with the stewards would arise through fans standing, with the stewards being accused of heavy-handed tactics, which lead to many arguments on message boards.

It seemed most visiting fans and visiting teams hated Valley Parade, but this was good for the Bulls point of view, as they went on to win the Grand Final to become Super League champions in October 2001. Also that month, Bradford Council said they would pass on the planned re-development to the Government in December of the same year. Sterling Capitol were completing a study of any effect the Tesco superstore could have on the city centre retailers and neighbourhood shopping centres, and also carried out traffic and environmental assessments. Bradford Chamber of Trade and Bradford Retail Action Group both said they had no objections to the development. However, in November, several supermarket chains wanted to bring a halt to the development. Morrisons, Asda and Somerfield Stores Ltd (owners of Kwik Save) all said that their own stores would be hit by the new Tesco superstore, and also increase traffic congestion.

December 2001 came. It seemed all systems go when Bradford Council's Planning Panel gave the Odsal development the all-clear. A few local residents did object who expressed fears of increased traffic congestion, construction noise and disruption to wildlife. The plans were then sent to the now 'infamous' Stephen Byers MP, who was then Secretary of State for Transport, Local Government and the Regions, who had an initial 28-day period to consider the application. Richard Carbon MP, the Minister for Sport gave his support to the project.

Then came the shock news. Environment Secretary Byers called for a public inquiry into the proposed development. There were concerns over traffic congestion, the effect it would have on the city centre trade, the environment, pollution and the need and leisure to make the stadium viable. What made this all the more astonishing was that Arsenal F.C. had submitted plans for their own new stadium at the same time, and their plans had been approved. Another case of anti-League bias?

Two months passed, Bulls waiting for any news. On 1 February 2002, Bulls won the World Club Challenge against the Newcastle Knights of the NRL. Then, on 1 March, the start of Super League VII, Stephen Byers MP promised he would speed up the public inquiry. Another objector, the Foster Square Development Partnership, who wanted to re-develop an area of Bradford city centre called Broadway, said they would send representatives to the inquiry. This Partnership included Caddick Construction, headed by Leeds Rhinos chairman Paul Caddick. The group claimed that the Odsal scheme could hit trade in the city centre. Also, Kirklees Council objected, saying that it would effect shopping in Cleckheaton.

Birth of BISA

About this time, Bradford Bulls supporters decided they needed a voice to show their concerns over what was happening. The Bradford Independent Supporters Association (BISA) was set up, the main priority at the time being the Odsal development. Newly installed members of BISA were asked to write letters to Stephen Byers MP, their local MPs, and their local councillors, urging them to keep the project alive. Bulls' supporters also expressed their views in the local newspaper, the *Telegraph & Argus*. Trevor Foster MBE, a legend of Bradford Rugby League, and Honorary President of BISA said he would walk to the Houses of Parliament to persuade them to give Odsal the go ahead. Soon it was announced that the public inquiry would not take place until September 2002.

On 14 June, the worst news so far happened. Both Sterling Capitol and Tesco decided to pull out, both claiming that the public inquiry would leave long delays and spiralling costs. It was a double blow to sport in Bradford, as Bradford City had been placed into receivership with debts of £30m. Bradford Bulls were now left in a dilemma. They could not go back to Odsal in the state it was in, and, even though they needed the money, City did not

184

want Bulls at Valley Parade. Indeed, the Bulls chairman, Chris Caisley admitted that he 'didn't know where we are going to play next season'. He said that Bulls could not go back to Odsal, as it was 'in a disgraceful state'. Bulls' fans had already voted with their feet about Valley Parade, with attendances down. The argument between Bulls and the Council spiralled. The Council actually owned Odsal, and was still in a contract with the Bulls to keep the stadium fit for a team to play there. The latest council report recommended that only the minimal repairs needed to be done, but the Bulls argued this would leave the stadium below the minimum standard required by Super League regulations. The council claimed that they would give the stadium new floodlights, and improve health and safety in a 25,000 capacity stadium. This would mean however that they would not spend money on facilities such as bars, proper toilets, and food kiosks. Health and safety alone needed £600,000 spending on it. The roof over the main stand had only a few more years left on its health and safety, so the attendances would be reduced.

BISA decided that enough was enough. A campaign to get the council to do their best for the Bulls was started. Banners were made, with the slogan 'Try harder Bradford Council'. BISA thought the power of television would help to spread the word. The Millennium Baton was due to arrive in Bradford. A few Bulls' fans made their way down to Centenary Square, just outside the City Hall where local television was filming the events. As the runner made his way along the path, banners could be seen lining the barriers. The first blow had been struck. The next opportunity arose on 28 June. Bradford were to be playing away at St Helens, a game that was to be shown on Sky television. This time, thousands of flyers with the new slogan of 'Try for Odsal' had been printed, and were distributed amongst the away support. Several Saints fans, who, having visited the Bradford message board, were aware of the campaign also took some. Saints fans had an intense dislike to Valley Parade due to the stewards, and longed to see us go back to Odsal. A phone call had been made to Sky, telling them of the campaign. Sky said that they would focus the cameras whenever the banners were shown. As the Bulls came out, Sky were true to their word. Every time Bulls scored, or they showed the crowd, the banners were waved. People at the ground received text messages from those watching saying that they had been spotted.

The follow week, Bulls were at home to Widnes. Bradford Council wanted to use this game to gain support for its bid of European Capital of

Culture 2008, and a few dignitaries they wanted to impress had been invited to the game. Bulls' fans, thinking the council had a cheek trying to use the club for a purpose whilst denying them a decent stadium, planned to continue the 'Try for Odsal' campaign, even though Sky would not be at the game. BISA members handed out A4 banners all around Valley Parade. These were again held up high as the teams appeared, and when ever Bulls scored. Other Bulls fans had also made their own banners, and had stuck them on walls and barriers.

Hull away was another opportunity for Bulls fans to get the message across via Sky, with the banners once again being shown during the games. A picture from this game appeared in *League Express*, with the now seemingly famous large 'Try for Odsal' banner being held up by several BISA and Bulls board members. Again, the support from away fans was fantastic. Hull fans had also complained about the treatment from stewards at Valley Parade. In seems ironic looking back that we were campaigning to go back to our spiritual home, in the same season that Hull were preparing to leave theirs to go to a new stadium.

Some fans came up with other ideas to show their support for Odsal. One Bulls fan, Li, set up her own petition to which she took around Valley Parade, to away grounds, and on the internet. She collected over 1,200 signatures, plus however many on the internet. Another fan from the message board, AndreaB, devised a survey to ask both Bulls' and visiting fans various questions regarding Valley Parade and Odsal. BISA thought about organising a march from Odsal to the City Hall, but unfortunately this had to be abandoned due to safety fears, closing of roads, police etc. Some fans did question as to whether we should return to Odsal or not. Valley Parade did have some redeeming features, mainly that it was covered (as anyone who has stood at Odsal when it was been lashing with rain, wind, or snowing will know how bad it can be), the atmosphere, when it got going, echoed throughout the ground. But the down sides were more prominent. Valley Parade was in the colours of City (claret and amber... maybe Huddersfield Giants could play there), nothing to say that Bulls played there. Most people preferred to stand, and did not like being told to constantly sit down by the stewards. Letters from both City fans and Bulls fans were published in the *T&A* having goes at each other. City fans said the Bulls were lucky to have a ready made stadium to play in, Bulls fans said how would City like to leave Valley Parade and play at Odsal? For someone like me, who supports both clubs, I could see both sides of the coin. There is

186

too much Rugby League history at Odsal, including the 1954 Challenge Cup replay between Halifax and Warrington, with officially 102,569 people cramming into Odsal (even though it was thought that 120,000 people got in!), the largest Super League gate (24,020 against Leeds Rhinos in 1999). Also, even though Valley Parade had been built for Manningham Rugby Club, it had too much football history, as well as being a memorial for the 56 people who died in the Bradford City fire.

The same day as the Hull game, Chris Caisley demanded that the Council sort out the crisis within the next month, but moving back to a patched up Odsal was not an option. Some sponsors threatened to stop funding Bulls if they moved back to Odsal, as the argued that they could not entertain their guests at Odsal as well as they could at Valley Parade. The Bulls were in talks with the council, to see if they could be paid out of the agreement that meant the council paid Bulls £300,000 a year while at Odsal.

Then, a month later, came the best news since the Bulls had won the WCC back in February… Bulls were going back to Odsal Stadium. A one of payment from the Council of £4.6m would be paid to the Bulls to release them from the contract, so Bulls would be able to develop Odsal themselves. The Council would still own the land, and Bulls would pay a peppercorn rent for 150 years. Bulls' fans were overjoyed! It was a victory for all the hard work that BISA, and other Bulls fans had done."

Rugby League's greatest strength

Originally taken from a debate on the *Totalrl.com* message board in early September, Steve May was happy to have his opinions published here:

"Rugby League's greatest strength is, I think, sheer bloody-mindedness. Right from the beginning, when the 22 clubs said 'Sod it then, we'll do our own thing, see you when you arrive in the 19th century' and took their collective bats home, bloody-mindedness has been the one consistent feature of Rugby League, its players, fans and, God bless them, its administrators.

Don't underestimate the extent of that rebellion in 1895. In a very class-ridden, constrained society, those 22 clubs turned the world of rugger, probably the sport closest to the hearts of the 'officer' classes and second only to cricket in its importance to the Empire, upside down. I do not for one moment believe that they were acting purely for moral reasons, as is often portrayed, but the fact remains that they took a stand and backed it to the hilt, putting their money right where their mouths were.

The actions of those 22 clubs were unquestionably a strand in the wider rising of the working classes from 1880 onwards, culminating in this country with the Labour landslide of 1945.

Like most of the elements of that movement, it took courage and a great deal of personal confidence, and was done with the understanding that there was no way back. This is, I believe, a major aspect of the treatment Rugby League receives from the media, and 'establishment'.

Strangely, just as it took the Conservative Party and the enormous social upheaval of Thatcherism to permit true social mobility for the working classes, it took Rugby Union to become professional for Rugby League to be able to come out and shine, spreading across the country.

I digress, but I come back now to this bloody-mindedness. It is why we play and watch Rugby League, it is why the game has survived against the odds for over a century, and it is also why those in control have enormous rows. Mainly, however, I think it is a strength, and something to use in the years ahead as Rugby League finds its feet once more and the peculiar relationship the sport has with Rugby Union changes and develops."

Bring on the cannon balls, or loose cannons

An article in *The Independent* on 6 September commented on the damp squib that has been Henry Paul's progress in Union, having been left out of an England training squad of 53 players. If he were to re-switch would it be met with a media 50-gun salute, or rather a damp sparkler? Likewise Iestyn Harris is going through the mill.

Spotted by Heez of the rlfans.com site, 6 September 2002: "Iestyn Harris has been relegated to the bench for Cardiff's Celtic League clash against Connacht in Galway on Friday night. The former Rugby League star is replaced by young fly-half prospect Nicky Robinson. Other players dropping out include scrum-half Ryan Powell and wing Anthony Sullivan."

I wonder if the penny is finally dropping with players and journalists alike that League and Union are indeed two different games, both deserving fair coverage and respect? Most Leaguies take no pleasure in seeing thoroughbred sportsmen struggle in an alien environment. It's like watching Paula Ratcliffe run in wellies or Michael Schumacher driving an Austin Allegro. I wonder if either Henry or Iestyn will coin September's catch-phrase and cry: 'I'm a Rugby League player, get me out of here'.

Reality check

A moment's pause for thought as the regular season draws to a close and what passed for a British summer fades towards autumn. Where is our game and where is it going?

For those who think the Rugby League game is irretrievably stuck 'up north', another of Tim's snapshot surveys, this time of the games played in week starting 7 September 2002 suggests otherwise.

Played at the Prince of Wales Stadium in Cheltenham, hats off to Coventry Bears who beat Hemel Hempstead Stags 31-18 (refereed by Paul Gluck of Northampton) in the final of the Rugby League Conference to win the Harry Jepson Trophy. Earlier, South London Storm beat Bedford Swifts 54-2 in the Rugby League Conference Shield Grand Final.

The concluding fixtures of the Australian NRL regular fixtures saw the New Zealand Warriors club finish top of the table.

On 9 September in Kazan, Tatarstan played the USA Tomahawks, winning 30-24 in front of 9,692 fans.

The game between two of the sport's developing nations was the first of two matches being held that week in the Russian federation, with USA Tomahawks playing Russia at Moscow's Olympic stadium on 13 September, Russia winning 54-10 in front of 35,000 spectators.

Advertising and press coverage for the event were strong. Local politicians and the Minister for Sport were in attendance. The game was televised live throughout Russia.

On 10 September England Students beat the British Army 32-20 in Germany, and on 11 September three Royal Navy teams (women, under-23 and open age) played their RAF counterparts at Portsmouth.

Would any of those unlikely fixtures, teams or locations have seemed possible as recently as 10 years ago? I think either my road atlas must be missing a few pages, or the M62 has been extended.

The structures that have enabled games such as these to now be commonplace have not just come about by accident, taking 'no' for an answer or listening to defeatists.

They are the direct result of hard work by the motivated individuals who have gone the extra mile to make them happen, laying the ground often for little if any reward other than the love of League.

Rugby League Conference - Vision of the Future

Another view on the Rugby League Conference, by Phil Cole:

"Cast your minds to the far future, Old Trafford. The Super League Grand Final has just finished. The Bradford players have sunk to their knees in despair while the Southampton team celebrate, their coach already contemplating the World Club Challenge showdown with the NRL champions at St Mary's Stadium, the home of Southampton F.C. In his acceptance speech, the captain thanks the board that started the club 20 years earlier from a local Union club and built the team from local kids. He remembers when he first played for Winchester under-11s and thanks the Hampshire Rugby League Development Board for their help and support.

Fantasy? The dreams of people who ought to get out more? Perhaps. Then again, it wasn't that long ago that a concept of a League of 30 clubs stretching from Newcastle to Cardiff and Manchester to Crawley would have seemed absurd. Yet in 2002 that dream has become a reality.

Welcome to the world of one of our great success stories, the Rugby League Conference. In 1997, Rugby League stood at the crossroads. The great explosion of southern amateur clubs in the 1980s had come to a halt, with many clubs collapsing and others struggling for players and fixtures. The advent of summer rugby offered an incredible opening to attract players from Union backgrounds to give League a go, while benefiting from the lull in local media football coverage.

The Conference owes its roots to four men. The initial idea came from discussions between Julian Harrison, Hector McNeil and former GB skipper Bev Risman, then a director of the London Broncos. The man who became synonymous with the Conference, Lionel Hurst, quickly joined them. The idea was to create a viable competition featuring well-structured clubs that could develop the game across the country. Many of the old MASWARLA clubs had been dominated by one individual, who ran the club, and quickly fell apart if anything happened to him. Harrison told *Open Rugby* in 1997: "We are very confident that with a professional and effective administrative structure, and with summer rugby, we can be successful in establishing a strong and viable Southern Conference. Running the Conference in summer opens up many exciting possibilities, notably promotional opportunities and the means of opening up Rugby League to a wider group of players and a wider audience."

A pilot League was played in 1997 featuring two Groups: A featured Leicester, Birmingham, Worcester, Oxford and Bedford; B featured Ipswich, Cambridge, North London Skolars, Kingston and West London. The Skolars, beating Leicester, won the Grand Final. Importantly though, all the clubs in the pilot are still competing today.

Inaugural competition

With the success of the pilot behind them, the organisers moved onto the inaugural Conference in 1998 with 15 teams from Chester to London and running from May to July. With a high profile launch at the Houses of Parliament, the competition saw the game getting publicity in the strangest of places. I remember driving through Oxford and hearing local radio station Fox FM plugging the Cavaliers' home games, while local papers offered support. The Conference has benefited from the industry of press officer Phil Caplan and the enthusiastic support of many in the game and none more so than Ray French.

A move to 20 teams in 1999 was followed by increases to 24 in 2000 and 30 in 2001, with the inclusion of the north-east sides, making it a truly national Rugby League Conference. 2002 has seen a period of consolidation, albeit with the introduction of a Shield play-off series to compliment the struggle for the Harry Jepson Trophy. The competition was also extended into September. Now we are in preparation for an explosion of new clubs expected for 2003. Names expected including Bristol, Liverpool, Blackpool, Lancaster, Ely, Taunton and Bath.

A whole new audience is also watching games. At this year's Grand Final, for example, it was clear that most of the crowd were new to the game. A mind-boggling array of accents could be heard, not to mention yelps of pain at the hits on the field.

There have been some great stories and none better than that of South London Storm's exciting fullback Corey Simms, who came to Rugby League while in prison for armed robbery. The Conference has given him a way to rebuild his life and its no wonder that both Sky and Dave Hadfield of *The Independent* picked up on his remarkable story.

It's perhaps not surprising then that *League Publications Ltd* took the naming rights from 2001, giving us the Totalrl.com Conference. They also host the Conference website.

All too good to be true? Well the Conference is not without its critics. The first is an understandable resentment from parts of BARLA at how

191

much coverage the competition gets. If you played for Leigh East, Thornhill or Walney Central, it must be frustrating to see a lower level getting greater attention than your efforts.

The second is the reliance on Rugby Union players. Let's be fair, these people have never had a chance to play League and while most will remain loyal to Union, some will spend greater time with their League club. Some conference players have gone onto a higher level, most notably Jon Breakingbury who left Cardiff Demons for Sheffield Eagles and has now broken into the full Wales squad.

The third criticism was the spate of cancellations that blighted the 2002 play-off series. Clubs struggled to get players to turn out, especially for games against superior teams and some distance away. As the Gloucestershire Warriors noted, it's hard to get players' families to accept them being away for three Saturdays running until late at night. Why travel from Cheltenham to London for League, when in Union you'd only travel to Painswick? The good news is the problems of cross-country fixtures is being addressed by the RFL.

The key is the development of young players who will come through junior sides and see themselves as League players first and foremost. Most Conference clubs are looking at junior development with more work expected in conjunction with the RFL's new development department. It is now recognised that all strands of the game must work together, be they Conference clubs, students or armed forces.

Ironically, the best way to reduce cancellations is to have more clubs. If each side plays in a conference of six local sides then travel time is reduced and more interest will be generated in the region. Niel Wood of the RFL is now attempting to bring together the interest that exists in towns around the country and channel it into setting up clubs. A recent meeting of the South West in Bristol, for example, has put in place the basis of a club in Bristol.

The stronger clubs will now also make up the bulk of the lower National Leagues, making the Conference the gateway for bigger things for the more ambitious. Hopefully some of these sides will remain in the conference with their second teams. The same must apply to the North London Skolars who make the biggest jump of all, into National League 2 alongside the likes of Gateshead, Chorley, Hunslet and Swinton. The boost to the game of a second professional team in the capital is incalculable and will no doubt spur on many of their old Conference rivals.

This leads to the most exciting prospects Rugby League has seen for years. 2002 has seen the advent of the Conference challenge match between the English / Welsh and Scottish Leagues – the Teeside Steelers taking the spoils against Edinburgh on Challenge Cup Final weekend. We've also seen the advent of an amateur Home Nations championship, won by Wales. While the Conference had a representative side in the Lionhearts, it has never caught the imagination. Anyone who saw the titanic finale between England and Wales at Cheltenham will know that now we have a mechanism to reward the best players with the ultimate accolade in sport, representing your country.

So that dream about a Super League Grand Final between sides from opposite ends of the country? Well nobody is kidding themselves that it is going to happen soon, maybe not in my lifetime, but roots are being planted. Rugby League has broken out of the north and is now spreading rapidly across Britain. Soon on a weekend, you'll never be further than half an hour from a game whether you're in Pontefract or Penzance. Can't wait."

With grateful thanks to the Gloucestershire Warriors media guide by Chris Wilson.

15 September 2002 - a new 'rugby' publication

As pointed out by MJM of the rlfans message board, the forthcoming publication from *League Publications Limited*, a venture into Rugby Union with a new weekly paper, *Rugby Times*, did not meet with universal approval. In fact Mr Sadler the newspaper's proprietor, got a bit of a going over, notably by the *Sunday Times*.

Calling anyone for anti-Union diatribes is a bit ironic given that the *Sunday Times*' chief 'rugby' (*sic*) correspondent's reputation for anti-League writings goes before him.

I suppose it does demonstrate that someone within the national media reads, or at least is aware of, the Rugby League trade press.

I wouldn't do your job...

As has been said before, there's no game without them. Top referee turned 'chief of whistlers' at Red Hall, Stuart Cummings kindly submitted a peice for us during September:

"'I wouldn't do your job...' has been said to me so many times over my refereeing career and even more since I finished refereeing to take overall charge of refereeing matters for The Rugby Football League. A strange statement from where I sit because I would think that any fan of Rugby League would love to be in a position to be part of the planning and processes that put our game together. Even when they talk about not wanting to referee, how can they not be envious of the referees' position, where he is taking part in a game alongside many of the great names that embellish the sport. Is the average supporter jealous of the man in the middle? I think some are.

OK, so no one likes to cop the abuse that comes their way but referees learn to cope with that. You develop a filter system for all 'advice'. Most of it is filed in the 'forget it' compartment while the rest is put in the 'they may have a point there' file or the 'they are absolutely right' file which will be acted on in the future.

Whitehaven roots

I learned very early on in my career that the abuse you receive is not personal. You are called various things because you are the referee. Very few people actually know you as a person. As I refereed out of Widnes and as every club programme had me listed as being from Widnes, the most common form of abuse I would receive would include a reference to the fact I was a scouser. Being called names never bothered me apart from this one and anyone who knew me would realise how ridiculous the statement was. I was born and bred in Whitehaven (and proud of it) and have no hint of a 'scouse' accent.

It was in my early years as a Whitehaven supporter that actually gave me a lesson later on in life that helped me tremendously in my career. The changing rooms at the Recreation Ground used to be situated outside the main gates of the ground. The players and officials therefore had to walk through the crowd after the game to get back to the changing rooms. Every referee in those days seemed to have it in for Whitehaven. Everyone always used to say they travelled up on the team bus with the opposition. So, in my formative years as a late teenager, I used to leave my position on the half-way line to take up a prime spot to shout at the referee as he would walk out. I would shout all sorts at the referee as he went past along with the whole Whitehaven crowd (well those who could be bothered anyway). Once I had said my piece, I walked home contented. I did not know the referee; all I knew was that he was a referee and traditionally that is what you do. You have a go at him and he is a convenient excuse when your team loses.

194

Fifteen years later I find myself on a Friday night at the Watersheddings, Oldham, a ground with fantastic charisma and a massive slope. It was a Friday night before Christmas and I was given a trial game (roughly translated as everyone else was on a works Christmas party) in the Alliance. Oldham were playing Featherstone Rovers and it was a crisp clear night. Fred Lindop, the then Controller of Referees, had just brought out an edict, stating that anyone who commits a head-high tackle has to be sent off.

The game was going well and extremely fast compared to what I was used to (I remember thinking after a 'length of the field' try that I had never seen a referee throw up before). On 27 minutes, Featherstone made a break down the slope and across to cover came the Oldham winger. He was a young man making his debut, who had been hyped up as the 'next Martin Offiah.' His name was Richard Blackman.

Sent off

Richard came across and tackled him high. I had no hesitation in sending him off. Oldham then conceded another couple of tries and went in at half time trailing by about 12 points. As I left the field for the break,, the then Oldham coach, Tony Barrow, was waiting for me by the dug outs. He had some advice for me and said: 'Cummings, this is your first game at this level, it will be your last'.

With 15 minutes to go, Featherstone were leading by 20 points and somehow lost by two points. Leaving the field at the end of the game, I was now faced with an angry Featherstone coach, Ken Loxton, who made no bones about the fact that his team's loss was entirely down to me.

As I walked under the stand and turned to walk up to the pavilion to the changing rooms, I was faced with a mass of people who had kindly lined the path all the way up leaving a nice little gap for me to walk up between them.

I turned round and noticed that my experienced touch judges had taken an alternative route. Luckily, my assessor, Sam Shepherd, knew the situation at Oldham (as well as most of the people) and guided me through the masses. They always used to get a healthy crowd for Friday night Alliance games at Watersheddings. There were 1,200 watching, but I reckon there were 2,000 lining the route to the changing rooms.

When I got to the changing rooms I sat down and asked myself, seriously, if this was what I really wanted. Sam was very good. I suddenly realised that they had done exactly what I used to do at Whitehaven. It wasn't personal it was because I was the referee. I could rationalise their behaviour so I could move on and not let that sort of thing effect me.

I have been very lucky in my career to have been involved in many great games. I have had the privilege of refereeing at Wembley. The 1996 Challenge Cup Final will always be in my memory, not just because it was my first Challenge Cup Final but because of the way the players in that game played. The spirit was tremendous.

I have refereed in Australia several times, including at Lang Park in Brisbane and The Sydney Football Stadium. The highlight was to referee the first international game to be held in the Olympic Stadium in Sydney. I have travelled to France, USA, Ireland, Scotland and Wales to officiate in games and have refereed in two World Cup Tournaments, refereeing both finals.

Refereeing has given me the chance to travel the world and be involved with a sport I love. It has enabled me to observe first hand many great players and interact with them. It has given me chance to meet many great people who work tirelessly behind the scenes in both the professional and amateur circles. So, you wouldn't do my job?"

Rugby League - the cultural anchor

To many people living away from their roots, it's important to have a cultural reference point, a reminder of who one is. For Michael Wall, and no doubt countless others, this is his favoured sport:

"Several years ago I made the decision to move away from my native St Helens, like many others I went in search of the better opportunities that lay in the south of England. My wanderings have taken me from the concrete features of Milton Keynes, to the ethnic melting pot of North London and more recently to the more sedate pace of life in commuter belt Surrey. Each step I took representing more than just a change of scenery, but a distinct change in culture.

Coming from St Helens, Rugby League was something I took almost for granted, my dad having taken my younger brother and myself to games from an early age. It is only when something is taken away from you that you realise its value and thus I was drawn towards the London Broncos. This was a move that went further than just a desire to watch a fine sporting product, it was also the desire for a cultural anchor, a link to things I didn't want to leave behind; camaraderie, belonging and acceptance.

It has been wonderful to see that Rugby League can thrive outside of its traditional heartlands, with the mix of great entertainment and a family

196

friendly atmosphere proving infectious. Just as once my dad took me to games, so now other fathers take their children along to enjoy the atmosphere.

The culture of Rugby League is one in which everyone is welcome, where rival fans can stand side by side regardless of any personal persuasion or circumstance.

In the Greater London area there are few, if any, sports as welcoming to newcomers as Rugby League, there are even fewer sporting events that the average family can afford to go to as a group. It is these qualities that are League's strength and its biggest opportunity.

The work of organisations such as London Broncos and the Rugby League Conference mean that the game is now accessible beyond the heartlands. Great news for exiles like me who were born into the Rugby League family, but even better news for a whole new audience of Rugby League fans just waiting to be discovered.

'Time for a Challenge' revisited

April recorded the stink caused by the RFL fining St Helens £25,000 for fielding a weakened team the week before the Challenge Cup Final, among a fair degree of acrimony and name calling between clubs and the RFL.

At the end of April Saints and the RFL went to arbitration, the fine was quietly dropped and each side paid its own costs. All that bother had been for nothing. At least everyone's slate is now clean, let's hope this doesn't happen again next year, in fact let's make sure it doesn't.

Ray, the new 'Man of Steel!'

During the month of September the *Daily Express* and *Sunday Express* gave Rugby League some very encouraging articles. In fact in one edition of the *Sunday Express* there was a one and a quarter pages of positive coverage. An e-mail campaign was started on various internet message boards in regards giving the papers some positive feedback. Richard Lewis, executive chairman of the RFL was also contacted to see if the he could also send in a positive response and John Huxley, media and public affairs executive duly responded on his behalf.

From the above John Huxley did receive a warm and encouraging reply that was honest in content. It is only right that we as a sport can give praise when it is due, as we have to be seen to be positive in trying to break down any media barriers. It isn't good practice just to dish out the negatives, as this then sends out the wrong impressions.

After sending in my e-mail to the *Daily Express* I then travelled down to the delightful Cotswolds for a mini-break. While relaxing in the hotel lounge I picked up a *Daily Express* and got quite a shock. In the letters page was my e-mail of praise. The only 'downside' being a true Lancastrian was that it credited me with being from the steel city of Sheffield. Still, Ray Gent, a 'Man of Steel' sounds good to me.

12. October 2002

The last of 12 eventful months. Contributions were received from two senior figures in the game, Richard Lewis, RFL executive chairman, and David Hinchliffe MP, secretary of the All-Party Parliamentary Rugby League Group. But we start with perhaps the senior campaigning body within British Rugby League, represented here by Geoff Lee and Cliff Spracklen.

The RLSA: Still going for the line after 12 years

In February 1990, six Rugby League supporters involved in the production of the fanzines, *The Steam Pig* (Bradford), *The Loiner* (Leeds) and *Flag Edge Touch* (Hull KR), met in Leeds and decided that 'enough was enough'. (watch out for copyright on 'enough is enough). For too long, the Rugby League authorities had ignored the voice of the ordinary supporter on the terraces. And for too long the game had squandered too many opportunities to become the national force it had the potential to be. At this 'historic' meeting it was agreed that to form a national organisation for Rugby League supporters. Six months later the Rugby League Supporters' Association held its founding conference at the George Hotel in Huddersfield, almost 95 years to the day that the game was founded, and in the very same location. One of the first actions of the new organisation was to produce a national fanzine, called *TGG*, *The Greatest Game*, still going strong today, with 44 issues now under its belt.

Since those early days, the RLSA has organised many campaigns. Pre-dating the writing of 'The Petition', in 1995, it produced an 'in-depth' survey into the amount and quality of media coverage of Rugby League. The main conclusion from Media Watch '93 was that the coverage of the game in the national press was at best poor, and at worst disgraceful.

It then instigated 'Stamping for 95', a successful campaign to encourage the Royal Mail to produce a range of commemorative stamps to mark one hundred years of Rugby League.

Previous to that, its first major document had been the *Fans' Charter*, a ten-point statement on the minimum requirements the RLSA believed all the professional clubs should implement. In 1991 came *Blueprint 2000*, an eight point statement of policy for the welfare and development of Rugby League. Before the 1992 General Election, it lobbied MPs to support a campaign to get Rugby League recognised as an official sport in the Armed Forces.

Always keen to encourage the expansion of the game both nationally and internationally, the RLSA supported the fledging South African Rugby League in the same year with a 'Shirts for Soweto' campaign, helping to supply playing gear for young black players in the townships.

Never afraid to be controversial, its two leading members at the time laid a wreath at the Headquarters of the RFL, paying its last respects for the 'Dream of Expansion' after the Rugby League Council had voted to kick out three clubs and return to a two division structure in 1993. And on the front cover of the following issue of *TGG* was a photograph of the Chapeltown Road HQ, with the headlines, 'The Lunatics have taken over the Asylum'.

1996 saw the first of the two surveys of the fans. The second followed two years later. Over 1,300 fans took part. Both provided valuable information about the fans' attitude on major issues and three points came across very clearly: support for summer rugby, support for one unified body for the game and total opposition to any form of merger with Rugby Union.

Always committed to expansion and the international game, the RLSA has always had close links with Russia and France. In particular the RLSA was involved in the setting up of the 'sister body' in France, XIII Actif, in 1997. This body, set up initially to campaign for a Government Inquiry into the banning of Rugby League in France by the Vichy Government, following the research work of Chairman Robert Fassolette, has now broadened its focus to work for aims similar to that of the RLSA, producing its own newsletter *La Tribune de XIII Actif*.

Following that dark period in 1999, when the mergers of Gateshead with Hull F.C., Sheffield Eagles with Huddersfield, and the closure of Bramley were all announced in the same week, fans were stunned. These were all carried out without any consultation with fans, and all fans were now vulnerable. They saw a common thread in these covert dealings. The dark days of the 'Calder', proposals were being replayed, with fans powerless to respond. As a result RLSA priorities changed, with commitments to help vulnerable clubs. The best way to do this was to encourage the creation of independent supporters' associations at every club, so that fans' voices could be heard. Following the Bramley experience and developments in soccer, this moved on a stage to encourage the development of supporters' trusts, where fans could have a real say and stake in the club, and prevent it from being closed or moved hundreds of miles down the road, on the whim of a Chairman looking for a better 'business opportunity'.

The RLSA does not claim to represent all fans, only its own members, but it has tried to present agreed views to the authorities, the most recent being a call for a unified administration, a coherent national league structure for the whole game, with promotion and relegation, and a planned international programme for all Rugby League playing nations. It cannot speak for independent supporters groups and trusts at individual clubs, but encourages their development. But it can act as a forum, through its meetings, *TGG* magazine, its' on-line access at rlfans.com, the largest fans' owned website in the world, to help fans crystallise their thoughts and work towards joint action. There have been serious issues of late, but the RLSA has not forgotten that Rugby League should also be fun. This is reflected in support for fanzines, however anarchic, and the continued lack of reverence and satirical humour in the pages of the magazine, remembering that this is where it originated. It firmly believes that the fan is as good as his master, and entitled to his view. But we are only as strong as the number of active enthusiasts. If you want to get involved in anyway and have your say, just see the RLSA membership details on rlfans.com or in *TGG* magazine.

The more things change, the more they stay the same, looking at these articles from past issues.

From issue 3 (October 1990): "The RLSA believes that the lot of British Rugby League supporters will only be improved alongside the development and expansion of the game. Only when the marketing strategy and the promotion of the game reaches the highest levels can we hope to attract the crowds and the money necessary to bring RL grounds into the 21st century. And to achieve that, supporters must be consulted at all levels"

From issue 4 (March 1991): "The failure of the RFL to enter into a dialogue with the RLSA which has friendly relations with BARLA, the Parliamentary Rugby League Committee and other supporters' groups, since its formation last August, indicates a lack of willingness to accept that the people who watch the game have any real value other than as turnstile fodder."

From issue 15 (June 1993): Press Bias Against League - Fact or Fiction. "For long enough many have suspected it, but is there any real evidence of a media bias against Rugby League and if so what can be done about it... The RFL must begin to stand up for the game. Fans are sick and tired of seeing League being presented as a poor relation of Union, just rugby you get paid for, rather than what it is; the ultimate in contact sports and as far removed from Union as it is possible to get while remaining on the same planet. Come on RFL, the message is clear, it's time to BITE BACK!!!"

From issue 22 (Summer 1995): "The challenge for Rugby League now is to harness the Murdoch whirlwind of change to the game's ultimate benefit. The results of the RLSA's consultation on this issue show that one of the biggest concerns amongst fans is the lack of quality administrators to ensure that whatever money flows into the game is spent wisely. It is an understandable fear...The RFL should distribute the money in the form of grants, with clubs having to submit proper business plans beforehand in order to get their hands on any of it. Priorities must be the improvement of conditions not just for those ordinary punters who have sustained the game through its hundred year history, but to win over the millions of people - potential fans, all of them - to whom Rugby League, at the moment, means nothing."

From issue 41 (Autumn 2001): "We have become our own worst enemy. Creeping appeasement, collaboration, private agendas by quislings who are merely servants of big capital, reduce the fan to nothing more than a cypher. Public consultation is cosmetic. The importance of organisations like the RLSA is diminished, so are referenda where over 80 percent of fans say they oppose collaboration with Rugby Union at the highest level, but are then ignored. So what is to be done? For me, it's simple. We mend ourselves or we end ourselves. But we do not stay as we are. Unless there is a move towards greater transparency in our game, and quickly, then the fans should be urged to involve themselves in direct action." From a Rugby League supporter in Swansea.

From issue 43 (Spring 2002): "The major sponsors of this great game, the supporters themselves, are desperately looking for strong independent leadership, which stands up for the game against its detractors, which wins over new support for the game, and which wins more ground against our competitors. But above all we want leadership independent of individual club interests."

History repeating itself - mergers

Matt Anniss writes about his beloved Sheffield:
"I'll let you into a little secret. The other Sunday I was reading the sports

202

supplement of a broadsheet Sunday newspaper, desperately trying to find some decent coverage of the Greatest Game. After a while I gave up and turned to an article about A.F.C. Wimbledon, the amateur football club set up by disgruntled fans of the Milton Keynes bound Dons.

As I read about the plight of the new, supporter run Wimbledon I couldn't help thinking about my club, Sheffield Eagles. In September 1999, the original Eagles club ceased to exist. With debts of around £1.7m (something that wasn't made clear to the fans at the time) Eagles plc ceased trading on the AIM Market. Their shareholding in the Eagles was passed to a new company, set up and run by several of the old Eagles' directors who agreed to merge with Huddersfield Giants. To a barrage of protest from both team's fans the Huddersfield-Sheffield Giants were formed.

At the time I was devastated. As a supporter of one of the games newest, most forward thinking clubs I never imagined such a thing would happen to my team. The likes of Cas, Fev and Wakey maybe, but Sheffield? We were a 'big city' club, the sort of side meant to be in Uncle Mo and Big Bad Rupert's Super Duper League. We were part of the big plan, or so I thought. As I sat in my Bournemouth home on that cold September evening back in 1999 my heart sank. Why did this happen to us? Didn't everyone know mergers just wouldn't work? It's obvious isn't it?

Sadly, it hadn't always been this clear to me. I think of myself as a bit of an expansionist, keen to see Rugby League spread out of its northern heartlands and into the consciousness, nay lives, of the Great British public.

When old Mo first brought up the idea of mergers in 1995 I found myself (somewhat surprisingly) agreeing with him. Having so many teams in such a small area just doesn't make financial sense. On paper one big club in Calderdale would be stronger than three struggling sides and one Hull club would be unstoppable. Makes sense doesn't it?

As I sat mourning the demise of my own club I realised how wrong I'd been. Sheffield may not have the traditions of a Castleford, Huddersfield or Hull F.C., but the roots of the game in the city are a lot stronger than many people think. To the 1,000 or so die-hard Don Valley regulars and assorted part time League enthusiasts in the city the merger was a major kick in the teeth. I can't quite describe how I felt when I first heard the news, though it felt like a mixture of anger, sadness and dismay.

It was sentiments like the fans of Wimbledon F.C. were expressing in my Sunday paper. Like us they felt great anger at their clubs board of directors (only one of the directors, Terry Sharman, spoke out against the merger), and expressed great dismay at the actions of their games governing body (personally I still feel that Super League's £1m plus offer to any two clubs that merged bordered on criminal.)

They refused, like us, to travel miles to see their team, arguing that their beloved club would lose its sense of identity and community. They could see, like we did, that such a move would be the death knell of the team they'd followed around the country for so many years. To the fans of Wimbledon F.C., like us Eagles' supporters a year later. Doing nothing was not an option.

Their club abandoned them, so what did they do? They set up a new club, just like we'd done in the winter of 1999. In our case being reborn was almost the best thing that could have happened to the Eagles. Sure, we'd lost our Super League place (sorry, franchise) and almost certainly consigned ourselves to an eternity eking out an existence in the lower regions of the NFP, but at least we had our own club again. A club that belonged to us and was run by fans (albeit rich and influential ones). A team that had a talismanic leader in Mark Aston, a man who believed wholeheartedly in Sheffield as an area of great Rugby League potential. A club that could be proud to call itself a team of the people, a sporting success story built on the dedication of ordinary fans.

At first the Eagles enjoyed something of a renaissance. Buoyed by the enthusiasm of the fans and a supportive local media (the *Sheffield Star* had previously largely ignored the Eagles, but were now one of the clubs' biggest supporters), the team started off with a succession of good performances. Attendances hovered around the 1,500 mark, better than average for a mid-table NFP team.

Sadly, it didn't last. Any momentum gained from saving the club soon faded away. As performances became worse, casual supporters drifted away, leaving only a hard-core support of 800 or so hardy souls. Now the club is desperately short of money, and has (privately) consigned itself to life in the newly formed National League Two. In the close season, it plans to get rid of many of its highest paid (and therefore most experienced) players, using instead a mixture of talented youngsters and locals. Recently, lack of funds led to the sacking of the one person the club desperately needed to survive in the long term, its Development Officer.

I genuinely fear for the survival of Sheffield Eagles. Each time I visit Don Valley, I get a horrible feeling in the pit of my stomach. Four years ago almost 10,000 turned up to see the Eagles parade the Challenge Cup before their home game against beaten finalists Wigan; these days were lucky to get 700 for a home game against Swinton.

When the club first merged with Huddersfield, they blamed the Sheffield public for their demise. Chairman Tim Adams confidently forecast that Rugby League will never work in Sheffield. I don't like to contemplate such sentiments, but maybe he's right. I mean the people of the Steel City haven't shown themselves to be massive supporters of the Greatest Game over the years; they're too wrapped up in the fortunes of Wednesday and United.

Yet Rugby League is stronger in South Yorkshire than its ever been. Sheffield's leading amateur club, Hillsborough Hawks, is looking stronger than it has for years, with a strong junior section backed up by two competitive open age teams (including one National Conference side), a women's team and a new girls side. More school children play the game in South Yorkshire than ever before, with a recent rally at Don Valley attracting some 500 kids from the across the city. The Eagles development team have been working hard in deprived areas of the city too, giving kids from poorer backgrounds the chance to play the Greatest Game.

But is all this enough? If the Eagles were to fold, would the roots of League in the city be strong enough to withstand such a major setback? Would the game be able to flourish without its figurehead, the peoples club, that has put so much into establishing Rugby League in the Steel City?

Basically, are the foundations solid enough? Its hypothetical of course, but one that relevant to clubs in other development areas, most notably London and Gateshead. The latter, with its small but nevertheless fan-run NFP club, is probably the closest to the Sheffield model. They are having problems; have concentrated their efforts on development, and like Sheffield were the victims of a merger that all but killed off top flight Rugby League in the north east for good. Clearly mergers just don't work.

But, of course Rugby League doesn't learn. I have to admit to feeling a shiver down my spine when I first heard of a proposed merger between the newly relegated Salford City Reds and Swinton Lions, another great Manchester club with a long and distinguished history. After the appalling events in Sheffield and Gateshead, were they seriously considering jeopardising the future of Rugby League in the area, not to mention alienating two of the most loyal sets of fans in the country? Apparently so.

Is history about to repeat itself? For the good of the game, let's all hope it never leaves the drawing board

On the home front

Unfortunately many in society do not enjoy the best of health that perhaps they were once accustomed to. This can lead to many problems, especially if one is house bound. Where once they could go shopping, enjoy trips to the countryside, or take in a live sporting event, this may now not be possible under the circumstances. We sometimes take our health and life for granted.

Kevin Maguire (a household name in the West Yorkshire media) sent Ray a letter in to say that he had suffered his first heart attack way back in 1986. Due to other problems it did change his world around. Unfortunately attending live Rugby League matches came to an abrupt halt that had been an integral part of his life for many years. So, how does Kevin now keep in touch with his favourite sport...?

Local radio played a big part in keeping the Rugby League diet going, including Radio Leeds and Radio Humberside. Restful holidays in Blackpool were no problem as Radio Lancashire and Cumbria were on hand to brighten up the sporting scene. Whilst the occasion letter to the media and Rugby League press gets his views across to a wider audience. Published letters can indeed be a welcome tonic.

The above does bear some quiet thought for the media in that for some it is the only way to keep in touch with their chosen sport that suddenly was taken away on a live basis. Many media outlets do indeed take pride of place in our sporting world, yet others sometimes let the side down.

I've not had the time

One thing that Tim and I have found out over the last couple of years is that writing and compiling a book is not easy and a great effort, over and above the 'day job', has to go in.

It is always important to try and get balance, cover serious issues, maintain the theme as well as having a laugh or two. However, as the potential articles take shape, one has to go back and back as stories develop, checking facts, spelling and much more. I suppose no book will ever be 100 per cent correct.

In a book such as *RL Fanpower*, it is even more important to check out articles contributed by other fans. On one side of the coin it is important not to disturb the contributors article too much, if at all, but there are often mistakes that have to be corrected and libel to consider. Another of the major problems is looking for the bit you're working on, like the proverbial needle in a haystack, when the text is 90,000 odd words.

Thanks, once again, has to go to all those who have contributed and helped tell the story and get another Rugby League book on the shelves of the bookshops.

Now what of the articles that have 'slipped the net?' Having promised, several potential contributors have received more than a dozen requests and reminders, yet nothing has transpired. This is a sad state of affairs in that I am sure many would have been a worthy inclusion. On the negative side it is disappointing when some of those people lead you on a merry dance with promises that are not delivered, although of course others may have genuine reasons.

One thing that can't be acceptable 99 per cent of the time is the excuse 'I have not had the time' covering possibly five months or more. If £1,000 was offered for an article, then I'm sure more would have come in. So in effect time is not the excuse, rather organisation and lack of motivation to not let anyone down.

There are no medals to be had for naming anyone, or any organisation in the above as this has been a voluntary project by the authors and contributors alike, yet a 'sorry can't do it' wouldn't have gone amiss. One philosophy that I have always upheld is never to let anyone down if at all possible. Still, on a bright note, thanks to all who have helped, as you have been appreciated and some of the surplus funds raised by the sale of this book (if it raises any!) will be ploughed back into the game.

A broad spectrum of levels and areas of the game are represented here, covering most angles from the corridors of power to the everyday fan on the bleak terrace. If any particular area interest is missing, sorry, but we did try! For those that did miss the boat, then maybe next time, eh…?

View from the top

Someone who could find the time was the executive chairman of the RFL. After 14 years as a professional tennis player and then successful coaching and administrative careers in the sport, Richard Lewis was appointed as the RFL executive chairman earlier this year charged with leading Rugby League into a new era. Here he gives the low-down on his first six months in charge and looks forward to the future.

"Becoming the executive chairman of the RFL was almost as if fate was telling me something. Purely by chance I'd been talking to a former Rugby League player who was the chief executive of a company in London on the

Wednesday. He was saying that Rugby League had been through a lot of turmoil but was starting to get itself into shape again. He talked about the sport's history, and how Rugby League had actually led the way compared to Rugby Union in many ways. It was just a fascinating discussion.

Then on the Friday, literally two days later, I was tipped off that the executive chairman job at the RFL was being advertised, and it was suggested that it might be an interesting role for me. I made some enquiries and it went from there.

I'd learnt all sorts of things about the game on that Wednesday, and then on the Friday someone was telling me about this job in Rugby League that might suit my background.

At the time I wasn't looking for a new job - when I left the Lawn Tennis Association I was the director of a company that gave one-to-one coaching to chief executives and MDs, enjoying the lifestyle and being my own boss.

But I thought the executive chairman role was a very interesting and exciting one, which is what got my attention. Since taking on the post, I have realised that Rugby League has two fantastic strengths. The first one is the players. There's what happens on the pitch and the product they provide, and also the way they conduct themselves generally speaking off the pitch.

The second strength is the fans. People talk about League's passionate fans and it's true, they are incredibly passionate. Those are two great assets to build on.

But I can see that the game hasn't marketed itself very well, and has failed to communicate in many areas. We can certainly improve on that. One other thing that has struck me is the lack of confidence in some aspects of the game as a whole. The game has a lot to be confident about, even though it has taken a battering over the last few years. I just think we should focus and be confident about what we're doing and not worry about that 'dreadful' other sport Rugby Union.

As I've said the communication from the RFL hasn't been what I would like it to be, and improving that has been frustrating at times. There were a number of things I could clearly see needed to be done when I first took over, but it has been frustrating that there are contracts in place that are proving difficult to extricate ourselves from. It has meant that some things are taking a lot longer to do than I would have liked. These have been mainly commercial things, with the website being a clear example.

But being realistic and looking back, there has been so much upheaval in the game and an awful lot of fire fighting gone on. I think we've done pretty well on that front, and people have worked hard. It's not been easy when we've also been swamped by day-to-day issues.

The new divisional structure is a big thing for the game, and I think it's right for the game. I also think it's right for the RFL and BARLA to unify, and it's something we're working hard on and negotiations are moving forward. It's been difficult, and for some people it will be a real quantum leap of faith. But I think it's really important for Rugby League.

As is the international game. I've yet to attend my first international meeting, and I think that is an indication of how few meetings there are. I want to encourage the organisation to have more meetings to move the international game forward. I'm lucky that my views coincide with a time when the Australians are more interested than they have been. Even without those meetings I've found that they are very positive and there's a genuine desire to come up with something.

As for media coverage of Rugby League, I probably have a slightly different view from some people. I tend to think we, as a sport, get what we deserve and it's up to us, particularly the RFL, to work harder to make it logical and right for sports editors to give us more space.

I'm not really in the camp that says the media is biased against us - I think what we've got to do is put together a very strong case as to why we should get more coverage, and that the sport is growing, putting down some hard and fast figures for them. We haven't done that over the last few years.

As for the next 12 months, I think progressing the marketing and commercial side is very important. The new appointment I inherited there didn't work out at all, and I had to sort that out, it wasn't working. The department is doing a very good job in a difficult situation at the moment.

A better marketing and commercial department will help us to improve communications, providing monthly newsletters, a proper website, things like that. There are a lot of things we can do better.

I think since I've been here we've improved communications with the clubs and people who are close to the RFL. But we need to improve communications to all parts of the game."

View from Parliament

A special thank you is extended to David Hinchliffe MP who has taken the time out to pen the article below in what is a very busy schedule for him. It is indeed very encouraging to have the All-Party Parliamentary Group active on our part. On a personal note I would like to extend my gratitude, and that of Cliff Spracklen for the warm welcome on 'petition' day. Your hospitality and friendship were top drawer, as well as those others in the Group. Not forgetting the wonderful meal, as well as drinks on the balcony.

"The All-Party Parliamentary Rugby League Group was formed in 1988 to draw MPs interested in Rugby League together in an organised lobby for the sport at Westminster. The group has around 80 MPs and Peers from the main political parties in membership and meets on a monthly basis. Key figures in the game attend the meetings as speakers and the Group's annual dinner in the Palace of Westminster has become one of the social highlights of the Rugby League calendar, bringing together personalities from the sport, representatives of the sporting media and politicians.

Since its creation, the group has focussed on many of the big issues facing the game, frequently bringing them to the attention of responsible Government Ministers and Government departments and agencies concerned with sport, such as Sport England.

Uniquely placed to highlight the concerns of those involved in Rugby League, the Group has championed the rights of sports men and women to be allowed to play the game of their choice. The basic right to play Rugby League was until very recently denied to members of the British armed forces and the Group's parliamentary campaign overturned this ban in 1994.

It took many years of pressure from the Group - through Parliamentary Questions, Private Member's Bills and Select Committee Inquiries - before the principle of free movement between Rugby Union and Rugby League was finally established in 1995. A number of the Group's members had the personal experience of being banned for life from Rugby Union for playing Rugby League - even as amateurs - and are proud to have played a part in contributing to the conclusion of the 'hundred year war' between the codes.

But some will say that the war is still a long way from over. And they may well be right for there are few meetings of the Group which do not discuss continuing discrimination against our code. Why did our Group have to fight to overturn a decision to exclude Rugby League from the Active Sports Programme? Why was our game outlawed at the Commonwealth Games in Manchester, when it is played in virtually every Commonwealth country? Why is Union's *Rugby Special* programme shown nationwide on BBC2, while the *Super League Show* on the same channel is confined to just the north of England?

It is this blatant media discrimination against the code, which so very clearly prevents our game from making a break through that the skills and qualities of those playing it so justly deserve. The simple fact is that our national media outlets are controlled by individuals with little, if any, idea or experience of the great spectacle of Rugby League. But if these media interests are not challenged about their treatment of our sport, then their grossly inaccurate coverage or non-existent coverage will continue.

The Parliamentary Group has been encouraged that the Rugby League supporters are not taking it lying down. I know from my own personal discussions with some London based sports editors that they have been frankly amazed at the vigorous response of our game's followers after the publication of hostile articles.

The supporters' media petition to Parliament was just the start. We need to keep up the pressure to ensure fair and accurate coverage for the Greatest Game. The Parliamentary Group will continue to champion the cause of Rugby League at a political level but grass roots initiatives such as the petition are essential in fighting for fair treatment of our game."

Births, Deaths and Marriages

6 October 2002 . It is with deepest regret that the game of Rugby League died in Australia today in front of 80,130 subdued Australian fans. No flowers please.

Well actually, this Grand Final was as big as any of its predecessors with massive TV audiences and widespread news coverage on both the Australian and New Zealand sides of the Tasman

Malcolm Andrews on Totalrl.com reported the facts that the biggest audience was in Sydney where 1.1 m tuned in. Brisbane had 709,000 viewers, astoundingly 35 per cent more than watched the Australian Rules grand final the day before when the Brisbane Lions beat Melbourne's Collingwood club. Incredibly 535,000 fans watched in the Australian Rules stronghold of Melbourne, greatly up on the 2001 figures.

In fact this prompted an outbreak of fanpower in Melbourne where the World of RL website reported that "Following the recent announcement on 3AW that over 535,000 Melburnians tuned into the Grand Final yesterday, Rugby League fans have started a campaign to not only seek an apology, but to get fair coverage of the 'Greatest Game of All'. In case you don't know, the Melbourne media seem to classify anything that rivals AFL as "enemy alien". Not only do they give no air time to our game, but in rude fashion, whenever someone calls in to discuss Rugby League on the Sports Program, they are put on hold, and after half an hour, cut off. This is the kind of

IF IT'S A DYING GAME HOW COME SO MANY PEOPLE
KEEP TURNING UP TO THE FUNERAL ?

attitude we, Rugby League fans, will not accept. Ladies & Gentlemen, it is time for action. We will not rest until we have achieved our goal of fair coverage of Rugby League in Melbourne, and the whole of Victoria. Therefore, to assist in our campaign, we encourage you to send e-mails to the radio station, 3AW"

The Russian Federation's Grand Final also took place the same week with 6,000 turning out to the Olympic Stadium in Moscow to see Moscow Lokomotiv beat Kazan Arrows 14-12.

The NFP Grand Final at Widnes on 12 October also proved a good day's work for all involved, a turnout of 9,051 being the largest drawn to the fixture to date with live TV coverage on Sky covering 80 enthralling minutes as Huddersfield emerged victorious and promoted.

The Super League Grand Final at Old Trafford on 19 October again topped the previous year's best turnout with 61,138 present, including the New Zealand Test team, having arrived ready for their eight match tour. In a marked contrast to last years event drew a comprehensive and positive preview in Friday's *Daily Telegraph* as the weekend's major event. No repeat of the *Times* disgraceful postscript to the 2001 Grand Final where

Simon Barnes' take on events bizarrely resulted in a piece entitled 'Final that signalled beginning of the end' and forecast the end of the game.

The Grand Final seems to finally have gained some acceptance as the major sporting event that it clearly is, but still no national profile on the BBC as its *Super League Show* pictures were still limited to northern regions. It seems there is still some work for fanpower to do, but last year's rumours of League's death seem to have been somewhat exaggerated.

As for Marriage, whatever our friends at the nationals were telling us last year, the proposal from the other code seems a distant, and hopefully receding, prospect. Anyway, I'm not sure they could afford the ring.

To end with a birth, Rugby League in Lebanon kicked off on 18 October 18 with the start of the inaugural season of the Lebanese Rugby League 2002-3 Championship. Containing four sides, (Lebanese Army, Balamand University, AUB and LAU), the competition will bring credibility to the Cedar's national team which played their first game of League in 1997 and is scheduled to play France in Tripoli, on 2 November 2002. May the new delivery thrive and prosper.

Bookmaking

A book is no use unless people get to see it, and no-one will buy it unless they know it exists. So midway through September, a month before the last articles were due to be finished, thoughts turned to converting the around 90,000 words on Tim's computer and the collection of cartoons and other odds and ends into a book.

There are countless considerations and decisions at this point, such as setting a price, obtaining an ISBN number, finding a printer, working cartoons and photographs into the text, copyright and disclaimers, common font, punctuation and grammar, format and proof reading for the umpteenth time. The list is nearly endless, but the line has to be drawn somewhere.

To gauge interest and raise some funds to soften the blow of the printer's bill, a subscribers list was started offering the opportunity to order a copy of the book, in exchange for a mention in the list at the end

Ray circulated his list of previous customers of *Enough is Enough* and Tim wrote with a summary to 35 'famous names' within the game offering the opportunity to subscribe to the project.

A summary was posted on various internet sites and printed leaflets were handed out by volunteers, at amateur games and with fanzines (Thanks to Sergei and Delboy) and circulated to 20 amateur and Conference clubs.

There is a balance between generating and maintaining a level of publicity needed to create any sort of public awareness and boring people rigid. Trade and local media were approached for publicity, such as the article kindly published in *TGG* magazine.

Making this happen is the sort of work that a publisher would do. First thoughts were to self-publish but in the end we decided to have our work published by London League Publications Ltd. The company is run by two Rugby League supporters, Dave Farrar and Peter Lush, who took on the project at very short notice. An established publisher has the distribution contacts and know how to reach wider outlets and get the book in front of the public, where it needs to be.

Setting a price is an anguished process. Keeping costs down to maximise the potential audience is key, but this increases the risk of leaving the authors out of pocket and minimises the margin available for donation back to the game. All in all, quite an experience.

Rugby Widows

It is often said that behind every great man is a strong woman. Well behind every Rugby League anorak is a Rugby League widow. Two of these are Ray's wife, June Gent and mine, Helen Wilkinson.

Often at the behest of the vagueries of television's requirements, summer Friday and Saturday nights are often spent alone, marooned at home whilst men folk are off at some match or other, each apparently more important than last weekends.

The briefest of off seasons soon rolls round to a new fixture list, seemingly longer and more unmissable than ever before, packed with crucial Derbies, elimination semi-finals, Ashes Tests, international friendlies and other oddly named events, with the year ahead planned to revolve around the Challenge Cup Final 'lad's weekend.'

For many rugby widows there is unsavoury kit to wash and a deaf ear is required for the accompanying moaning and groaning about the growing list of injuries and afflictions caused stumbling round the local park with an oval ball, as if 20 years younger. Still, boys will be boys.

Worse still, the constant search with a fine tooth comb for any scrap or morsel of Rugby League information on telly, radio or newspapers, internet and magazines whilst researching the lunacy of a book.

And what is the inexplicable appeal of the accumulation of multi-coloured shirts, ticket stubs and dusty piles of programmes. And "do you have to have that sticker in the rear window of the car?"

Yes, the lot of the Rugby League widow would indeed test the patience of a saint. Talking of which, Ray tells me of his recent star billing in the *St Helens Reporter*, announcing some forthcoming book on Rugby League fanpower or other, complete with beaming photograph.

Leaving for work he left the paper open at the key page in the kitchen for June to admire when she arrived home. Oblivious, in the bin it went with the rest of the rubbish, never to be seen again. Who can blame her.

Ray reports that June loves nothing better than to wave goodbye on match days, unless it is Leeds away, a weekend at the Challenge Cup final or the promise of a cup of soup from a friendly Whitehaven supporter and a delightful trip through the lakes- all at Ray's expense of course.

The value of a bunch of flowers brought home on a matchday has long since lost its currency.

Rugby League 'ere, signing off

Awwwight mates, Rugby League 'ere again to sum up events. Seeing as the game is spreading into the 'heartlands' of London like the Great Fire of 1666, and the Media Petition went same way, I've taken on a bit of a Cockney accent what wiv all me new southern Rugby League mates.

First and foremost what a book! Handsome, ain't it? Certainly some literary talent around, and plenty of blindin' ideas and passion. Makes me proud as punch to think that Rugby League has some fine writers. As for the cartoonists. Really did give me a laugh or two. The one about my funeral is a 'dead' cert to make me want to carry on. And we also now know where Brighouse is. Rumour has it that Tim is re-drawing the world map to highlight all the 'heartlands.' M62 game? More like an M25 game ain't it.

And another thing, do you think Belgian stilt walking will take off?

Thanks to everyone who made the effort, now immortalised in print.

As for the fairer sex, we have a right couple of Pearly Queens! Gorblimey, Trish has a heart of gold and Claire ain't on a high horse. Two charmers to boot and can take me down the rub a dub any time. Mind you it is nice to see plenty of gals at the games, makes a change from when it was 'men only.'

Good to see me Fleet Street adversaries calm down wiv the negatives. However, a writer from the *Evening Herald* published in Plymouth has got a cheek, ain't he? Describing Rugby League as "played only by whippet breeding northerners"? I'll tell that to me mates down Crawley way, that'll cause a pen and ink!

Sorry, let you down with the one off Test in Oz. Hardly had time to get me coat off and used to time travel before facing me cousins. Like greyhounds straight off Walthamstow dog track, those blokes.

Up the apples and pears to Red Hall, our Richard looks like sorting it out after 100 years of trial and error. More a trial I reckon.

Something fishy at the BBC with Peter Salmon and co. Caught 'em hook, line and sinker. If they ever get their story straight, everyone may get the same excuse instead of all being led up and down the Old Kent Road.

I still can't understand why my telly can't get the *Super League Show* down here. Has to be on a future agenda at the RFL, cos all the investigation in 'ere shows it's worth its place. Fair play to all those that campaigned and continue to do so. Champion!

The final hooter

The end of a long and eventful year for Rugby League. Whatever your individual view, these are indeed interesting times for the Greatest Game. Hopefully, this book shows that fans don't have to silently accept the status quo, they can help influence events by getting involved in a myriad of ways.

Will we go through writing another of these books again? Would you read it if we did? Trouble will beckon if we don't get on with publishing this text, getting it printed and distributed and trying out a concept found to be alien to many in Rugby League - marketing!

One things for sure, with fanpower like Rugby League fans have got in abundance, the ups are bigger than the downs. The fans make sure of that.

Yours in Sport, Ray Gent

Best of British, Tim Wilkinson

Subscribers List

Thanks to our 250 or so subscribers who showed faith! Ladies first...

Aberdeen
Phil Stockton
Ainstable, Cumbria
Eleri & Alan Brown
Ashford, Middlesex
Chris Gallagher
Baliffe Bridge
Tim Hardcastle
Barking, Essex
Jeff Catley
Baildon
Jacky, Alan, Shawna &
Rhys Tranter
Pat & Paul Waters
Bangor, N. Ireland
Barry Scarth
Batley & Dewsbury
Lee Carson
Gary Clarkson
June & Kevin McGuire
Lauren Rose
Bedford
Amanda & Ben Barker
Belfast, N. Ireland
Suzanne Hamilton
Brian McKnight
**Billinge, Upholland &
Garswood**
Janette & Colin Anderson
Joan & Gill Cross
Sandra & Brian Davies
Edna & Nigel Deakin
Margaret & Jim Diffley
Maurice Gaskill
Christine & Andy
Hamilton
Bernard Higham
Shirley & Graham Morris
Angela Mullen
Wendy Neal

Marjorie & John
Shufflebottom
Eileen & John Taylor
Pam & John Turner
Julie & Derek White
Tom, Josh & Elliot White
Chris & George Wiswell
Bolton
Vera & Peter Gregory
Boston Spa, W Yorks
Simon Outten
Bradford
James Abbott
Kevin Field
Andrew Fleming
Adrian Goodrich
Aiden Greasley
Sam Grundy (BISA)
Linda & Phil Oates
Kathryn Owen
Gill & Toni Witeszczak
Bridgnorth, Salop
Emma Beales
Bristol
Phil Cole (Bristol Sonics RLFC)
Bromsgrove, Worcs
John & Ali Fairhurst
Cardiff
Dr. Jack Whittaker MD,
FRCP, FRCpath
Castleford
Nigel 'Delboy' Bennett
(*Aye of the Tigers*)
Donna & Neil Harvey
Chippenham, Wilts
Mr E Gallagher
Cleckheaton
Peter Benson
The Bod Family
Clitheroe
Nic Etchells-Skeat

Coventry
Andrew Barnett
Cottingham, East Yorks
Craig Penny
Croydon
Eamonn McNulty
Deganwy
Mamie & Harry Gent
Doncaster
Katherine and Adrian
Lodge
Durham
Malcolm Ferguson
Featherstone
Ben Dyas
Stephen Parker
Gomersal
George Timberley
Halifax
Mike McCunniff
Tony Ackroyd
Harlow, Essex
Keith Hodgson
Harpenden, Herts
David Lyons
Hartlepool
Neil Williamson
Heckmondwike
Cris Tout
Heywood
David J Smith
Hazel Taylor
Hounslow
Bill Drinkwater
Huddersfield
Ken Craven
Patrick Walsh
Hull
Jo & Gary Collinson
Harry 'Chops' Collinson
June & Don Marshall

217

Paul & Phil Newsom
Anne Newsom
Cindy Russell
Wayne Russell
Ilford, Essex
Lloyd Anderson
Kendal
Shaun McMullen
Keighley
James McGrath
Kirkburton
Brian Firth
Lancaster
Richard De-La-Riverie
Leeds, Farsley & Morley
Fred Bolderson - Hunslet
Ged Carr
Duncan Elsey
John Emsley - Farsley
Richard Grindrod
Michelle Holliday
Janet and Andrew
Holliday
Tim Huntley
David Jagger - Morley
(mexicanpenguin.com)
Gemma Jagger - Morley
Peter Kelly
Richard Lewis
(Executive chairman RFL)
Mark Lockwood
omebull - Churwell
Cliff Spracklen
(RLSA) - Bramley
Brenda & Geoff
Wilkinson
Leigh & Lowton
Stephen Barrow - Lowton
Peter Bentham
Lorraine & David Pasquill
Amy Wood
Leicester
Helen & Mick Dyer
Stephen Morris
Liverpool

Carol & David Bleasdale
Thomas Patterson
London
Sarah & Stuart Hogg -
Lee
Tim Finch - Kentish
Town
Gemma & Sam Moore -
Tottenham
Gareth Kelsey - Ealing
Geraldine Grobon - Ealing
Manchester & Radcliffe
Martin Alcock
Stephen Fox - Radcliffe
Paul Worthington
Matlock
Ant Finch
Norley, Cheshire
Pauline & David Glenn
Nottingham
Nick Evans
Catherine, Wayne,
Rebekah & Owen Tyler
Oswaldtwistle
Ashley Kenyon
Otford, Kent
Barry Davies
Otley
Paul Hancock
Dennis Houseman
Rainhill
Phil Speakman *(Haloman)*
Praze-an-Beeble,
Cornwall
Christine & John
Middleton
Preston
David Richards
Ripponden
Martin Harrison
Runcorn
Ste Jones
Ronnie Williams
Margaret & Tony
Williams

St Helens
Paul Appleton
Mary Appleton
Eric Beck
Linda & Neville Bond
Kath & Eric Culliford
Jim Bridge
Sheila Cheyne
Judith Critchley
Emily & James Cross
Laura & Conor Denning
Carla Doran
Harry Gee
Lynn & Russel Gent
Marjorie & Eric Gent
Olive Gent
Paula & David Gent
Alan Gordon
Pat & Paul Greenall
Paul Grime
John Grime
Ann & Roger Grime
Michael Grime
Jean & Bob Haddock
Pauline & Ken Harding
Willem Hendriksen
Phylis & John Holmes
Leonnie & Michael
Hough
Lynn & Sam Howard
Claire & Lee Innes
Barbara & David Jones
Chris Joynt
(St Helens RLFC)
Adrian Kay
Terry Kilgallon
Nicola Kilgallon
Hanna Kilgallon
Sandra McCormick
Robert Martindale
Linda, Karen & Ste
Pownall
Elaine & Keith Rankin
Nora Robinson
Sue & Geoff Sarsfield

Lynn & Bernard Smith
Debora & Simon Speight
Christine & Anthony Stuchberry
Ivy, Sue & Ron Sumner
Cath & Keiron Traynor
Karen Walker
Kerry Walmsley
Margaret & Denis Whittle
Julia & Tom Wood
Maureen & Joe Woods

Salford
Sandra & John Byrnes

Sealand, Deeside
Allan McKeown

Sheffield
Sarah and Darren Eccles

Shipley
Lynne & Laurie Hopkinson
Sue & Geoff Lee

Solihull
Darren Broadhurst

Southport
Beryl & Eric Bond

Stone Staffs
Dave Beales

Sutton, Surrey
Michael Wall

Swinton
John Barnes

Thomastown, Mid Glamorgan
Anthony Jenkins

Tingley
Liz & Steve Barnes

Upper Ballinderry, N. Ireland
Ciaran & Marie McCormick

Wakefield
Mick Hartley
Mark Smith

Wallasey
Rita Favager

Iain Stewart

Warrington
Mike Dolan
Andrew Fisher
Liam Gent
Carole & Bob Kiernan
John A Mitchell (jonnysaint)
Brenda Neary
Kate & Barry Robinson

Westwood, Notts
The Woodcocks

Whiston
Mattew Davies

Wigan
Anne & Alan Bithel
Pat & Sam Blackledge
Sue & Barry Bridge
Marian & Phil Brown
Anita Cobourne
Anthony Crook
Sandra & Ste Dermott
Louise Fairhurst
Jonathan & Joseph Francis
Barbara & Roy Ganderton
Jean & Tom Gibbs
Tony Higham
Val & Dennis Houghton
Angela & John Hulstrom
Howarth Johnson
Elaine & Keith Johnson
Michelle & Natalie Johnson
Janice Johnson
Dorothy & Billy Jones
Joe Marcroft
Allison Moore
Don Pritchard
Adam Read
Norma & John Scott
Ann & Albi Shields
Margaret & Denis Slater
Lynsey & John Smith
Betty & Peter Southworth
Rosemarie & John Terry

Avril Wilkinson
Sue & Ste Winstanley
Shane Wison
Karen & Mark Witherington
Lucy Megan Woods
Janine Woodward
Doris & Terry Wynn MEP

York
Peter Brown
Stuart Evans (York RLFC historian)
Mark Hinman

Australia
Brisbane
Anne & Bill Abernethy,
Caringbah NSW
John Camroux,
Newtown
Glen 'Bumper' Dwyer,
Sydney
Bob Payne,
France
St. Martin de Crau
J P Gerin
Caumont-sur-Durance
Jacques Guigue
Germany
Guetersloh
Margaret & Brian Hughes
Russia
Moscow
Valeri Kartsev
Koptyevo, Moscow
Dima Komar
Luxembourg
Jonathan Flynn
Spain/Wigan
Maureen & Ray Green
Switzerland
Bern
Andy Hallas

219

Rugby books from London League Publications Ltd:

The Great Bev
The rugby league career of Brian Bevan
By Robert Gate

Brian Bevan is one of the few Rugby League players to rightfully be called a legend. He scored 796 tries in British Rugby League, a record that will never be passed. He had remarkable fitness, pace, side-step and try-scoring skill.

The book covers his early days in Australia, his war-time experiences, joining Warrington and his triumphs there, including the 1950 and 1954 Challenge Cup victories. Also included are his international appearances with the Other Nationalities team, his time with Blackpool at the end of his career, and memories of him from fellow players and supporters.

Lavishly illustrated, the book also has a comprehensive statistical record of Bevan's career. This is the first book on Brian Bevan.

Published in August 2002 at £14.95. ISBN: 190365906X
Special offer to readers of this book: £14.00 post free (UK), add £3.00 overseas.

I, George Nepia
The autobiography of a Rugby legend
By George Nepia and Terry McLean
Foreword by Oma Nepia

George Nepia is arguably New Zealand's greatest ever Rugby Union player. This new edition of his autobiography, first published in 1963, also has new and reprinted material that gives a full picture of Nepia's life and Rugby career.

It has a new chapter by Terry McLean on New Zealand's other great Union full-backs. Other new material includes Huw Richards on the 1924-5 All Black tour, Peter Lush and Robert Gate on Nepia's time in Rugby League with Streatham & Mitcham, Halifax and Manukau, Dave Farrar on his Hawke's Bay Ranfurly Shield career and a review of the 1986 *This is Your Life* programme made three months before he died.

The book is fully illustrated and of interest to followers of both Rugby codes.

Published in September 2002 at £13.95. ISBN: 1-903659-07-8
Special offer to readers of this book: £13.00 post free (UK), add £2.00 overseas.

Please send your order to:
London League Publications Ltd, PO Box 10441, London E14 0SB
Cheques payable to London League Publications Ltd - no credit cards.
(Sterling cheques only)